THE WICKED + THE DIVINE

VOL. 4, RISING ACTION

GILLEN

McKELVIE

WILSON

COWLES

KIERON GILLEN
WRITER

JAMIE McKELVIE
ARTIST

MATTHEW WILSON
COLOURIST

CLAYTON COWLES
LETTERER

SERGIO SERRANO
DESIGNER

CHRISSY WILLIAMS
EDITOR

DEE CUNNIFFE
FLATTER

THE WICKED + THE DIVINE, VOL. 4, RISING ACTION
First printing. October 2016.
ISBN: 978-1-63215-913-7
Published by Image Comics Inc.
Office of publication: 2001 Center St, Sixth Fl, Berkeley, CA 94704.

For information regarding the CPSIA on this printed material call: 203-595-3636
and provide reference # RICH – 507826. Representation: Law Offices of Harris
M. Miller II, P.C. (rights.inquiries@gmail.com).

This book was designed by Sergio Serrano, based on a design by Hannah
Donovan and Jamie McKelvie, and set into type by Sergio Serrano in Edmonton,
Canada. The text face is Gotham, designed and issued by Hoefler & Co. in 2000.
The paper is Escanaba 60 matte.

GILLEN McKELVIE WILSON COWLES

THE WICKED + THE DIVINE

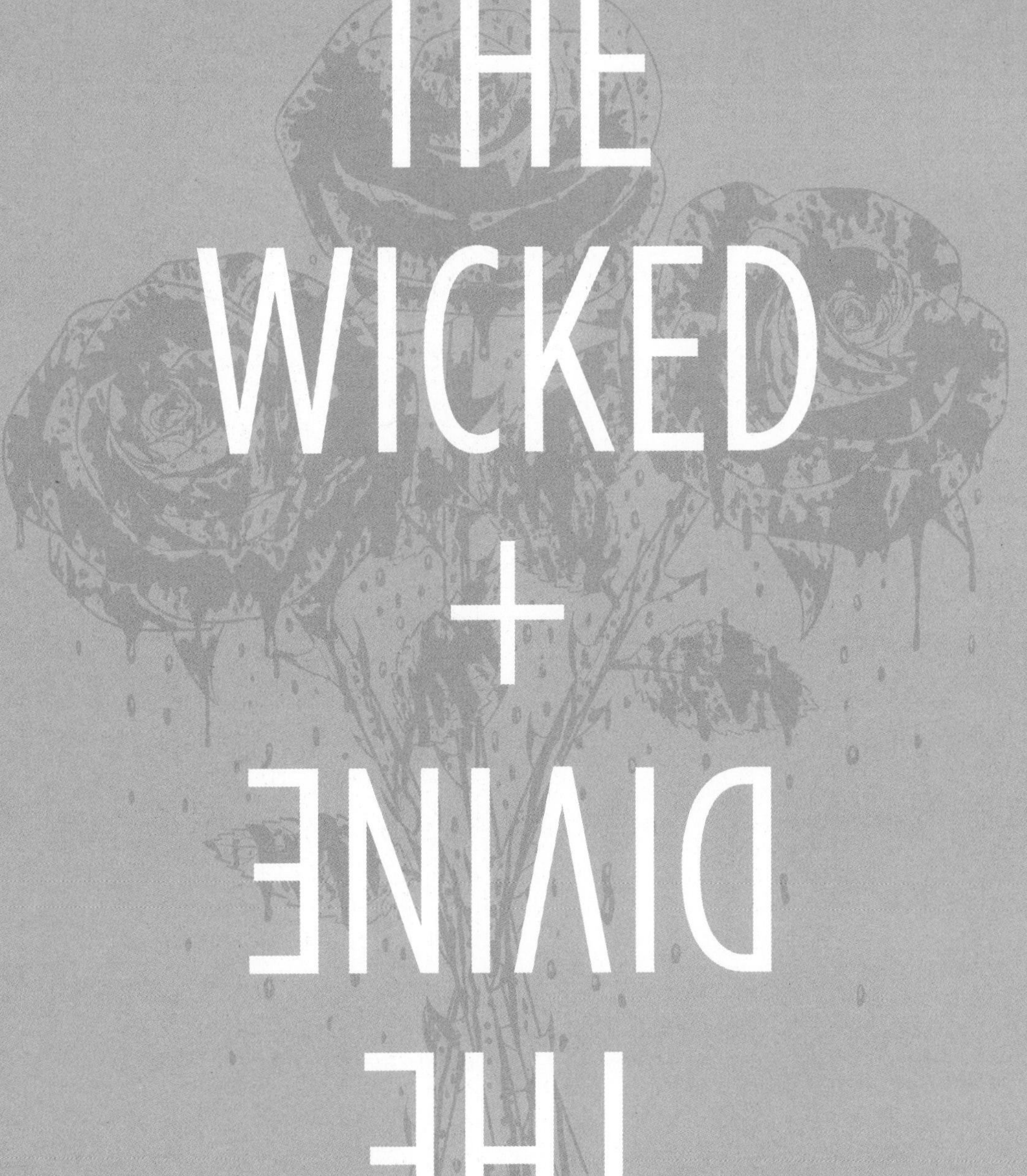

VOL. 4, RISING ACTION

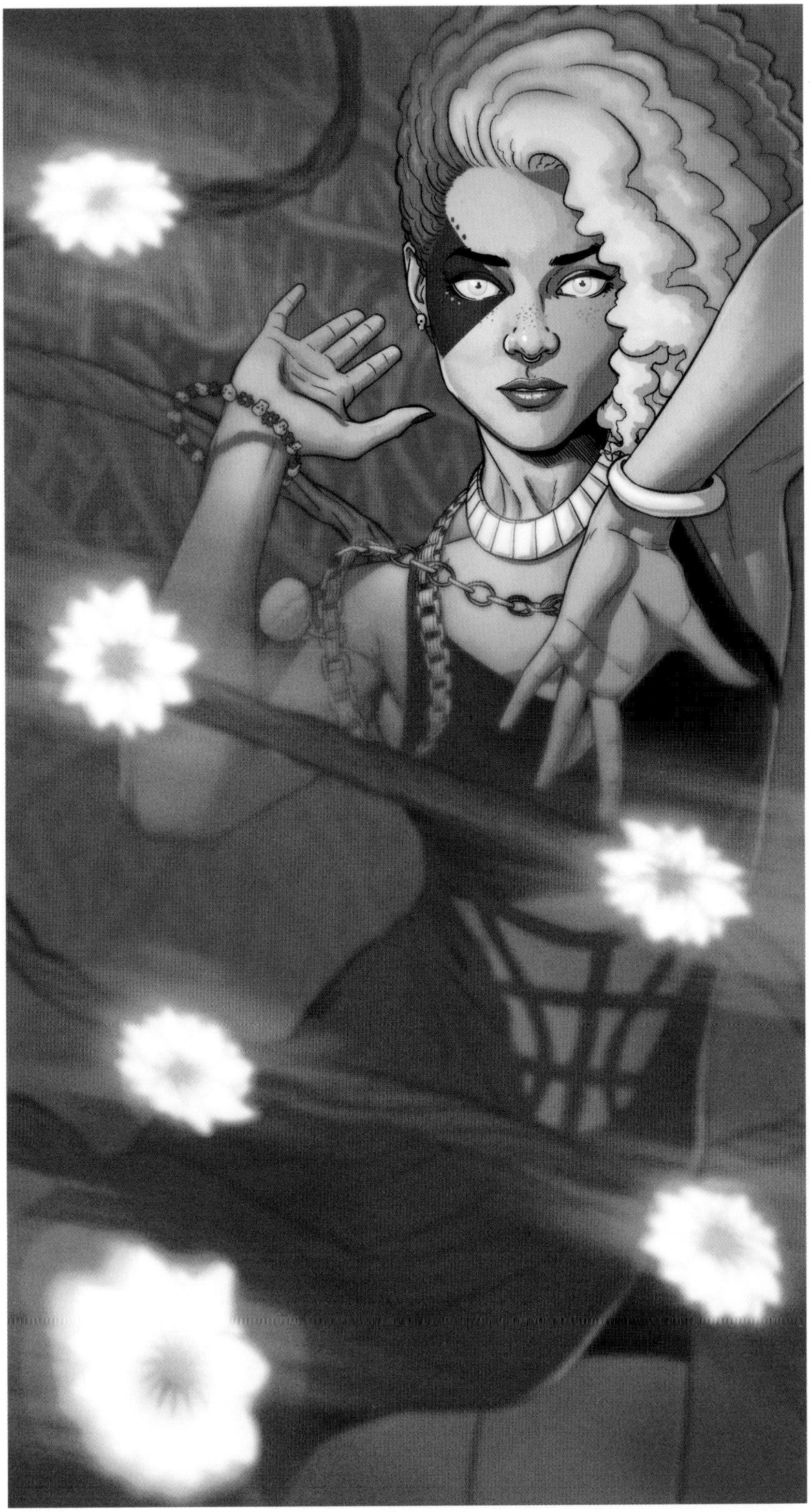

THE WICKED + THE DIVINE

Every ninety years twelve gods return as young people. They are loved. They are hated. In two years, they are all dead. It's happening now. It's happening again.

Unknown to all, Ananke revealed fangirl Laura to be a thirteenth god, Persephone, before killing her family and presumably Laura too. Except now a gig has been booked in London, with a "Persephone" set to perform...

Life goes on.

Persephone. Seemingly ascended fangirl Laura. Seemingly killed by Ananke.

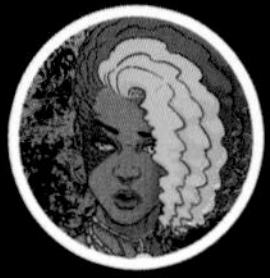

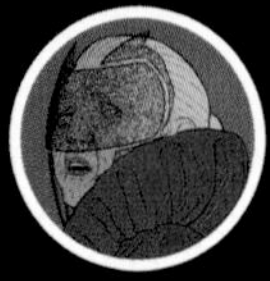

Ananke. Immortal god of destiny. The Pantheon's warden. Totally dodgy.

THE PANTHEON

Lucifer. Underworld god. Framed for murder. Killed when escaping prison.

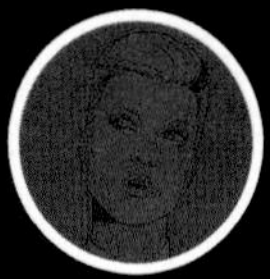

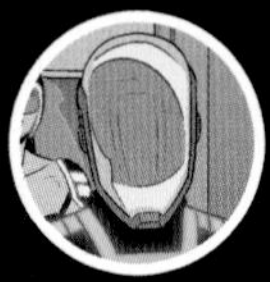

Woden. Shithead god, master of Valkyries. Ananke's secret semi-willing assistant.

Baphomet. Underworld god. Wanted criminal. The Morrigan's lover. Gothy. Secret geek.

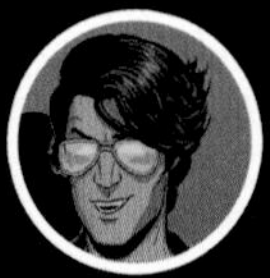

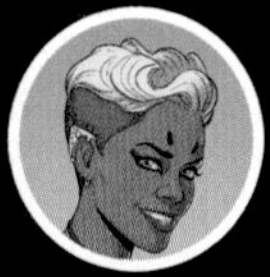

Sakhmet. Feline war god. Emotionally blank hedonist. Ate her dad. No, really.

The Morrigan. Triple-formed underworld god. Imprisoned. Baphomet's lover. Also geeky.

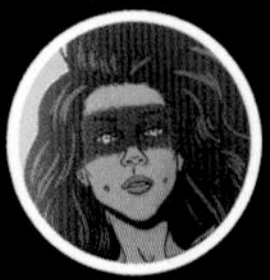

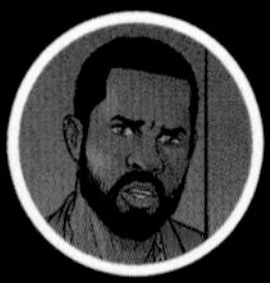

Baal. Storm god. Ex-lover of Inanna and Laura. Thrashed Morrigan when capturing her.

Dionysus. Hivemind dancefloor god. Doesn't sleep. Loyal to The Morrigan. Hates Woden.

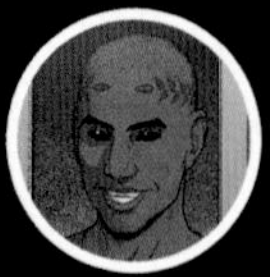

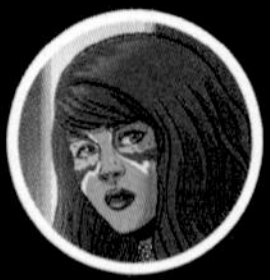

Amaterasu. Sun god with sunny disposition. Mostly. Friends with everyone. Almost.

The Norns. Cynical journo Cassandra and crew turned triple soothsaying-gods.

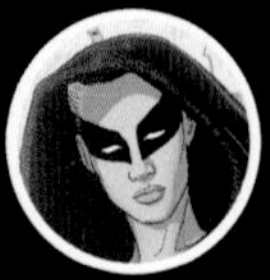

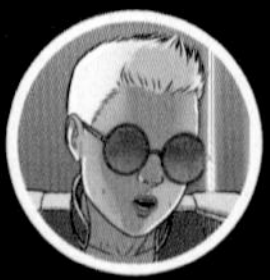

Minerva. God of widsom. Twelve, going on thirteen with increasing speed. Has owl. Yes.

Inanna. Queen of heaven. Ex-lover of Baal. Baphomet is wanted for his murder.

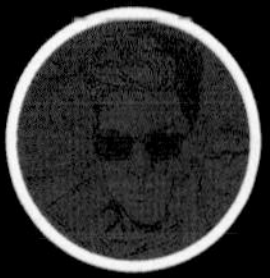

Tara. God knows what god. Secretly killed by Ananke in assisted suicide.

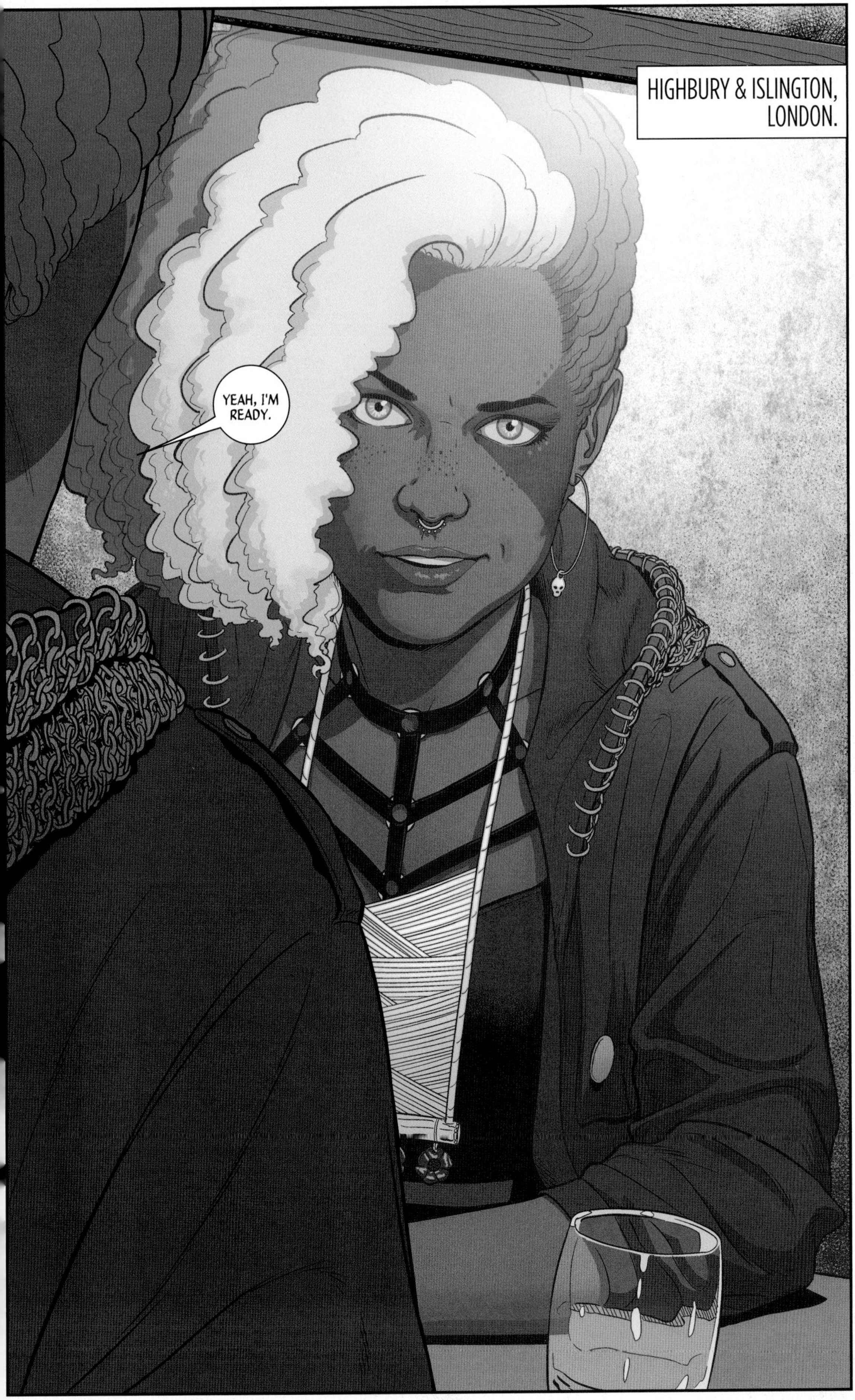
HIGHBURY & ISLINGTON, LONDON.
YEAH, I'M READY.

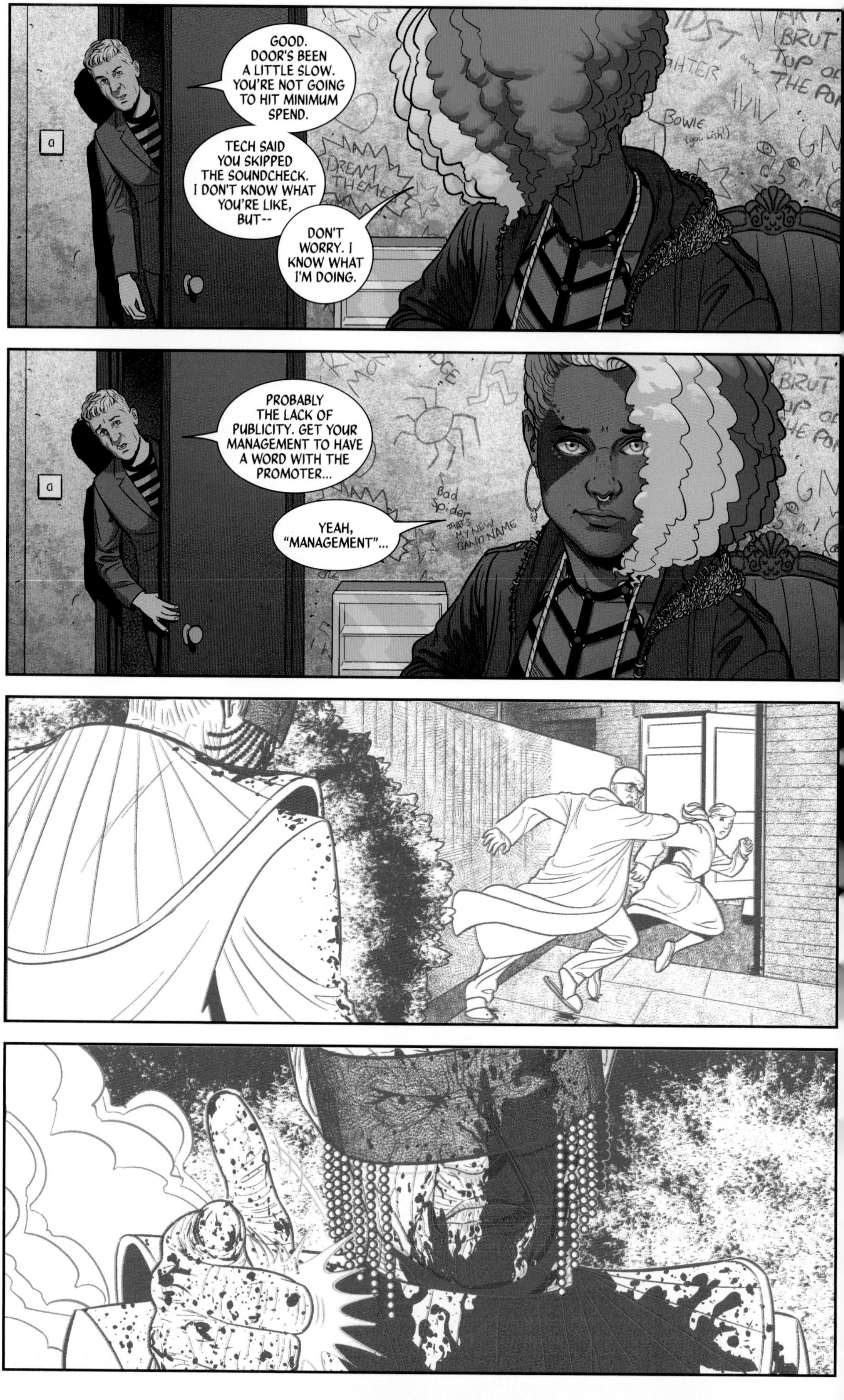
GOOD. DOOR'S BEEN A LITTLE SLOW. YOU'RE NOT GOING TO HIT MINIMUM SPEND.
TECH SAID YOU SKIPPED THE SOUNDCHECK. I DON'T KNOW WHAT YOU'RE LIKE, BUT--
DON'T WORRY. I KNOW WHAT I'M DOING.
DREAM THEMES
Bowie (you wish!)
PROBABLY THE LACK OF PUBLICITY. GET YOUR MANAGEMENT TO HAVE A WORD WITH THE PROMOTER...
YEAH, "MANAGEMENT"...
Bad Spider
THAT'S MY NEW BAND NAME

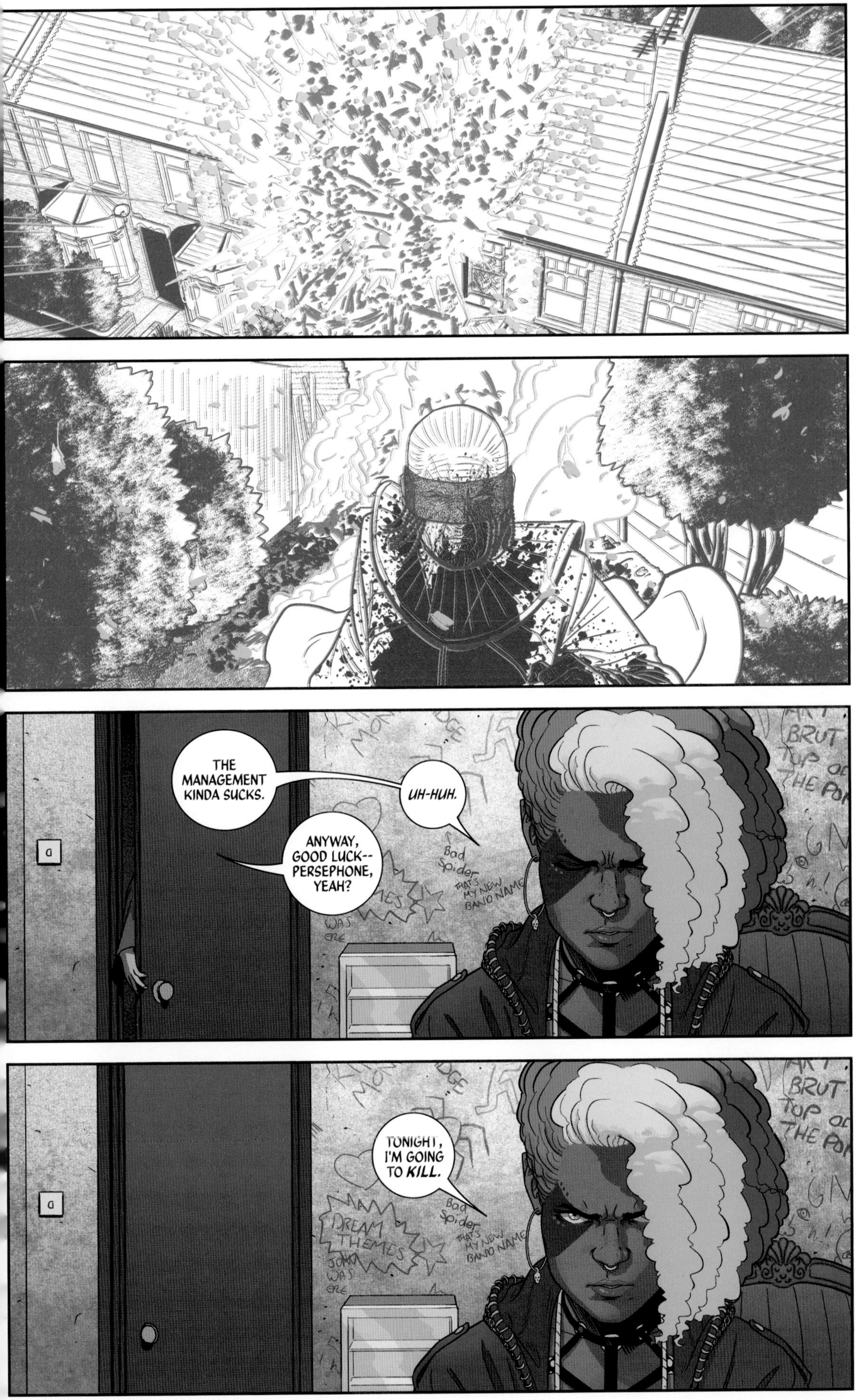
THE MANAGEMENT KINDA SUCKS.
UH-HUH.
ANYWAY, GOOD LUCK--PERSEPHONE, YEAH?
Bad Spider THAT'S MY NEW BAND NAME
TONIGHT, I'M GOING TO ***KILL***.
DREAM THEMES

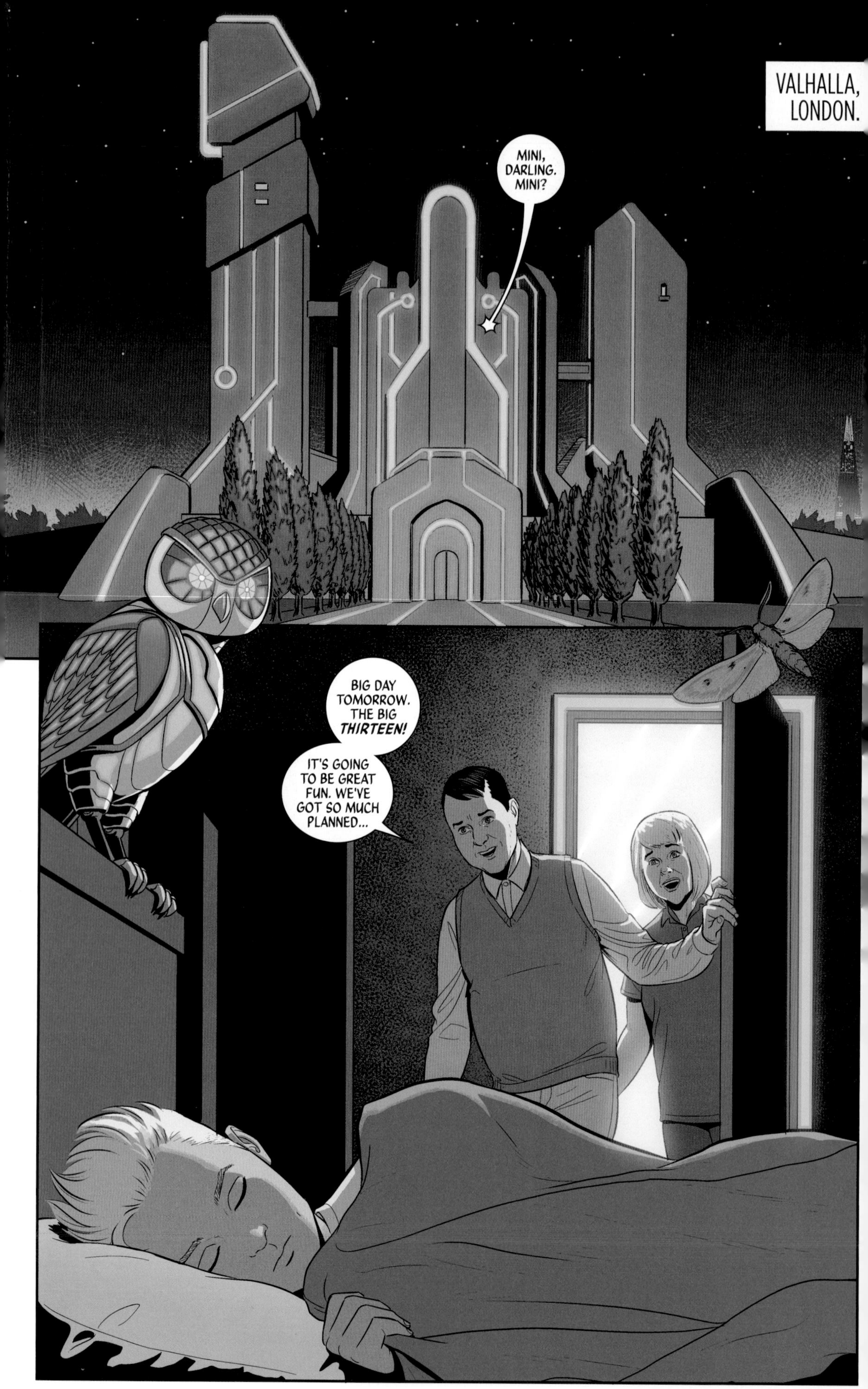
VALHALLA, LONDON.
MINI, DARLING. MINI?
BIG DAY TOMORROW. THE BIG THIRTEEN!
IT'S GOING TO BE GREAT FUN. WE'VE GOT SO MUCH PLANNED...

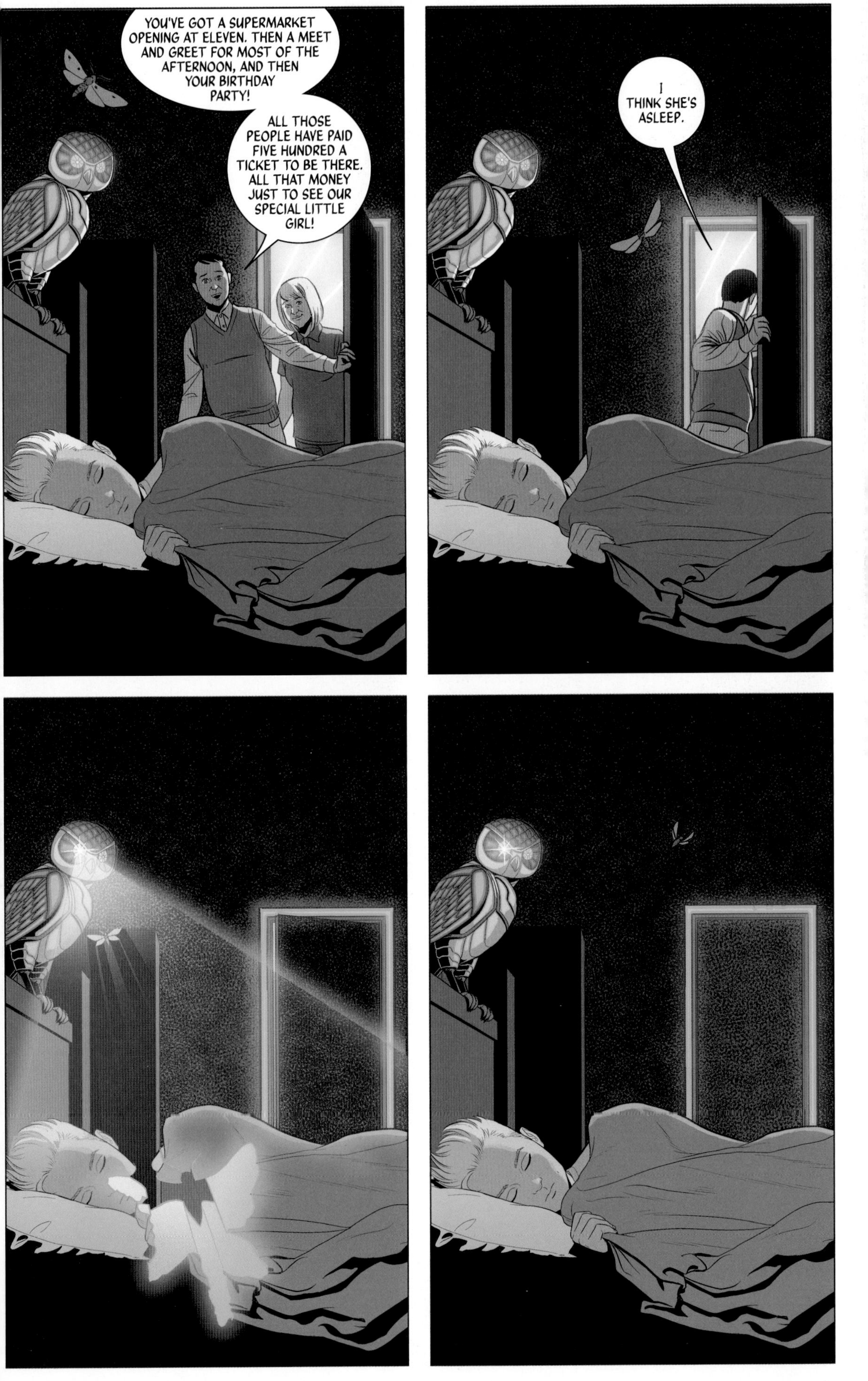
YOU'VE GOT A SUPERMARKET OPENING AT ELEVEN. THEN A MEET AND GREET FOR MOST OF THE AFTERNOON, AND THEN YOUR BIRTHDAY PARTY!
ALL THOSE PEOPLE HAVE PAID FIVE HUNDRED A TICKET TO BE THERE. ALL THAT MONEY JUST TO SEE OUR SPECIAL LITTLE GIRL!
I THINK SHE'S ASLEEP.

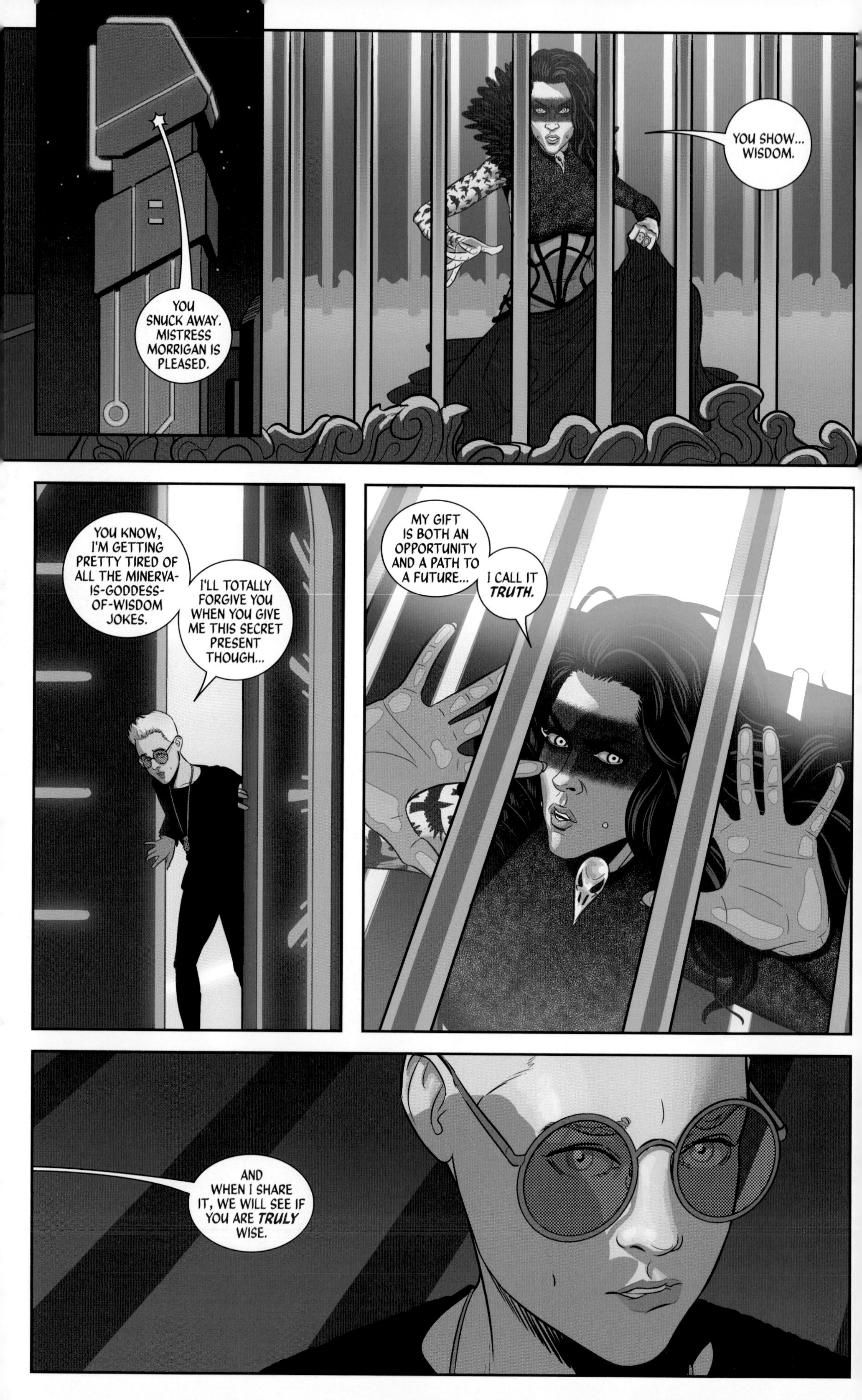
YOU SNUCK AWAY. MISTRESS MORRIGAN IS PLEASED.
YOU SHOW... WISDOM.
YOU KNOW, I'M GETTING PRETTY TIRED OF ALL THE MINERVA-IS-GODDESS-OF-WISDOM JOKES.
I'LL TOTALLY FORGIVE YOU WHEN YOU GIVE ME THIS SECRET PRESENT THOUGH...
MY GIFT IS BOTH AN OPPORTUNITY AND A PATH TO A FUTURE...
I CALL IT TRUTH.
AND WHEN I SHARE IT, WE WILL SEE IF YOU ARE TRULY WISE.

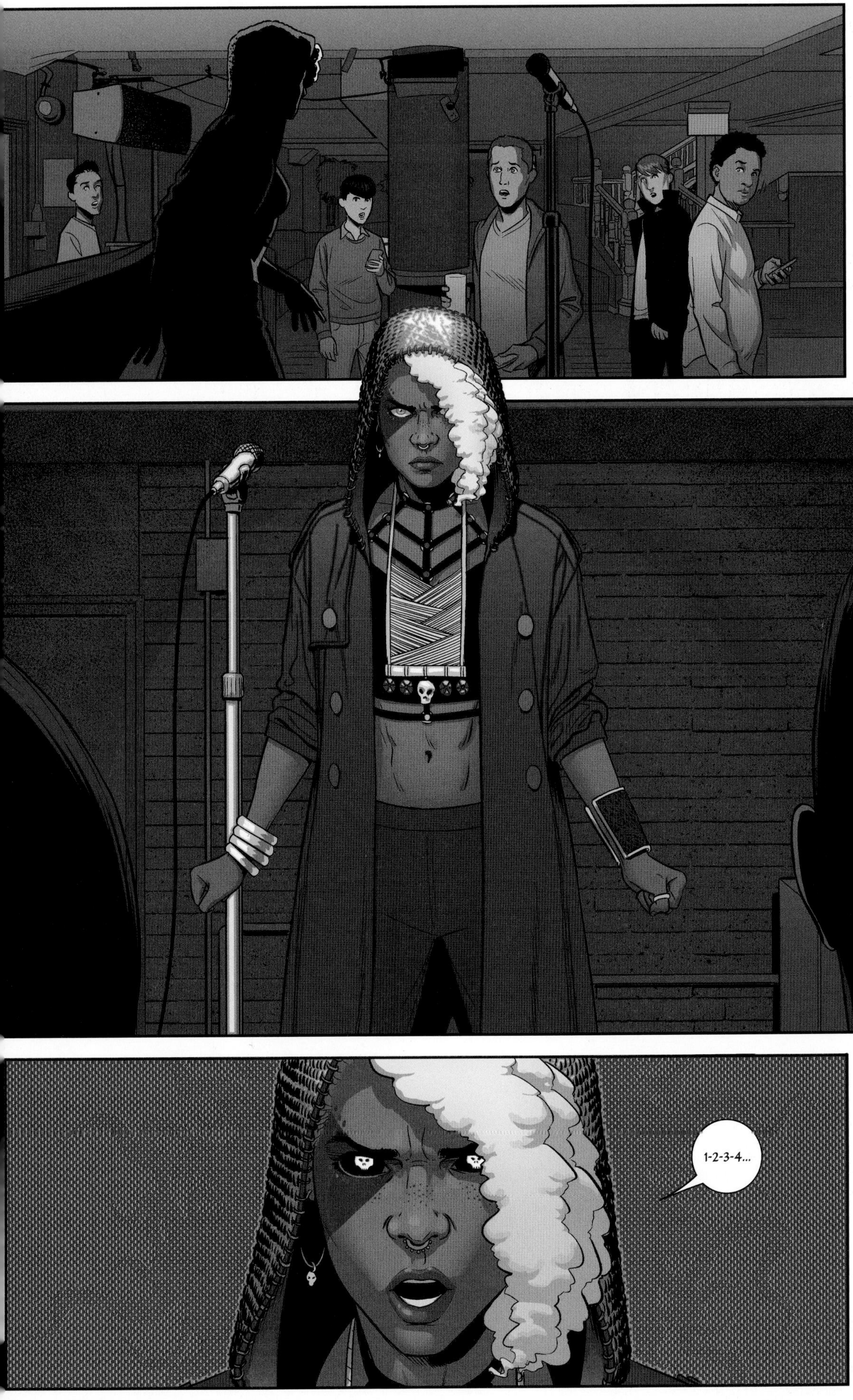
1-2-3-4...

PERSEPHONE'S
IN HELL.

PERSEPHONE'S
IN HELL.

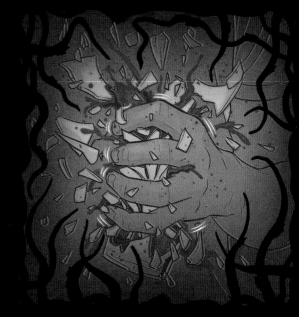

PERSEPHONE'S
IN HELL.

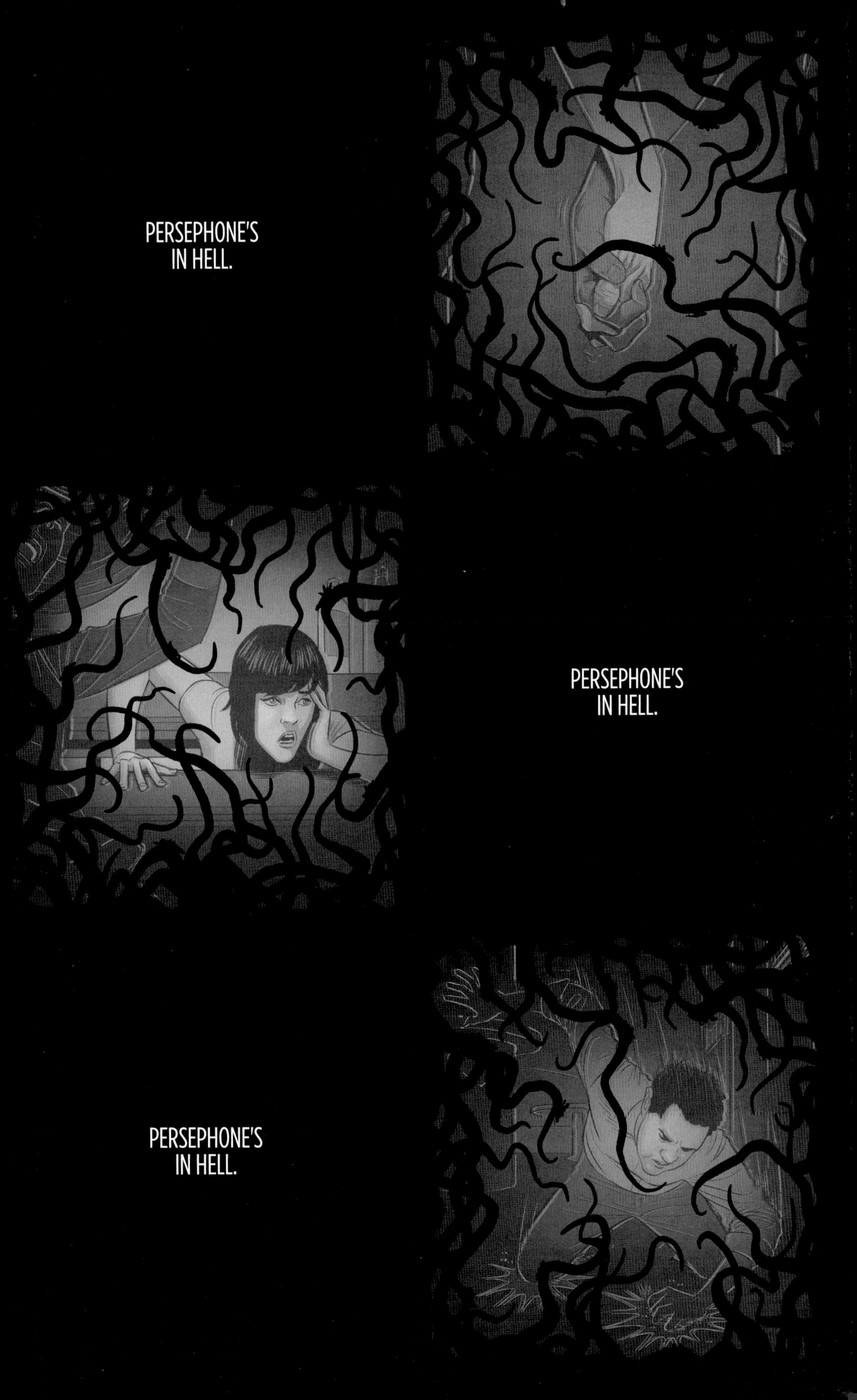
PERSEPHONE'S IN HELL.
PERSEPHONE'S IN HELL.
PERSEPHONE'S IN HELL.

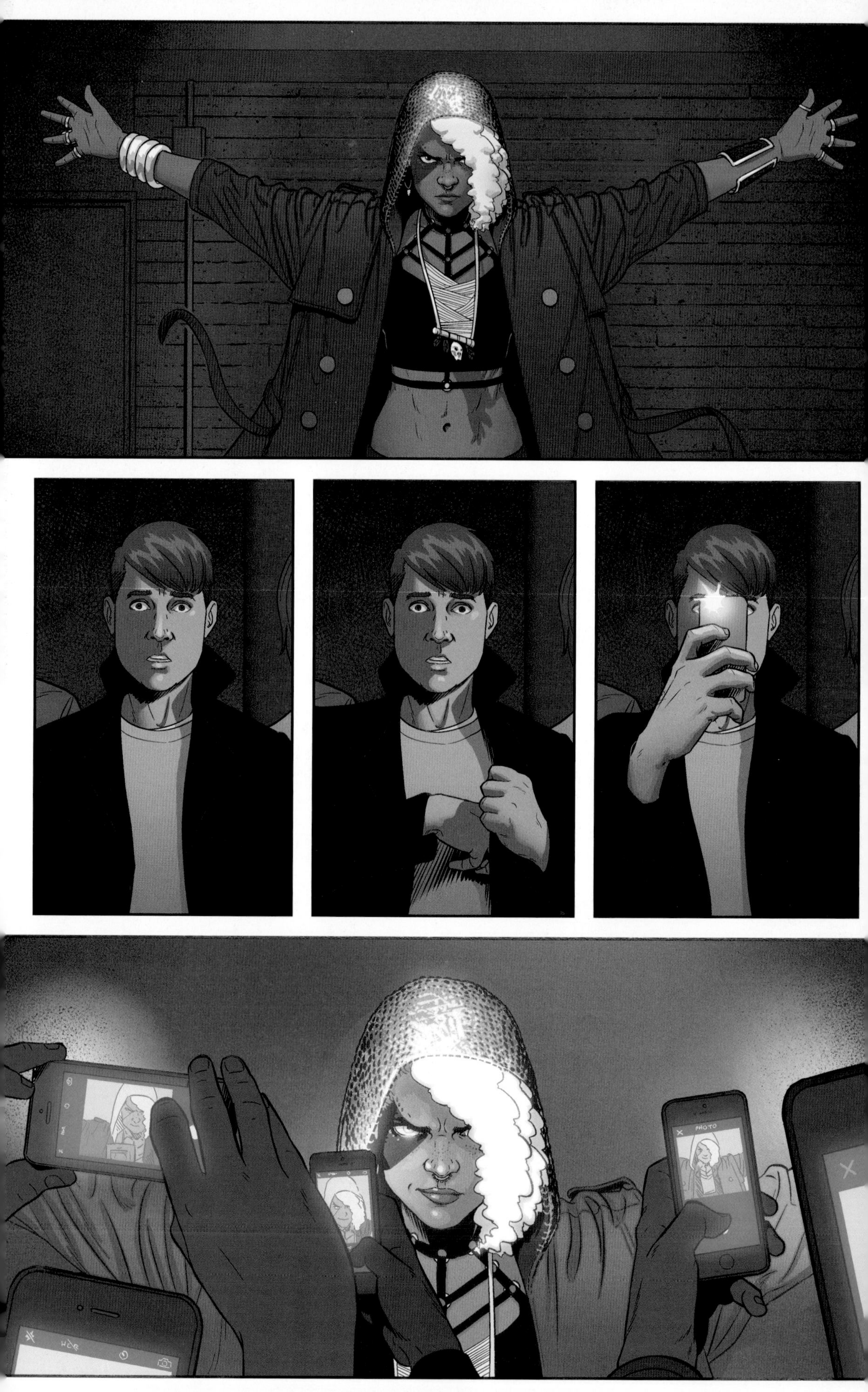
PHOTO
HDR

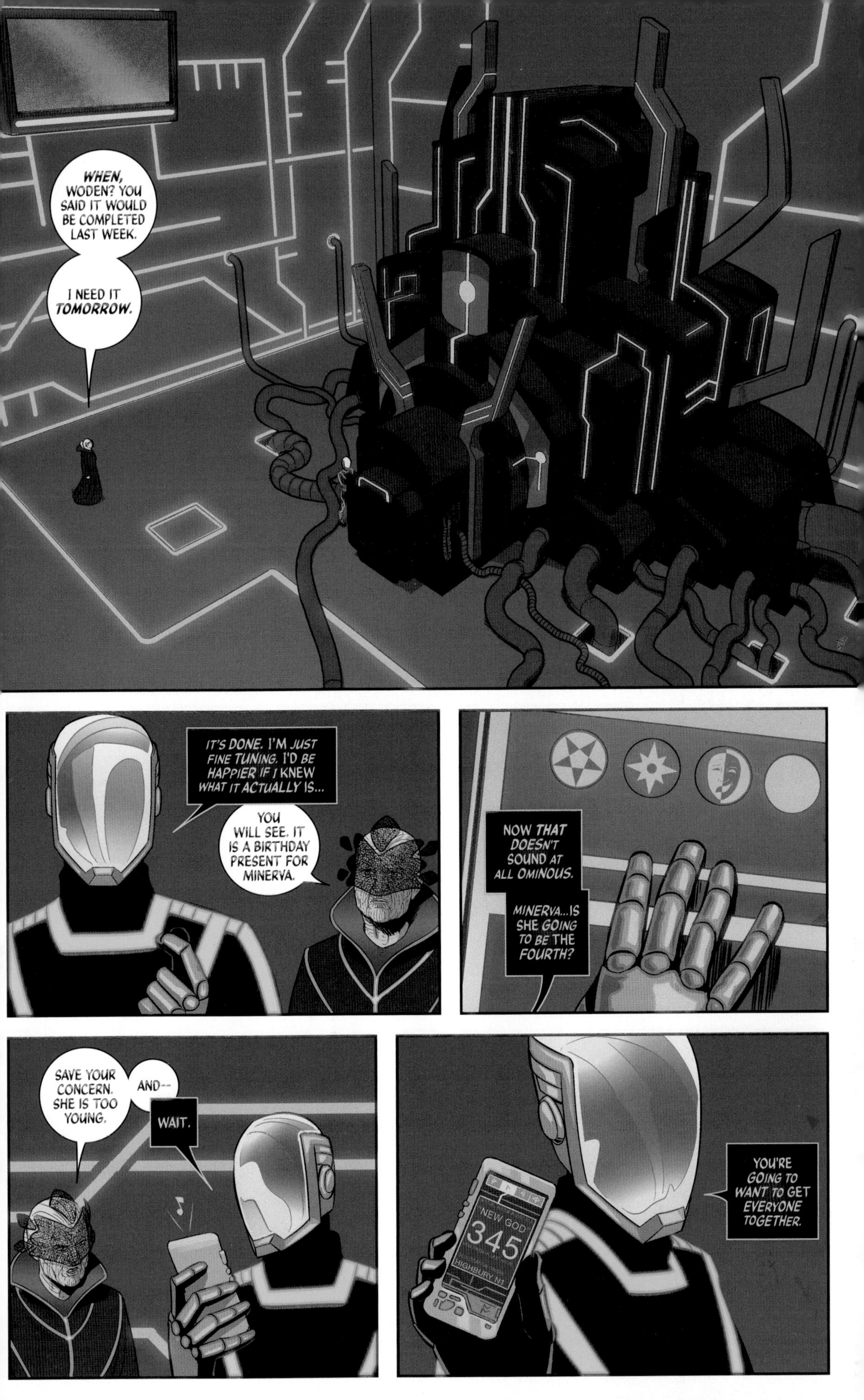
WHEN, WODEN? YOU SAID IT WOULD BE COMPLETED LAST WEEK.
I NEED IT TOMORROW.
IT'S DONE. I'M JUST FINE TUNING. I'D BE HAPPIER IF I KNEW WHAT IT ACTUALLY IS...
YOU WILL SEE. IT IS A BIRTHDAY PRESENT FOR MINERVA.
NOW THAT DOESN'T SOUND AT ALL OMINOUS.
MINERVA...IS SHE GOING TO BE THE FOURTH?
SAVE YOUR CONCERN. SHE IS TOO YOUNG.
AND--
WAIT.
NEW GOD
345
HIGHBURY N1
YOU'RE GOING TO WANT TO GET EVERYONE TOGETHER.

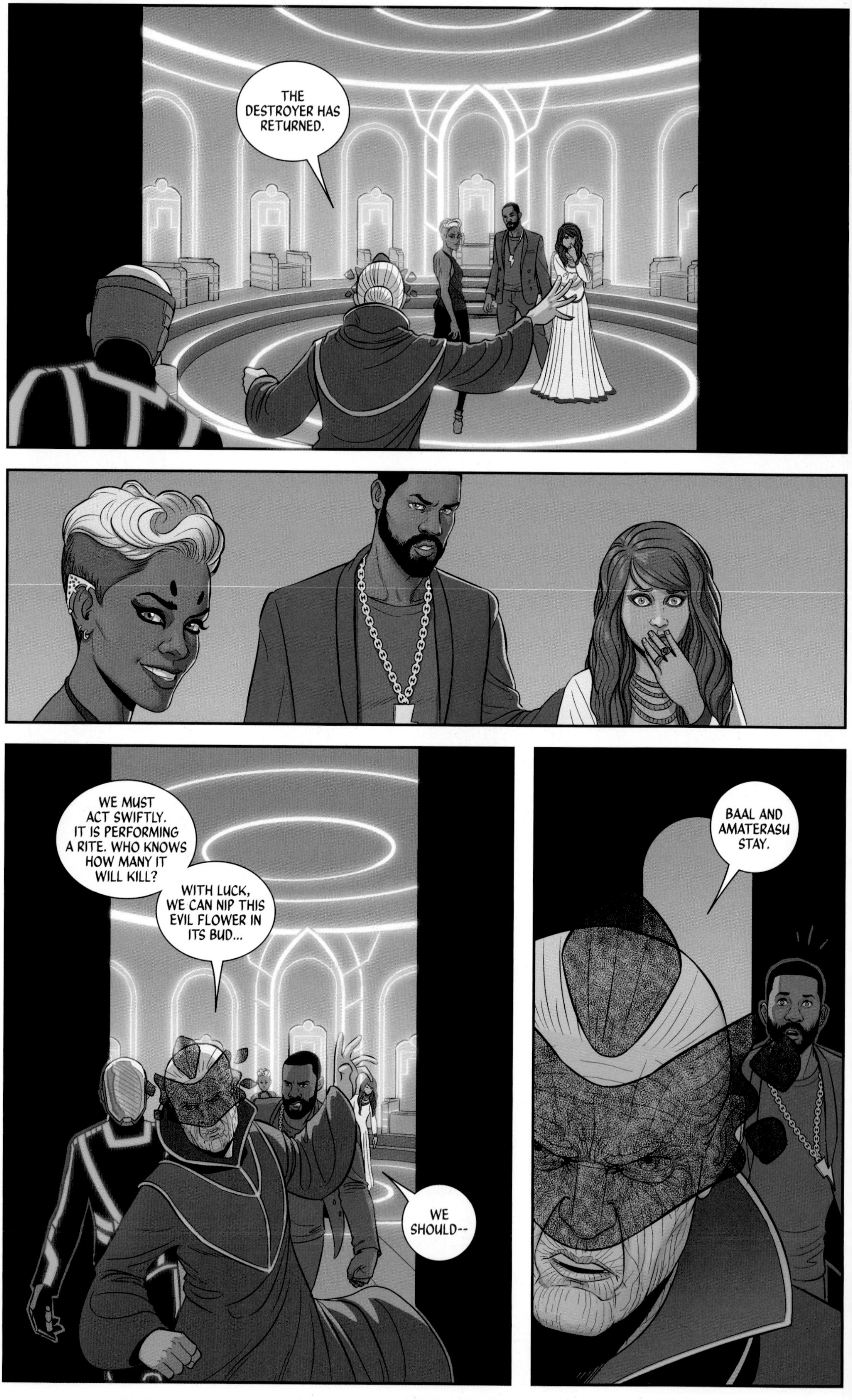
THE DESTROYER HAS RETURNED.
WE MUST ACT SWIFTLY. IT IS PERFORMING A RITE. WHO KNOWS HOW MANY IT WILL KILL?
WITH LUCK, WE CAN NIP THIS EVIL FLOWER IN ITS BUD...
WE SHOULD--
BAAL AND AMATERASU STAY.

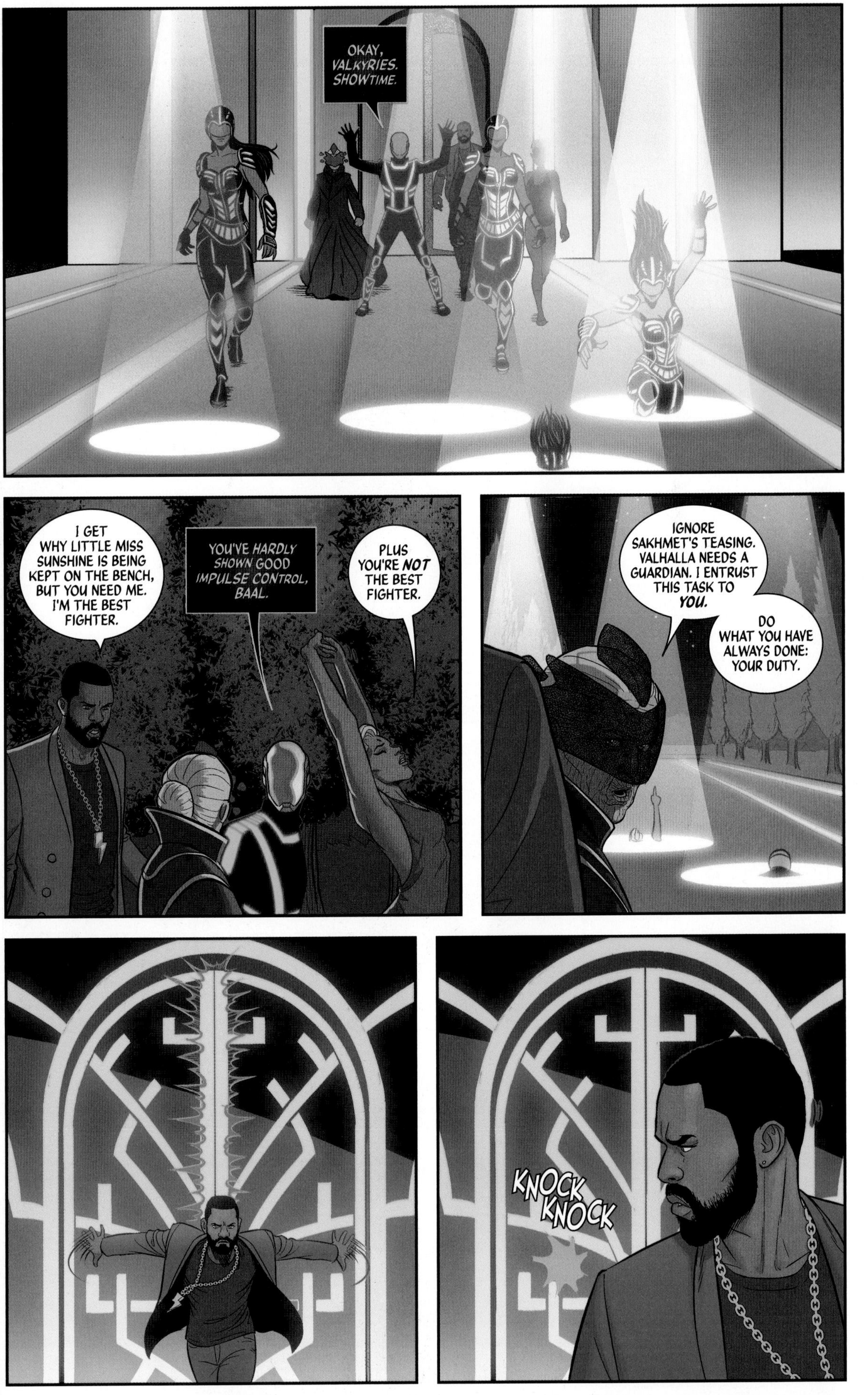
OKAY, VALKYRIES. SHOWTIME.
I GET WHY LITTLE MISS SUNSHINE IS BEING KEPT ON THE BENCH, BUT YOU NEED ME. I'M THE BEST FIGHTER.
YOU'VE HARDLY SHOWN GOOD IMPULSE CONTROL, BAAL.
PLUS YOU'RE NOT THE BEST FIGHTER.
IGNORE SAKHMET'S TEASING. VALHALLA NEEDS A GUARDIAN. I ENTRUST THIS TASK TO YOU.
DO WHAT YOU HAVE ALWAYS DONE: YOUR DUTY.
KNOCK KNOCK

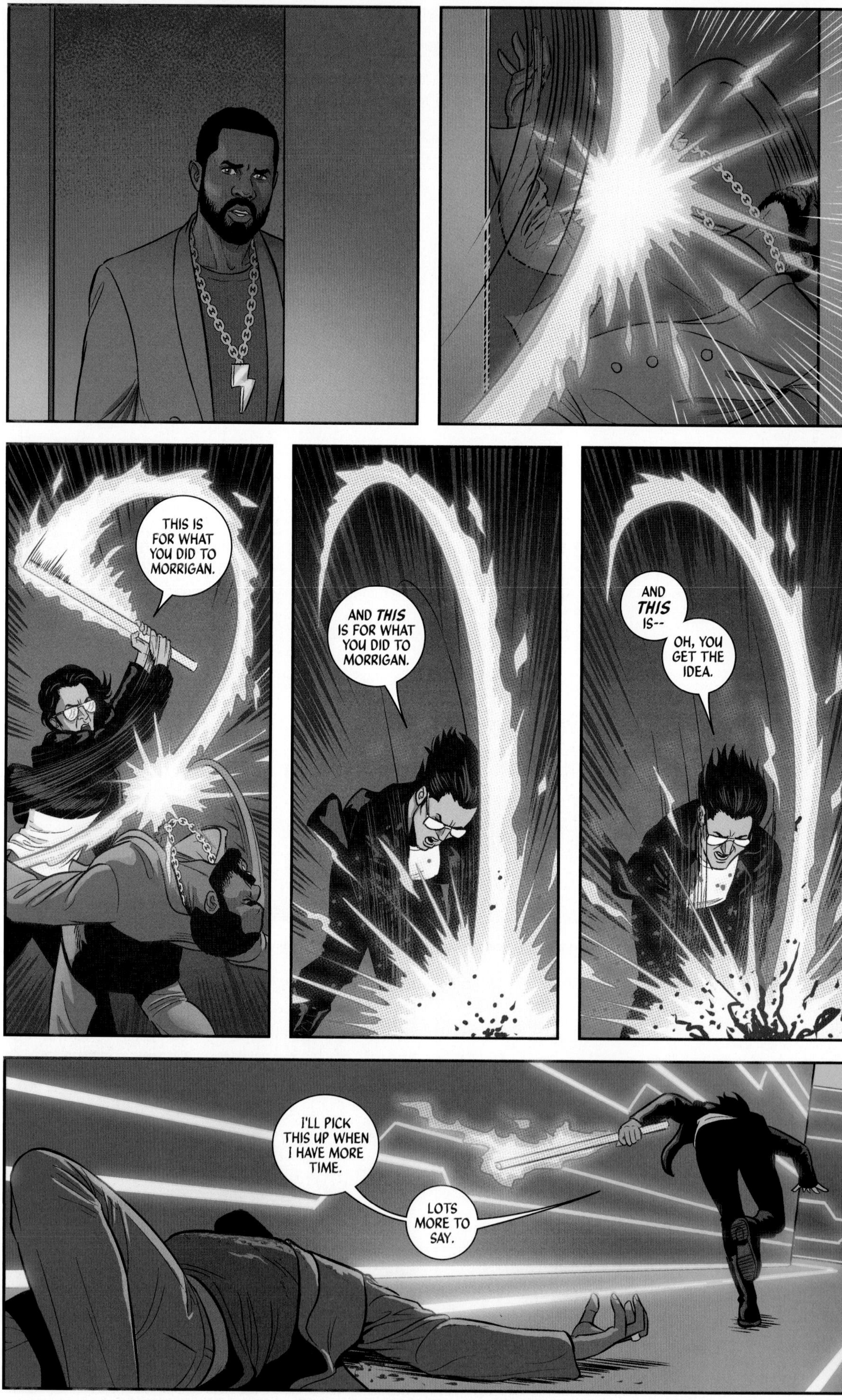
THIS IS FOR WHAT YOU DID TO MORRIGAN.
AND *THIS* IS FOR WHAT YOU DID TO MORRIGAN.
AND *THIS* IS--
OH, YOU GET THE IDEA.
I'LL PICK THIS UP WHEN I HAVE MORE TIME.
LOTS MORE TO SAY.

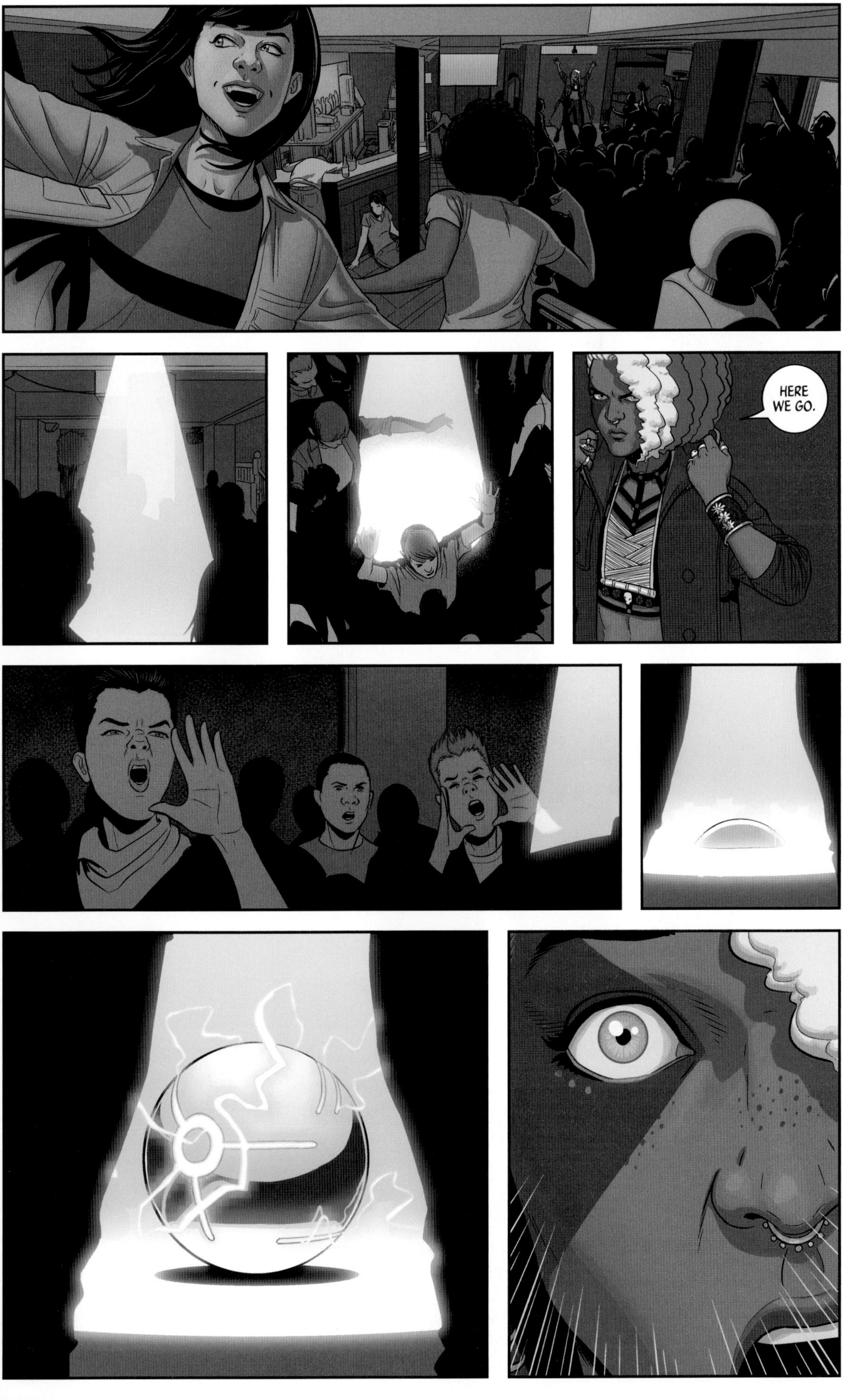
HERE WE GO.

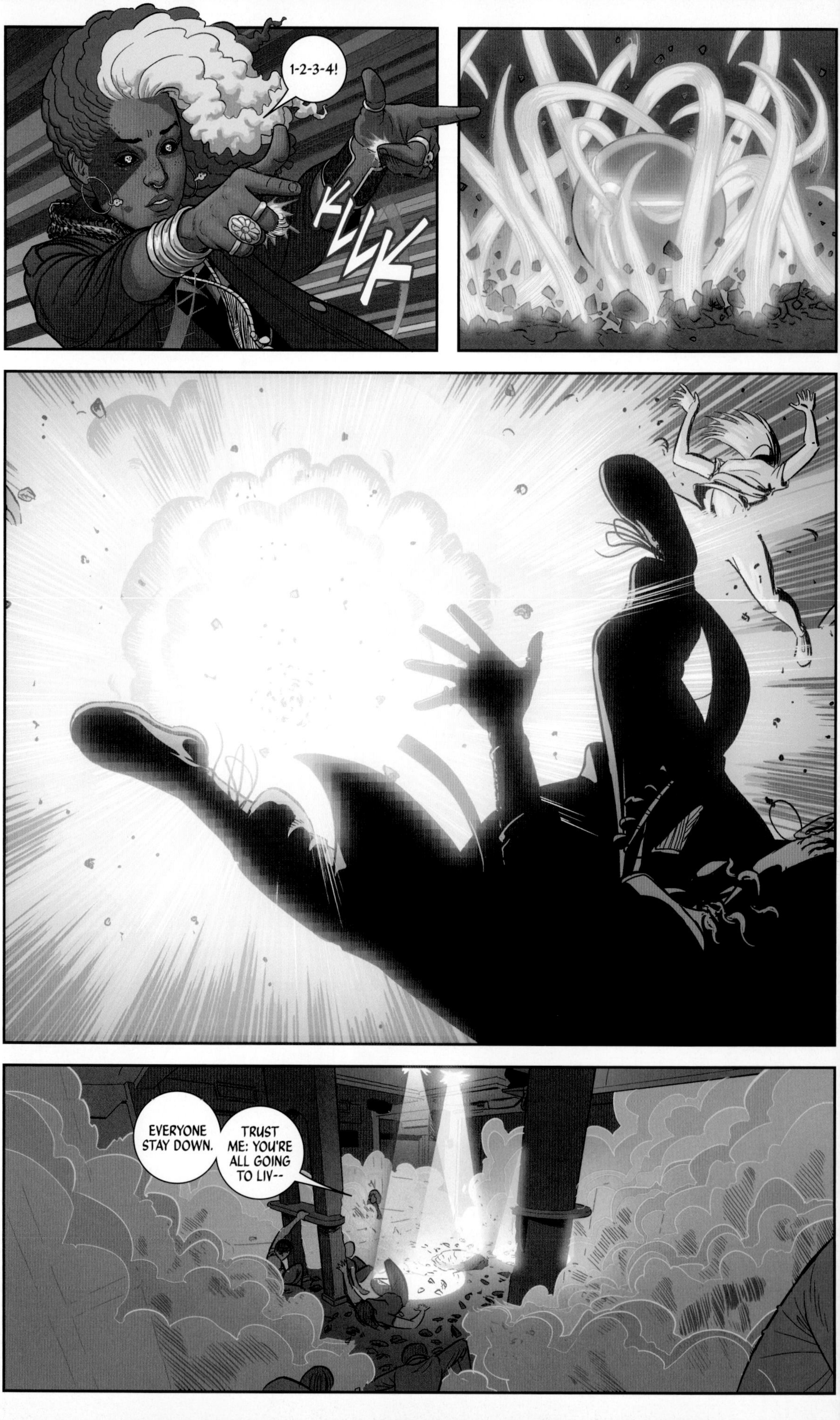
1-2-3-4!
KLLK
EVERYONE STAY DOWN.
TRUST ME: YOU'RE ALL GOING TO LIV--

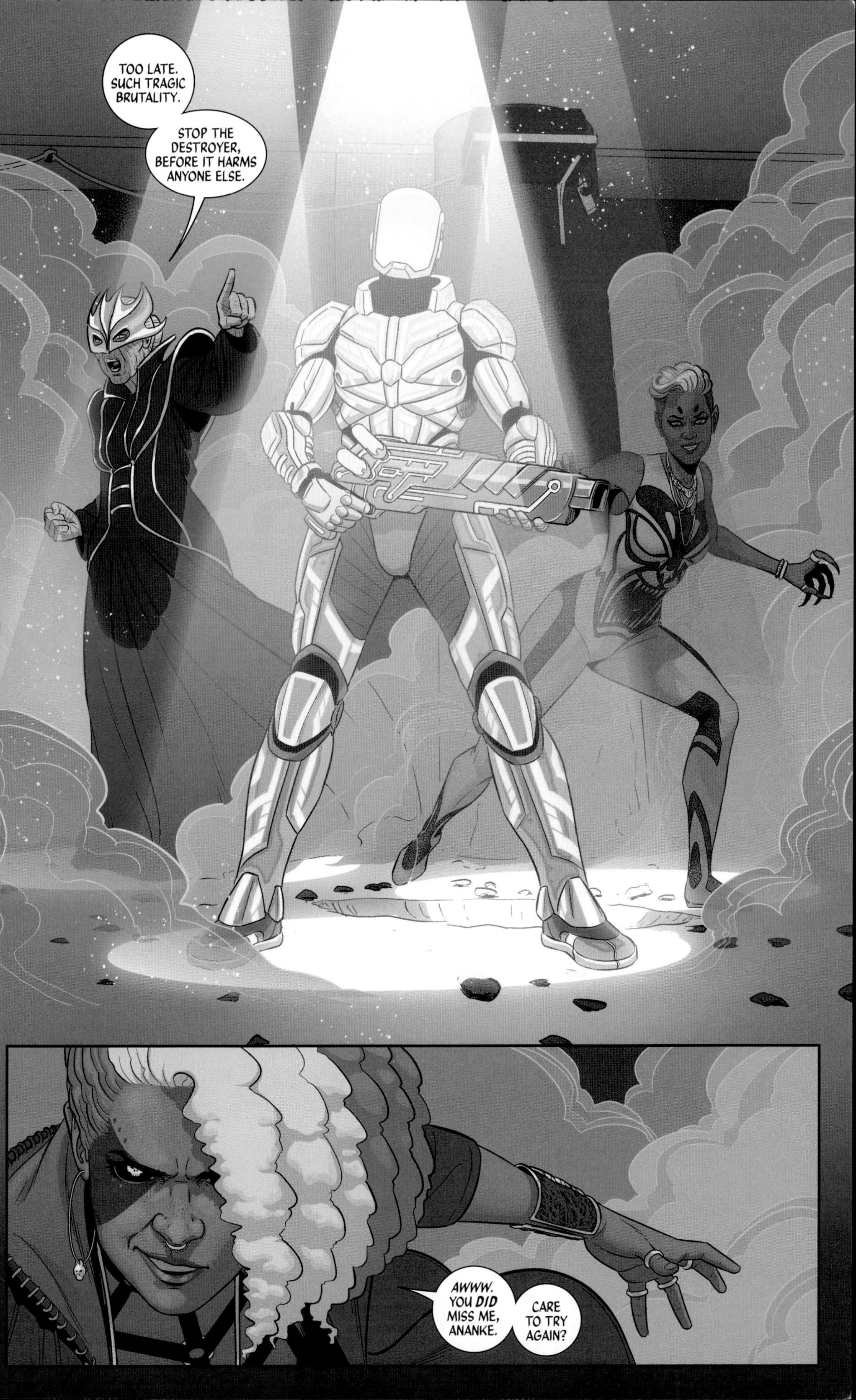
TOO LATE. SUCH TRAGIC BRUTALITY.
STOP THE DESTROYER, BEFORE IT HARMS ANYONE ELSE.
AWWW. YOU *DID* MISS ME, ANANKE.
CARE TO TRY AGAIN?

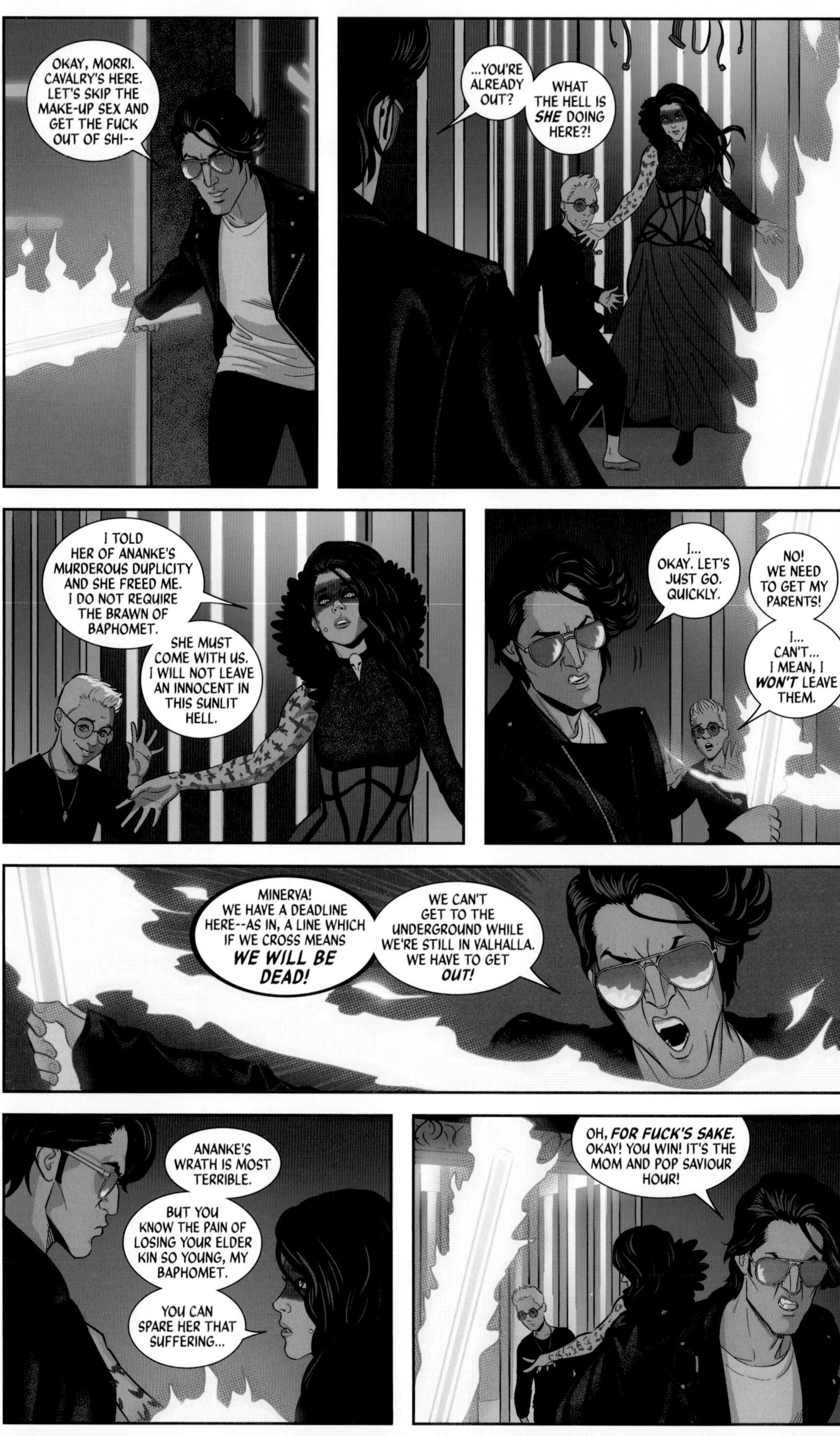
OKAY, MORRI. CAVALRY'S HERE. LET'S SKIP THE MAKE-UP SEX AND GET THE FUCK OUT OF SHI--
...YOU'RE ALREADY OUT?
WHAT THE HELL IS *SHE* DOING HERE?!
I TOLD HER OF ANANKE'S MURDEROUS DUPLICITY AND SHE FREED ME. I DO NOT REQUIRE THE BRAWN OF BAPHOMET.
SHE MUST COME WITH US. I WILL NOT LEAVE AN INNOCENT IN THIS SUNLIT HELL.
I... OKAY. LET'S JUST GO. QUICKLY.
NO! WE NEED TO GET MY PARENTS!
I... CAN'T... I MEAN, I *WON'T* LEAVE THEM.
MINERVA! WE HAVE A DEADLINE HERE--AS IN, A LINE WHICH IF WE CROSS MEANS ***WE WILL BE DEAD!***
WE CAN'T GET TO THE UNDERGROUND WHILE WE'RE STILL IN VALHALLA. WE HAVE TO GET ***OUT!***
ANANKE'S WRATH IS MOST TERRIBLE.
BUT YOU KNOW THE PAIN OF LOSING YOUR ELDER KIN SO YOUNG, MY BAPHOMET.
YOU CAN SPARE HER THAT SUFFERING...
OH, ***FOR FUCK'S SAKE.*** OKAY! YOU WIN! IT'S THE MOM AND POP SAVIOUR HOUR!

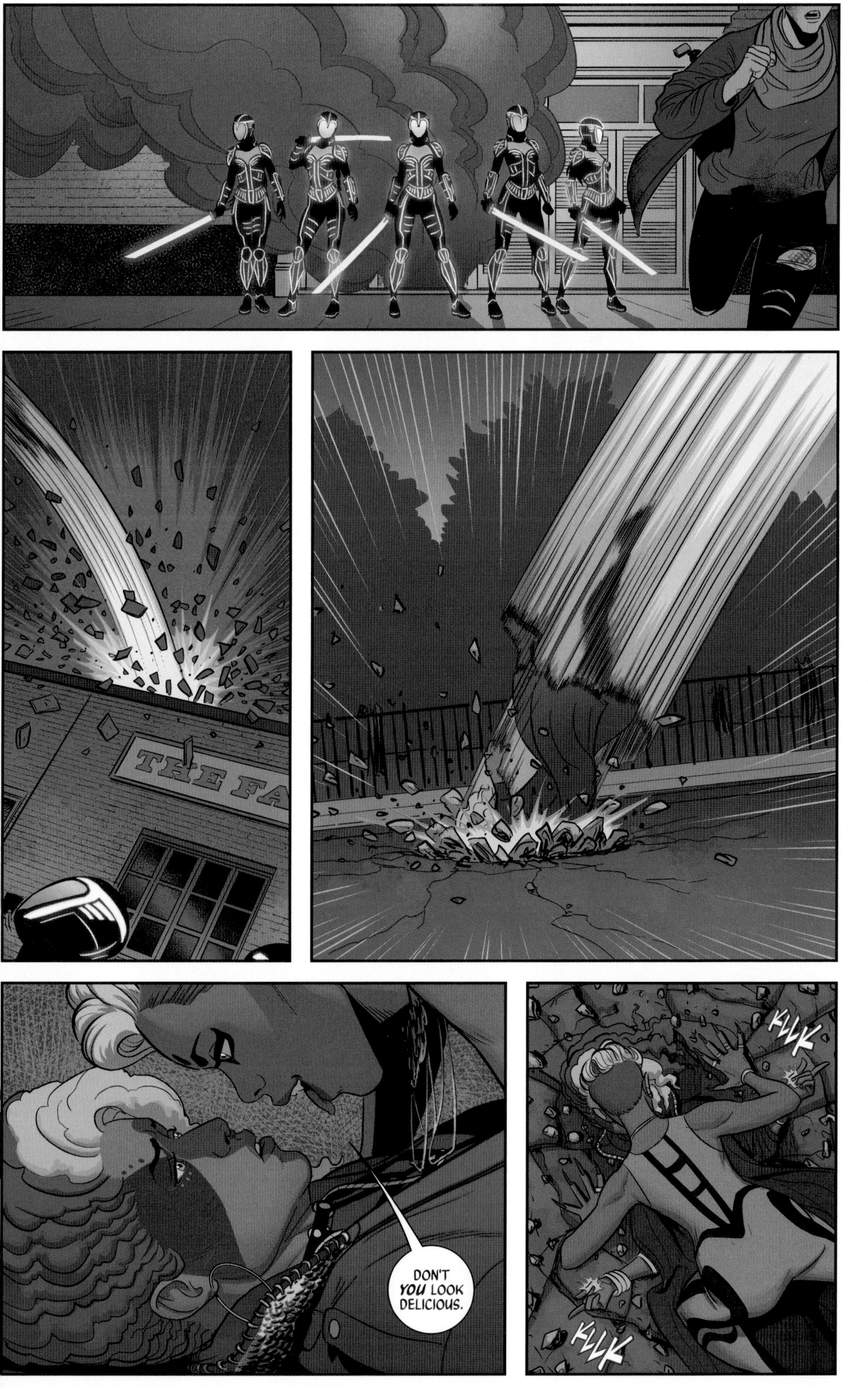
THE FA
DON'T YOU LOOK DELICIOUS.
KLLK
KLLK

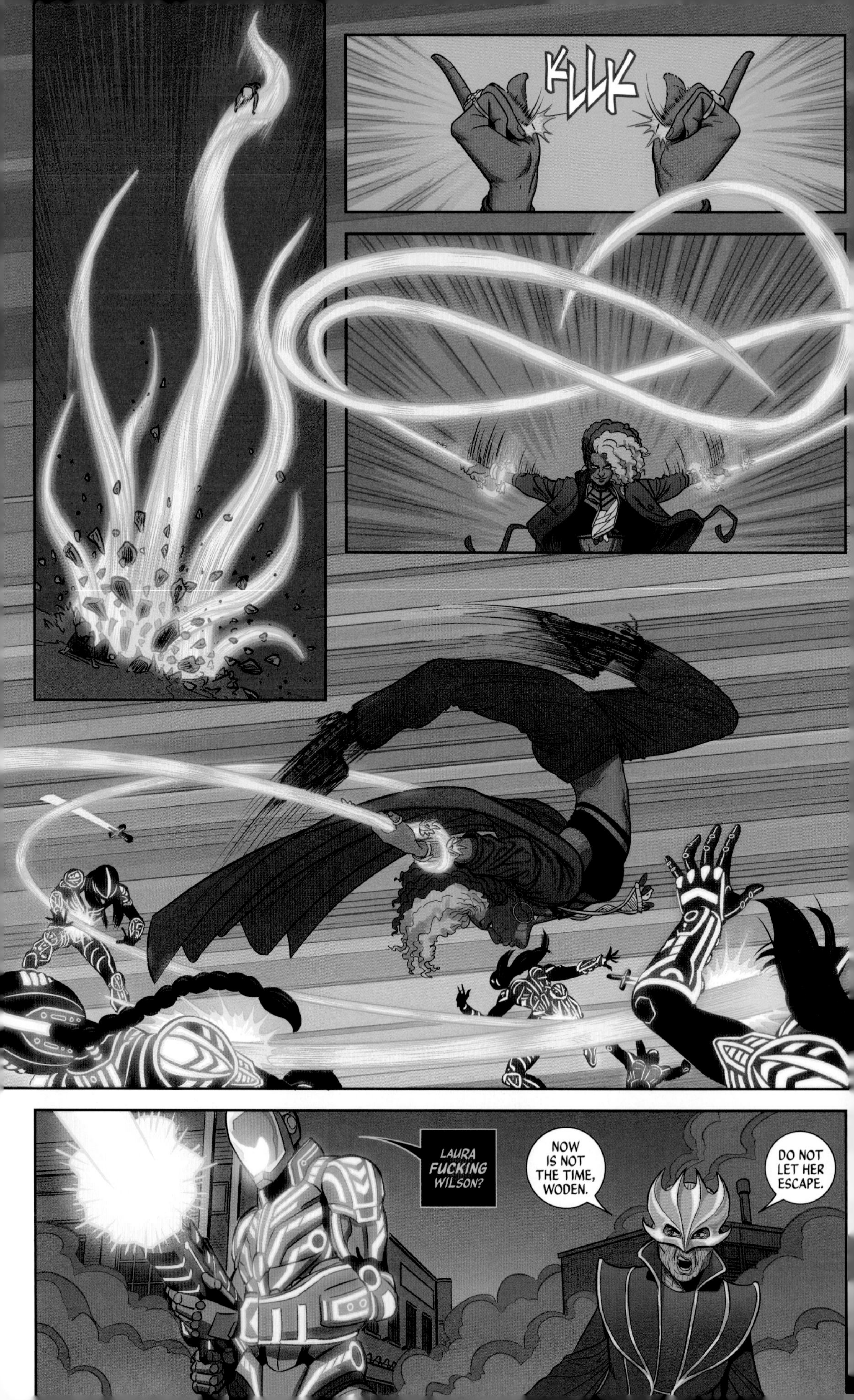
KLLK
LAURA FUCKING WILSON?
NOW IS NOT THE TIME, WODEN.
DO NOT LET HER ESCAPE.

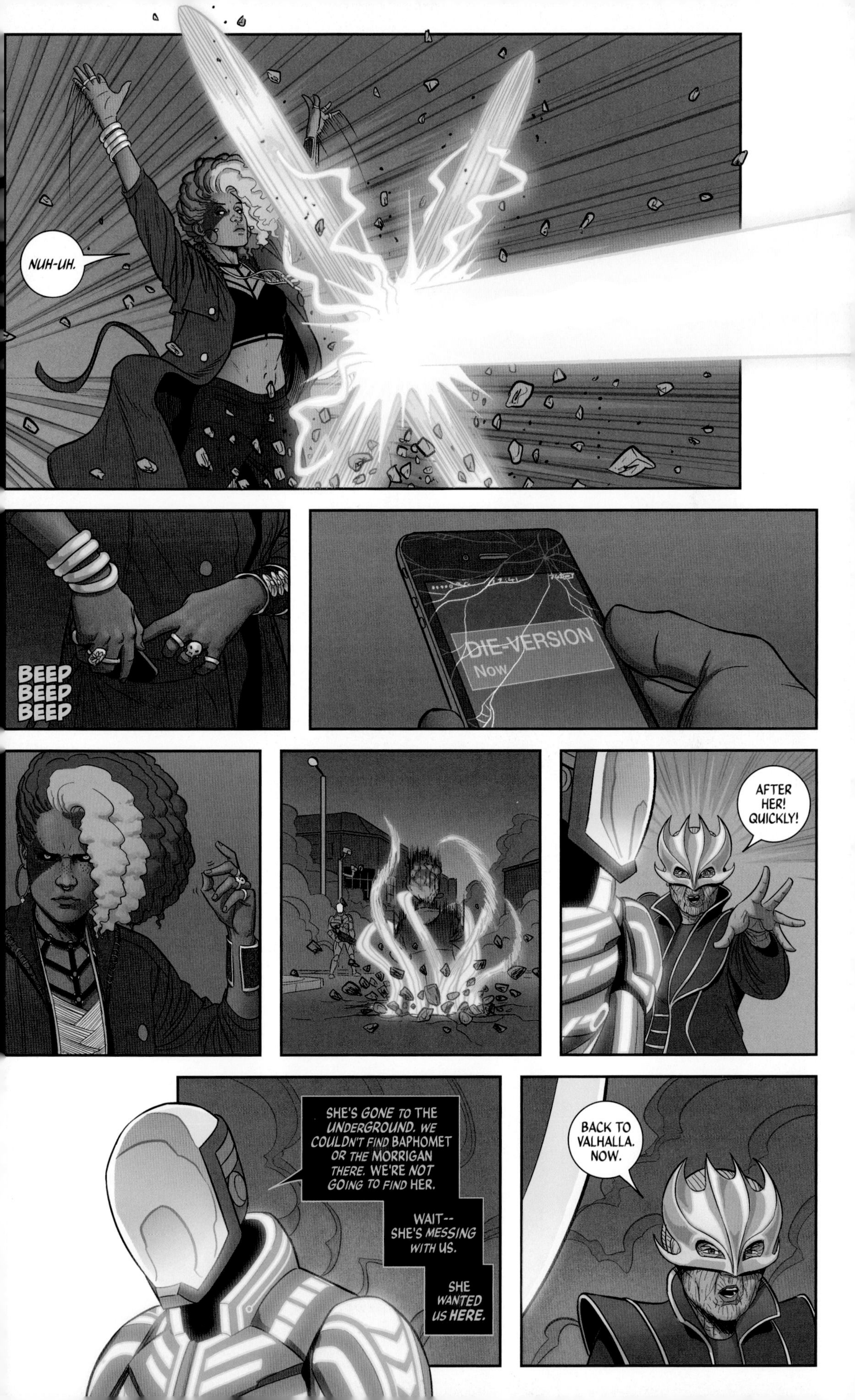
NUH-UH.
BEEP
BEEP
BEEP
DIE-VERSION
Now
AFTER HER! QUICKLY!
SHE'S GONE TO THE UNDERGROUND. WE COULDN'T FIND BAPHOMET OR THE MORRIGAN THERE. WE'RE NOT GOING TO FIND HER.
WAIT-- SHE'S MESSING WITH US.
SHE WANTED US HERE.
BACK TO VALHALLA. NOW.

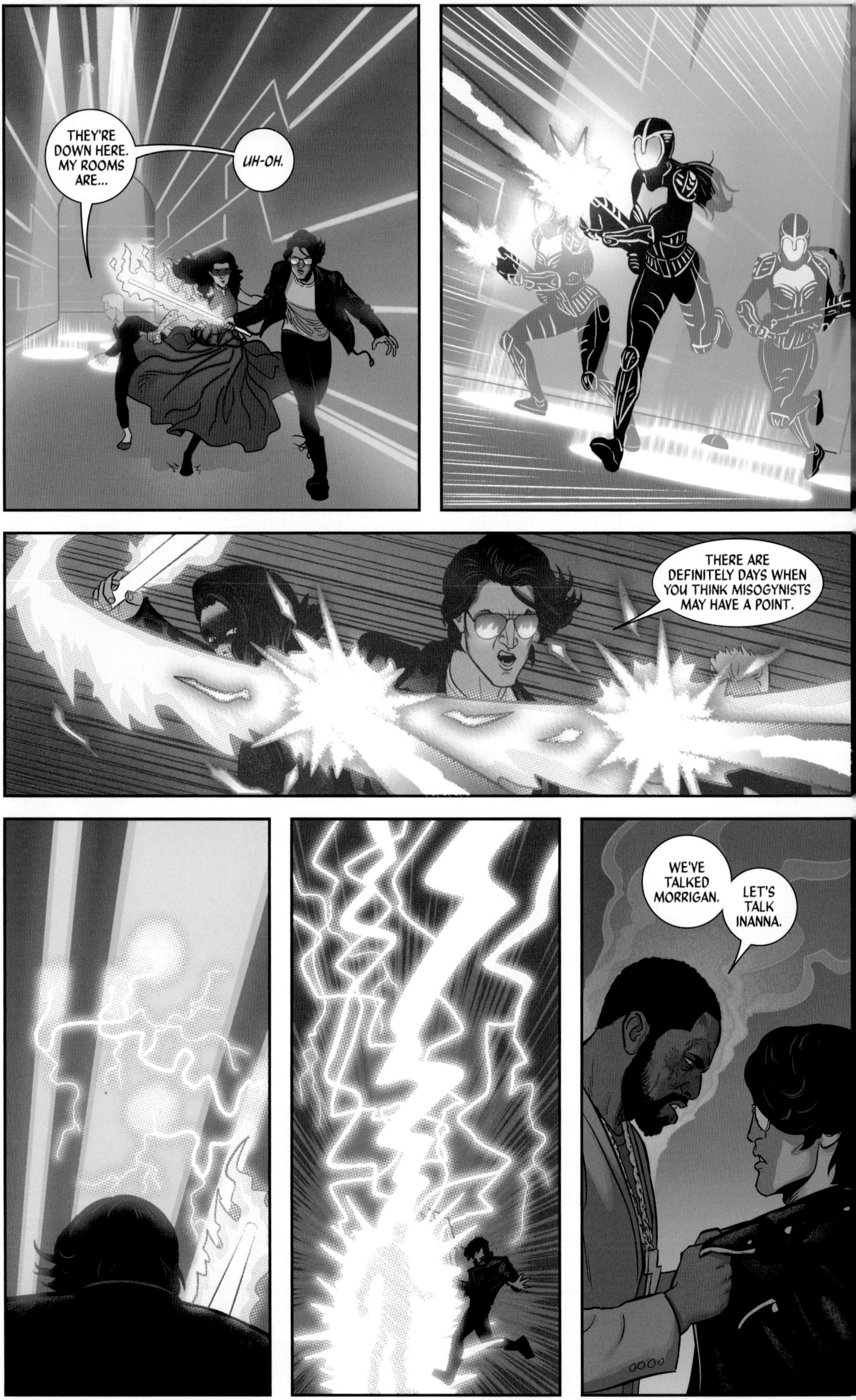
THEY'RE DOWN HERE. MY ROOMS ARE...
UH-OH.
THERE ARE DEFINITELY DAYS WHEN YOU THINK MISOGYNISTS MAY HAVE A POINT.
WE'VE TALKED MORRIGAN.
LET'S TALK INANNA.

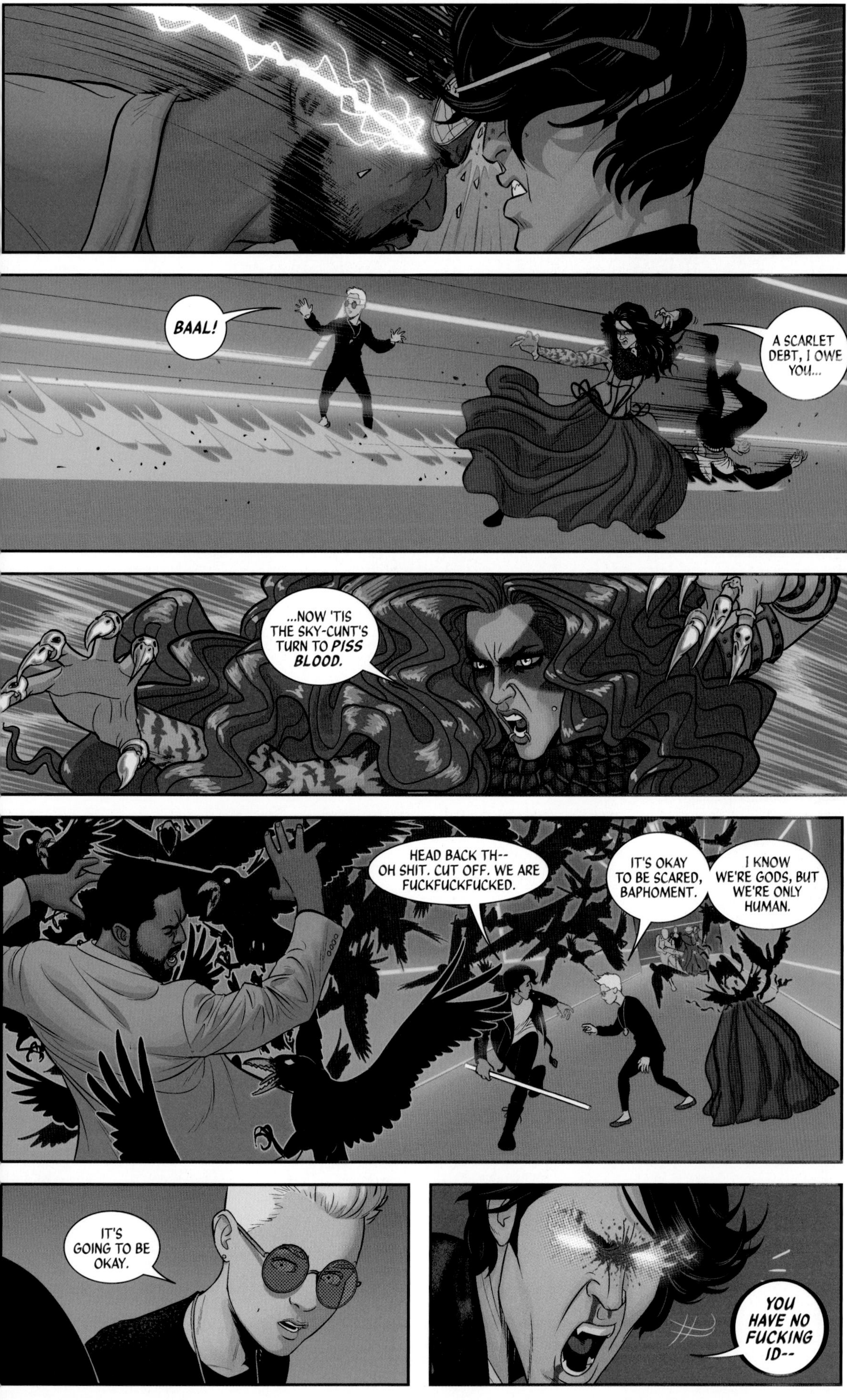
BAAL!
A SCARLET DEBT, I OWE YOU...
...NOW 'TIS THE SKY-CUNT'S TURN TO *PISS BLOOD.*
HEAD BACK TH-- OH SHIT. CUT OFF. WE ARE FUCKFUCKFUCKED.
IT'S OKAY TO BE SCARED, BAPHOMENT.
I KNOW WE'RE GODS, BUT WE'RE ONLY HUMAN.
IT'S GOING TO BE OKAY.
YOU HAVE NO FUCKING ID--

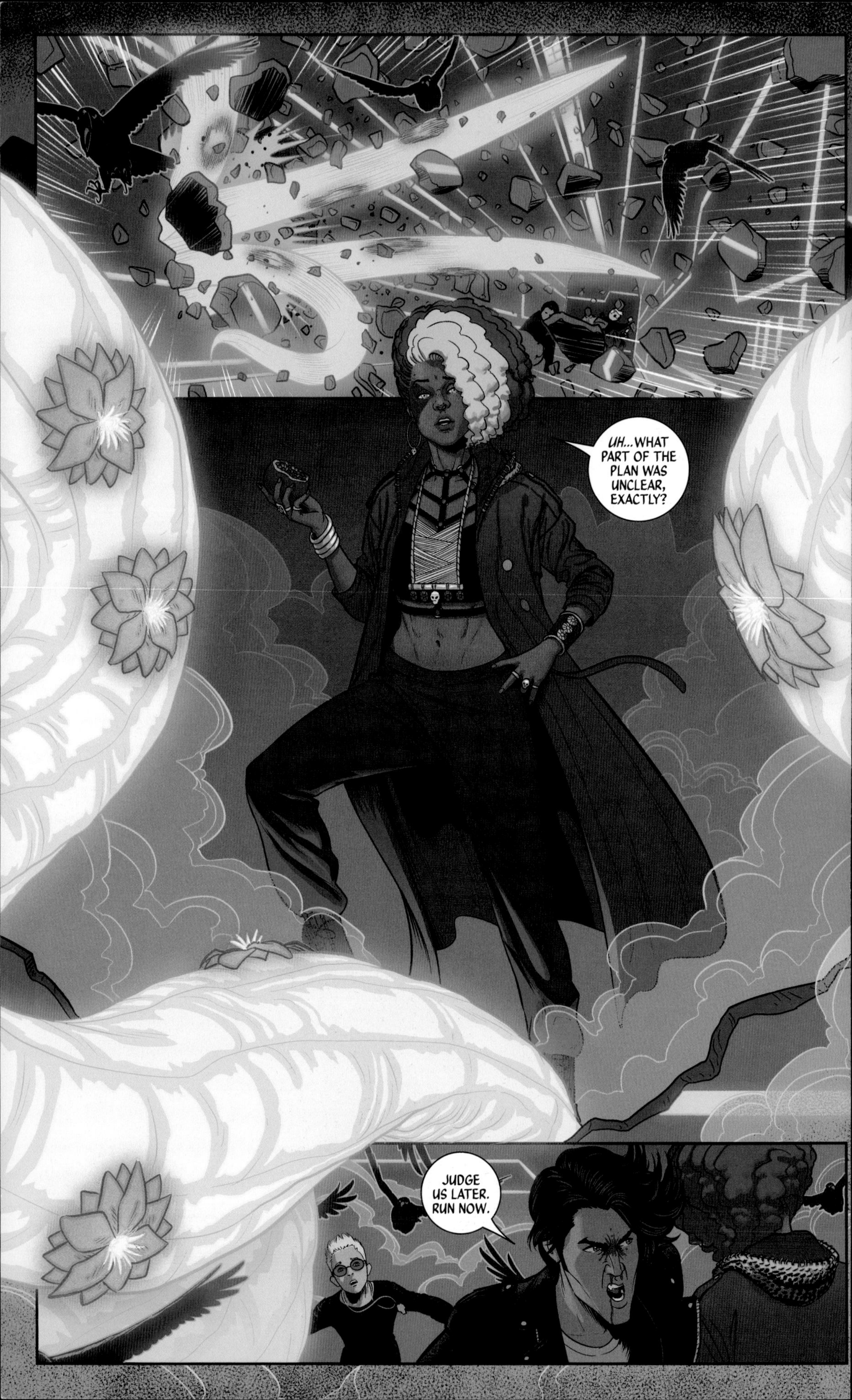
UH...WHAT PART OF THE PLAN WAS UNCLEAR, EXACTLY?
JUDGE US LATER. RUN NOW.

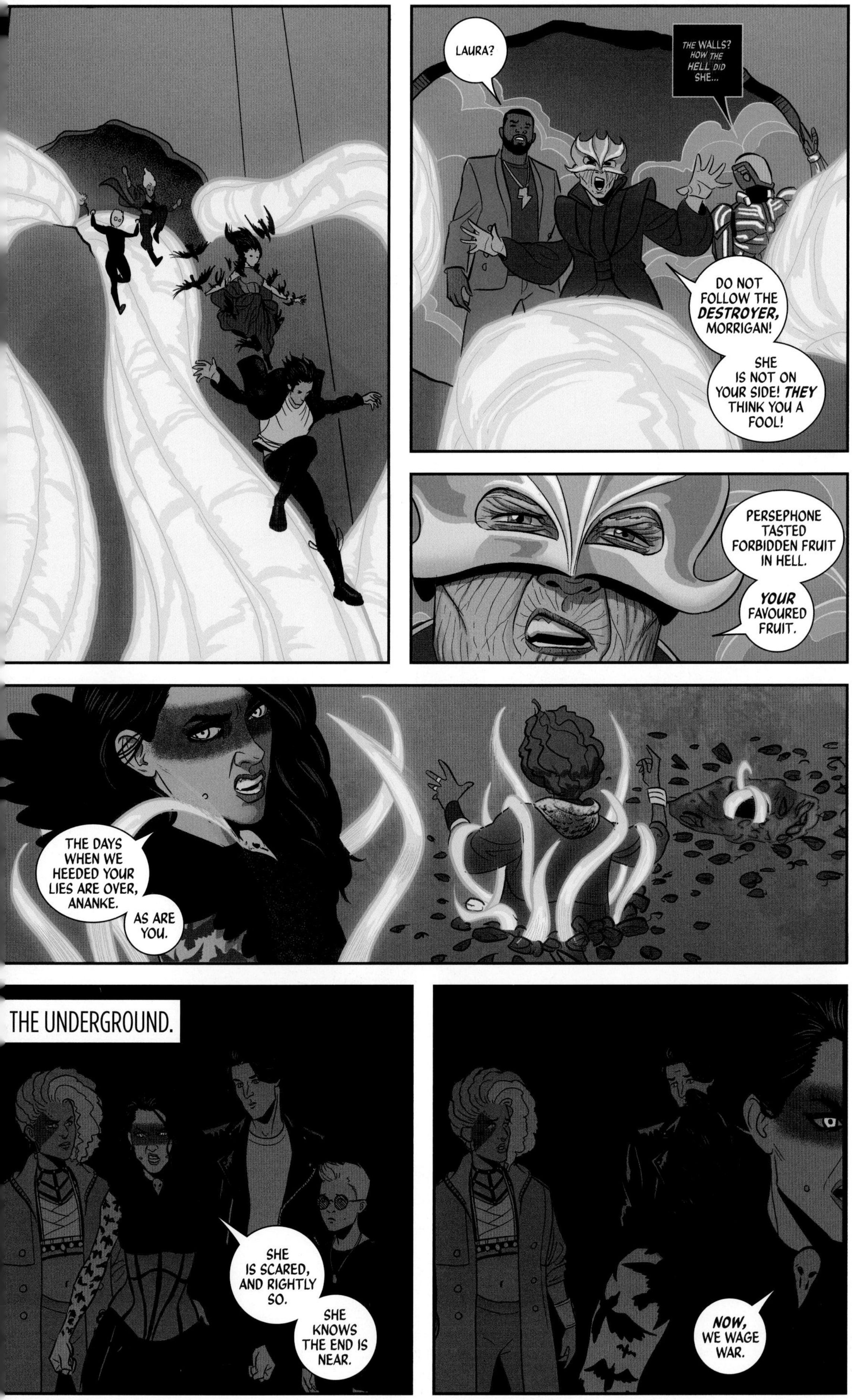
LAURA?
THE WALLS? HOW THE HELL DID SHE...
DO NOT FOLLOW THE DESTROYER, MORRIGAN!
SHE IS NOT ON YOUR SIDE! THEY THINK YOU A FOOL!
PERSEPHONE TASTED FORBIDDEN FRUIT IN HELL.
YOUR FAVOURED FRUIT.
THE DAYS WHEN WE HEEDED YOUR LIES ARE OVER, ANANKE.
AS ARE YOU.
THE UNDERGROUND.
SHE IS SCARED, AND RIGHTLY SO.
SHE KNOWS THE END IS NEAR.
NOW, WE WAGE WAR.

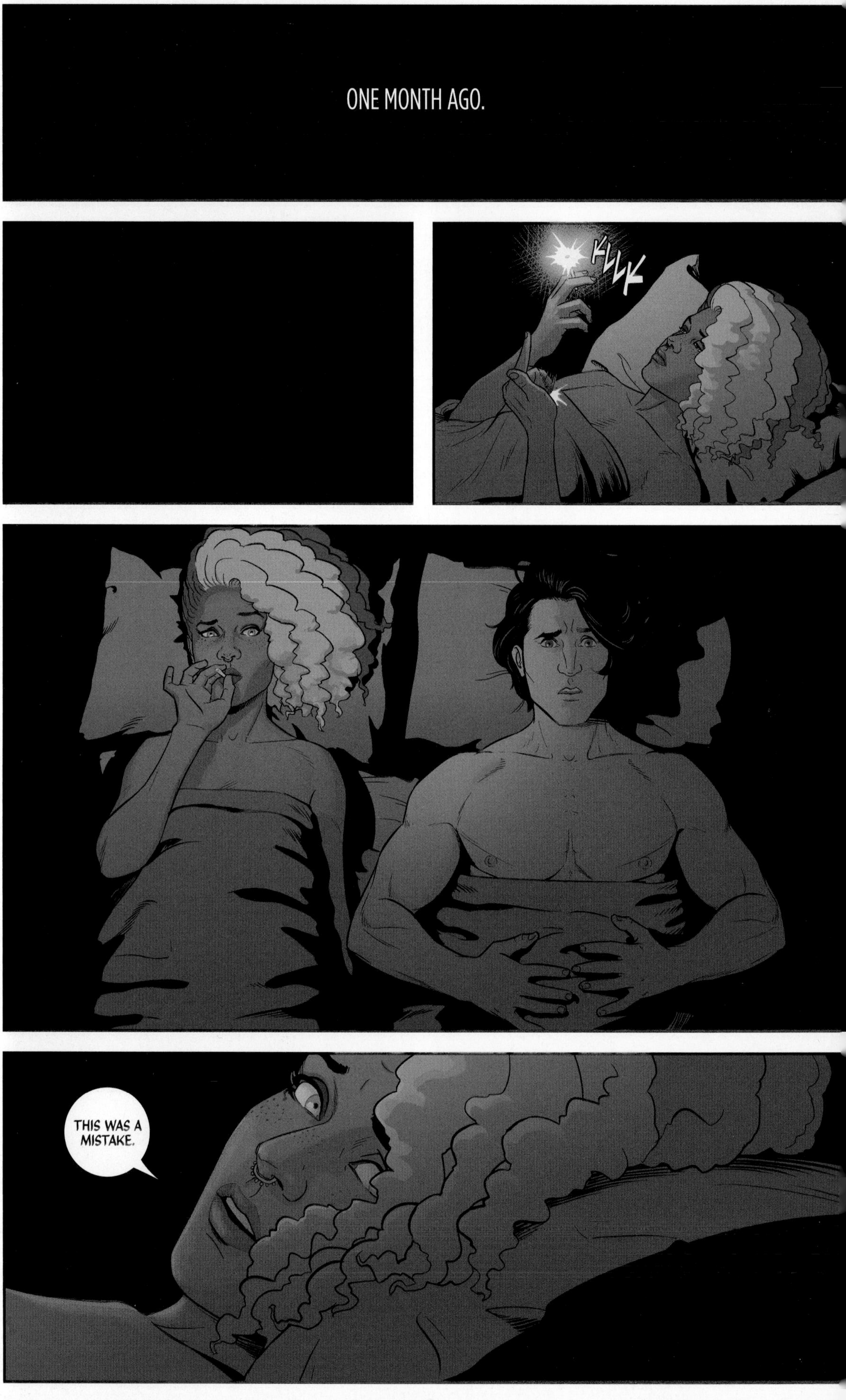
ONE MONTH AGO.
KLLK
THIS WAS A MISTAKE.

DON'T CALL IT
A COMEBACK

23 SEPTEMBER 2014

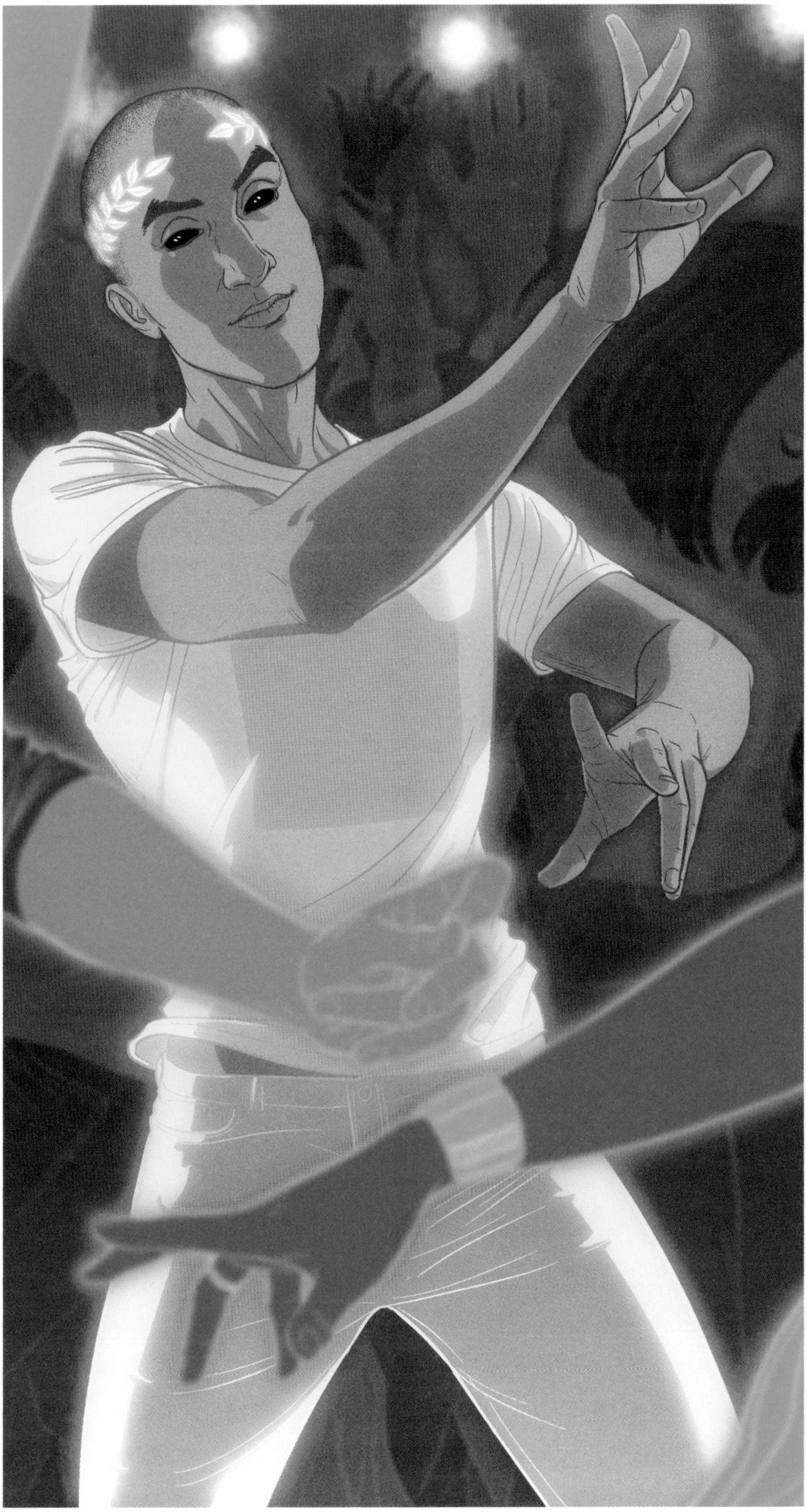

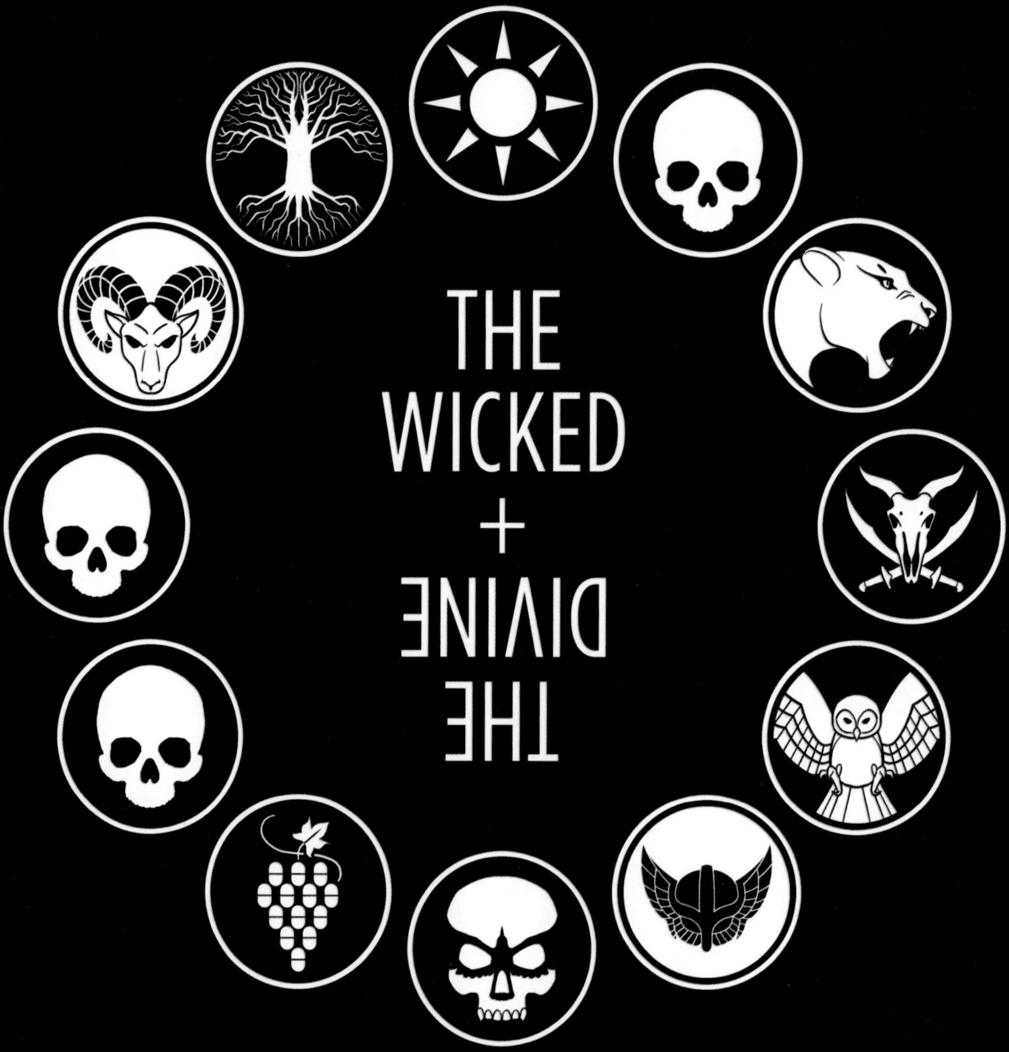
THE
WICKED
+
THE
DIVINE

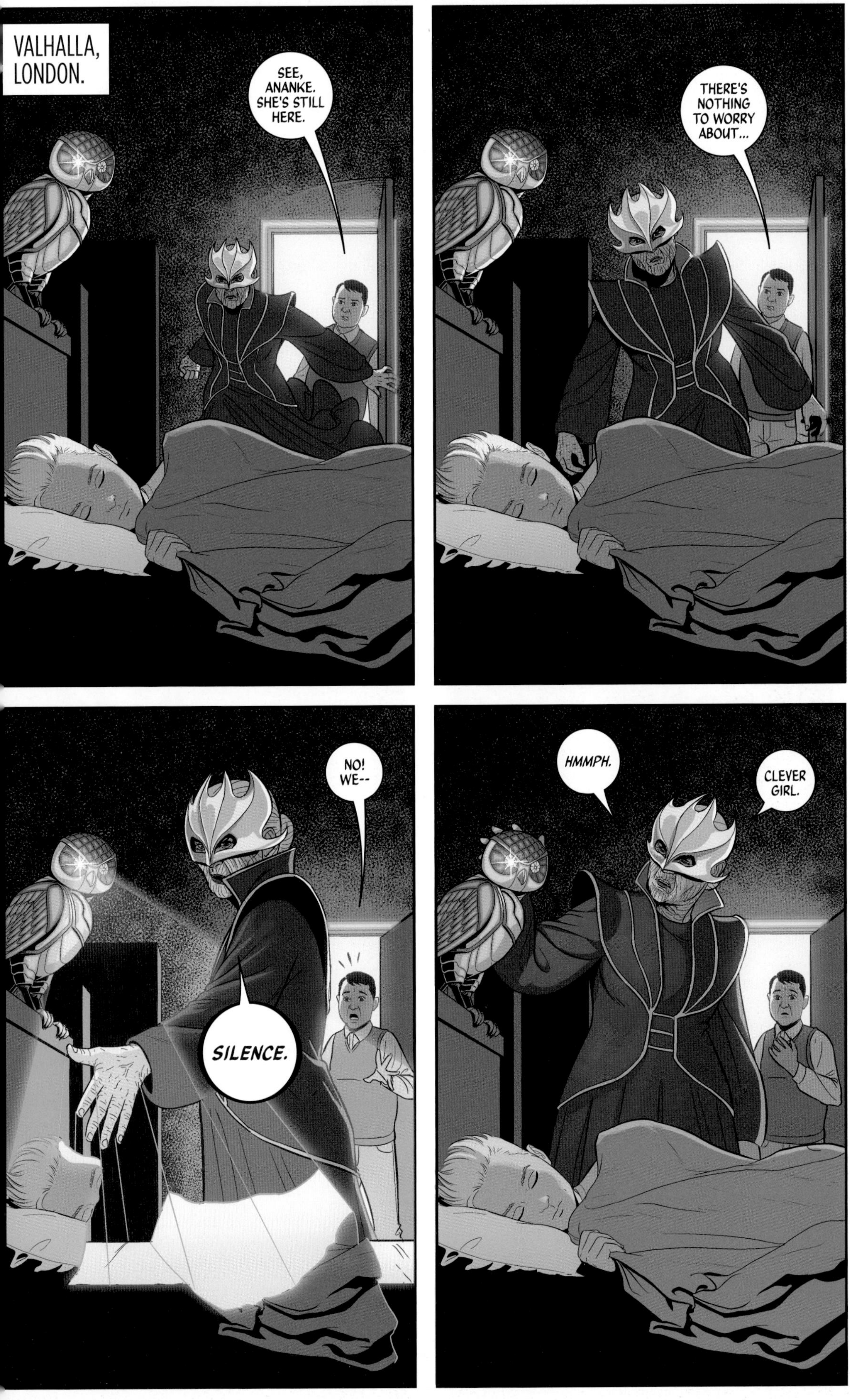
VALHALLA, LONDON.
SEE, ANANKE. SHE'S STILL HERE.
THERE'S NOTHING TO WORRY ABOUT...
NO! WE--
SILENCE.
HMMPH.
CLEVER GIRL.

WISDOM IS
MY DUMP STAT

24 SEPTEMBER 2014

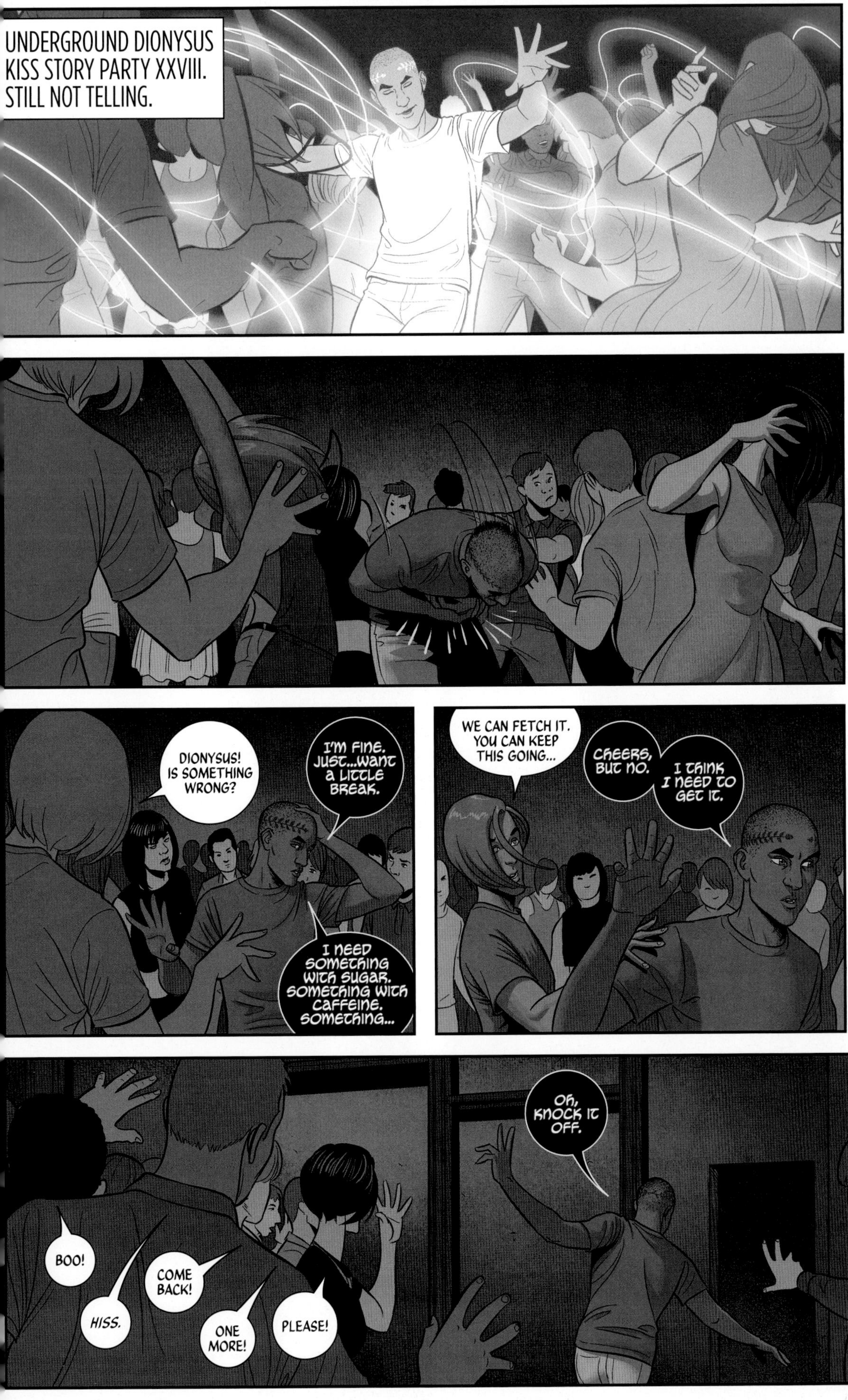
UNDERGROUND DIONYSUS KISS STORY PARTY XXVIII. STILL NOT TELLING.
DIONYSUS! IS SOMETHING WRONG?
I'M FINE. JUST...WANT A LITTLE BREAK.
I NEED SOMETHING WITH SUGAR. SOMETHING WITH CAFFEINE. SOMETHING...
WE CAN FETCH IT. YOU CAN KEEP THIS GOING...
CHEERS, BUT NO.
I THINK I NEED TO GET IT.
OH, KNOCK IT OFF.
BOO!
HISS.
COME BACK!
ONE MORE!
PLEASE!

BREAKING NEWS OF AN EXPLOSION IN HIGHBURY & ISLINGTON. NO FATALITIES HAVE BEEN REPORTED. "PANTHEON" INVOLVEMENT IS SUSPECTED.

DON'T FREAK OUT.

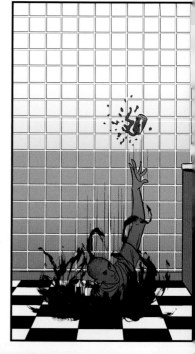

YOU FUCKER! I DROPPED MY DRINK!

I'M SORRY, DIO, BUT I'VE UNHEALTHIER THINGS FOR YOU THAN YOUR TASTE IN LIQUID SUGAR...

GIVE ME A SECOND.

HE'S CLEAN.

BAPH! WHAT'S GOING ON?

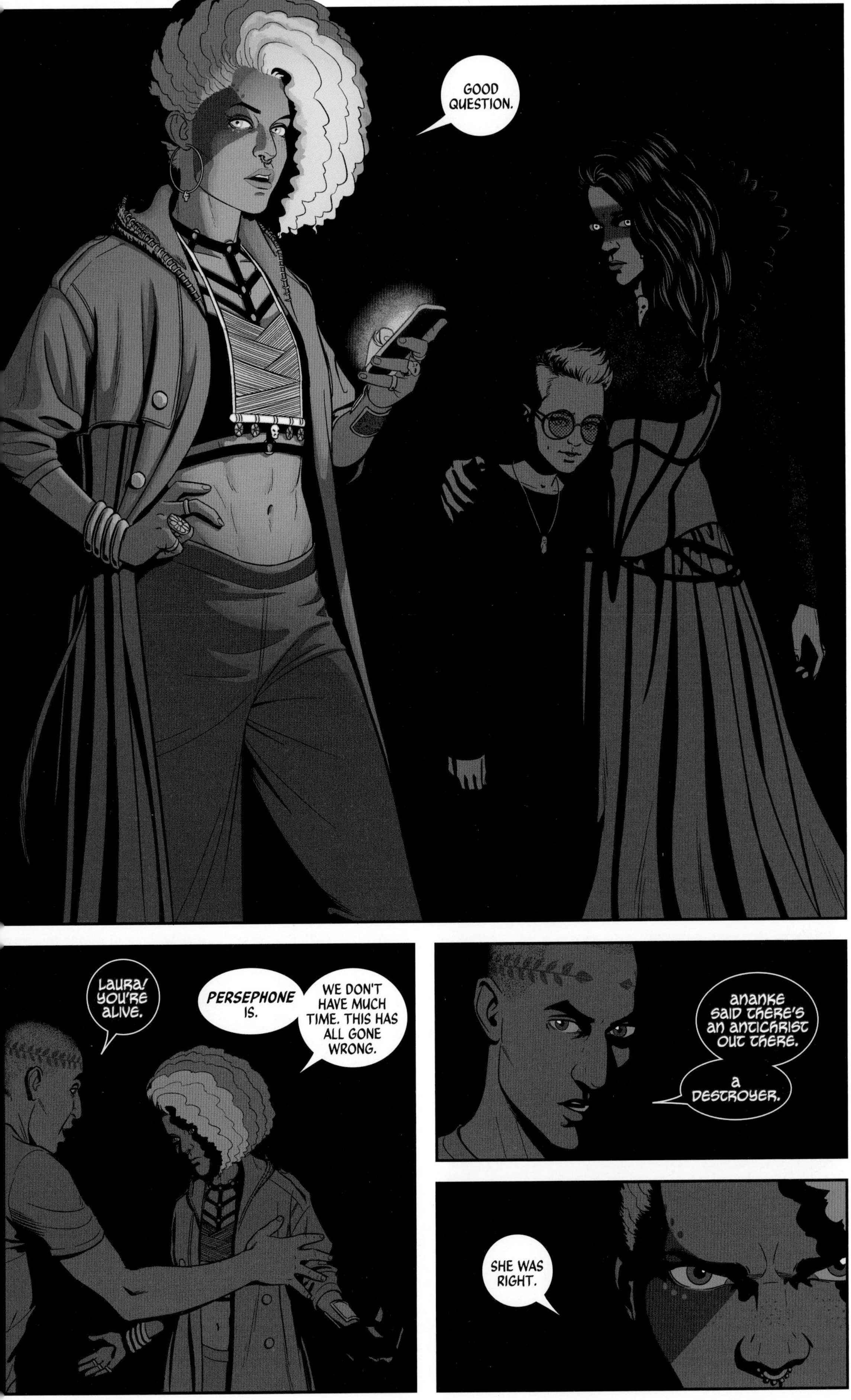
GOOD QUESTION.
LAURA! YOU'RE ALIVE.
PERSEPHONE IS.
WE DON'T HAVE MUCH TIME. THIS HAS ALL GONE WRONG.
ANANKE SAID THERE'S AN ANTICHRIST OUT THERE.
A DESTROYER.
SHE WAS RIGHT.

NECESSITY.

IT IS ALL NECESSITY.

ANANKE? *EVERYONE'S READY* FOR THE PEP TALK.

HAVE *TO SAY,* THIS *ISN'T A GOOD* TIME TO *START TALKING* TO YOURSELF.

I LIKE INTELLIGENT CONVERSATION.

GIVEN THE AVAILABLE OPTIONS, YOU CANNOT BE TOO SURPRISED IF I CHOOSE TO TALK WITH MYSELF.

WOW. *CATTY.*

WHILE WE'VE *GOT* OUR CLAWS OUT, WHEN WERE YOU *GOING* TO TELL ME THAT LAURA *WILSON* WAS ALIVE?

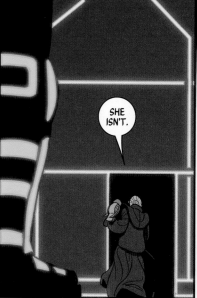

SHE ISN'T.

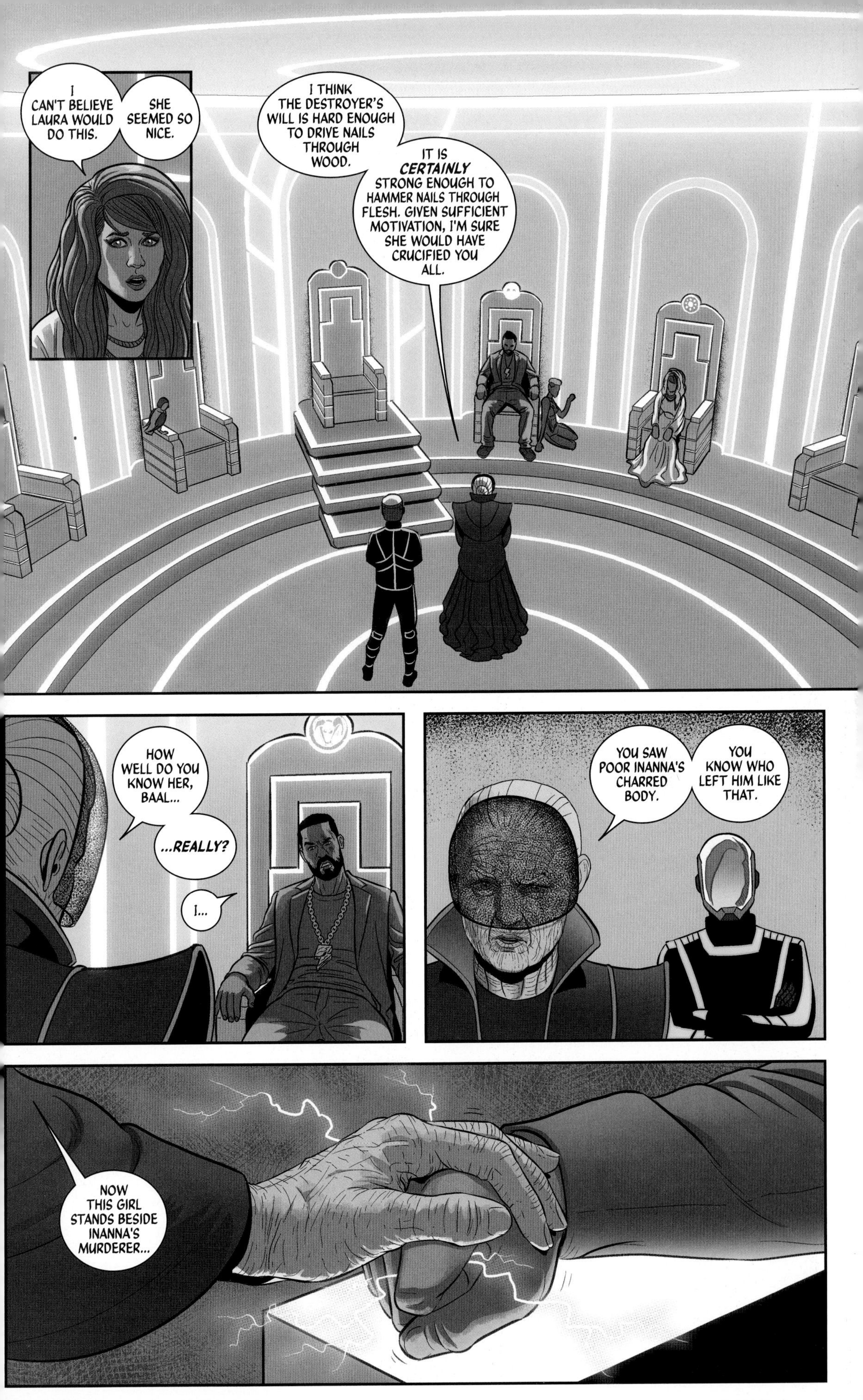

I CAN'T BELIEVE LAURA WOULD DO THIS.
SHE SEEMED SO NICE.
I THINK THE DESTROYER'S WILL IS HARD ENOUGH TO DRIVE NAILS THROUGH WOOD.
IT IS *CERTAINLY* STRONG ENOUGH TO HAMMER NAILS THROUGH FLESH. GIVEN SUFFICIENT MOTIVATION, I'M SURE SHE WOULD HAVE CRUCIFIED YOU ALL.
HOW WELL DO YOU KNOW HER, BAAL...
...REALLY?
I...
YOU SAW POOR INANNA'S CHARRED BODY.
YOU KNOW WHO LEFT HIM LIKE THAT.
NOW THIS GIRL STANDS BESIDE INANNA'S MURDERER...

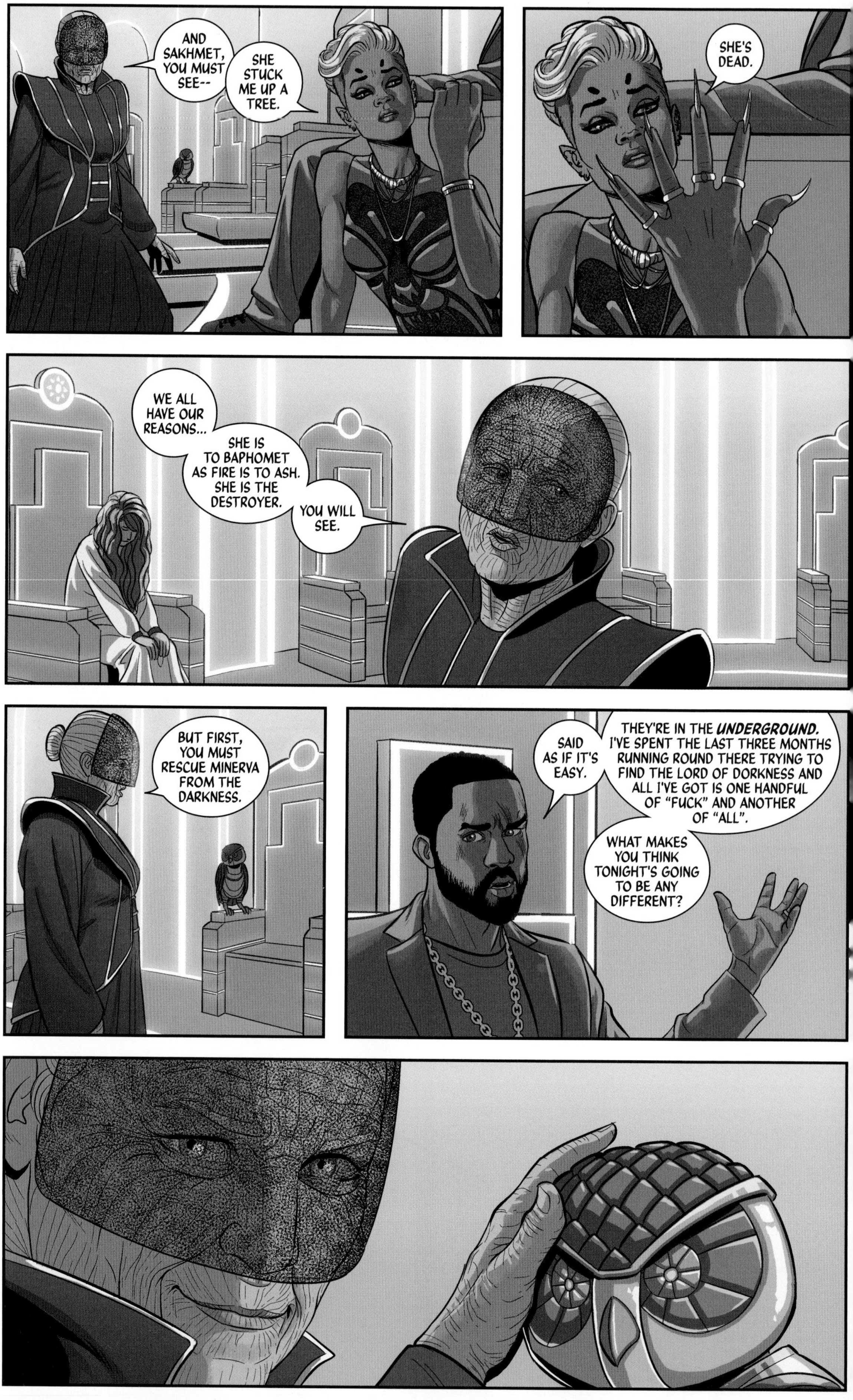
AND SAKHMET, YOU MUST SEE--
SHE STUCK ME UP A TREE.
SHE'S DEAD.
WE ALL HAVE OUR REASONS...
SHE IS TO BAPHOMET AS FIRE IS TO ASH. SHE IS THE DESTROYER.
YOU WILL SEE.
BUT FIRST, YOU MUST RESCUE MINERVA FROM THE DARKNESS.
SAID AS IF IT'S EASY.
THEY'RE IN THE *UNDERGROUND.* I'VE SPENT THE LAST THREE MONTHS RUNNING ROUND THERE TRYING TO FIND THE LORD OF DORKNESS AND ALL I'VE GOT IS ONE HANDFUL OF "FUCK" AND ANOTHER OF "ALL".
WHAT MAKES YOU THINK TONIGHT'S GOING TO BE ANY DIFFERENT?

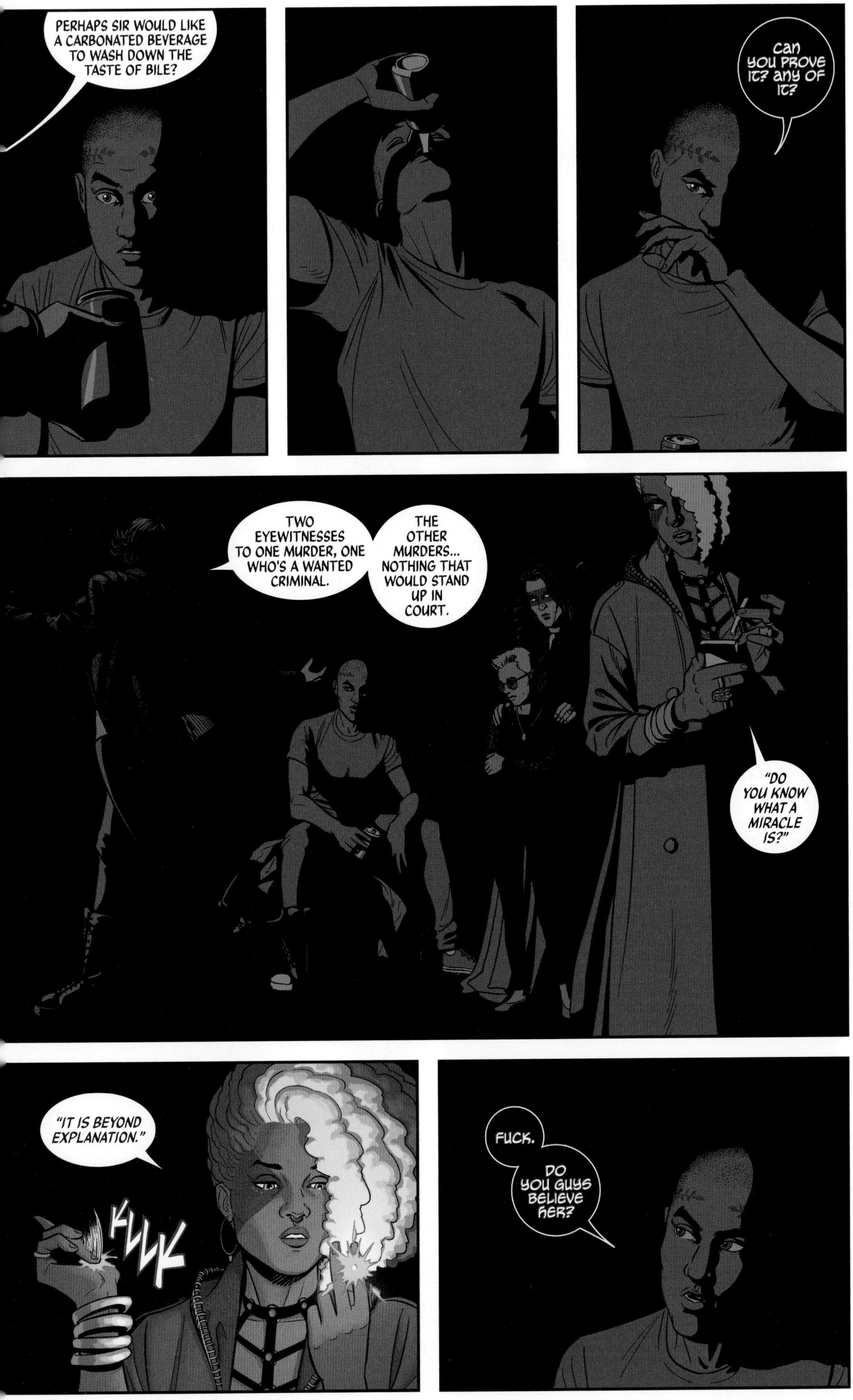
PERHAPS SIR WOULD LIKE A CARBONATED BEVERAGE TO WASH DOWN THE TASTE OF BILE?
CAN YOU PROVE IT? ANY OF IT?
TWO EYEWITNESSES TO ONE MURDER, ONE WHO'S A WANTED CRIMINAL.
THE OTHER MURDERS... NOTHING THAT WOULD STAND UP IN COURT.
"DO YOU KNOW WHAT A MIRACLE IS?"
"IT IS BEYOND EXPLANATION."
KLIK
FUCK.
DO YOU GUYS BELIEVE HER?

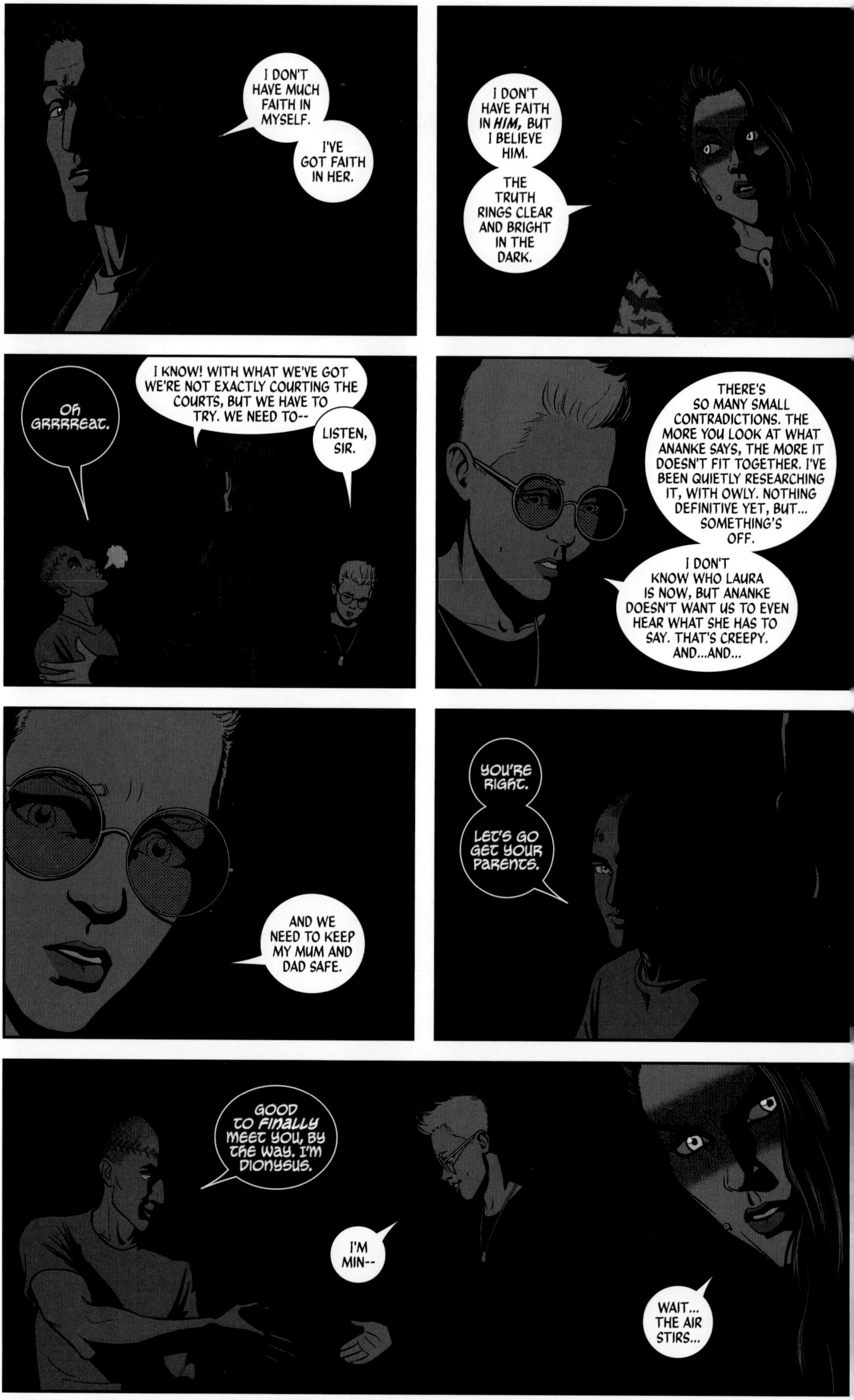
I DON'T HAVE MUCH FAITH IN MYSELF.
I'VE GOT FAITH IN HER.
I DON'T HAVE FAITH IN HIM, BUT I BELIEVE HIM.
THE TRUTH RINGS CLEAR AND BRIGHT IN THE DARK.
OH GRRRREAT.
I KNOW! WITH WHAT WE'VE GOT WE'RE NOT EXACTLY COURTING THE COURTS, BUT WE HAVE TO TRY. WE NEED TO--
LISTEN, SIR.
THERE'S SO MANY SMALL CONTRADICTIONS. THE MORE YOU LOOK AT WHAT ANANKE SAYS, THE MORE IT DOESN'T FIT TOGETHER. I'VE BEEN QUIETLY RESEARCHING IT, WITH OWLY. NOTHING DEFINITIVE YET, BUT... SOMETHING'S OFF.
I DON'T KNOW WHO LAURA IS NOW, BUT ANANKE DOESN'T WANT US TO EVEN HEAR WHAT SHE HAS TO SAY. THAT'S CREEPY. AND...AND...
AND WE NEED TO KEEP MY MUM AND DAD SAFE.
YOU'RE RIGHT.
LET'S GO GET YOUR PARENTS.
GOOD TO FINALLY MEET YOU, BY THE WAY. I'M DIONYSUS.
I'M MIN--
WAIT... THE AIR STIRS...

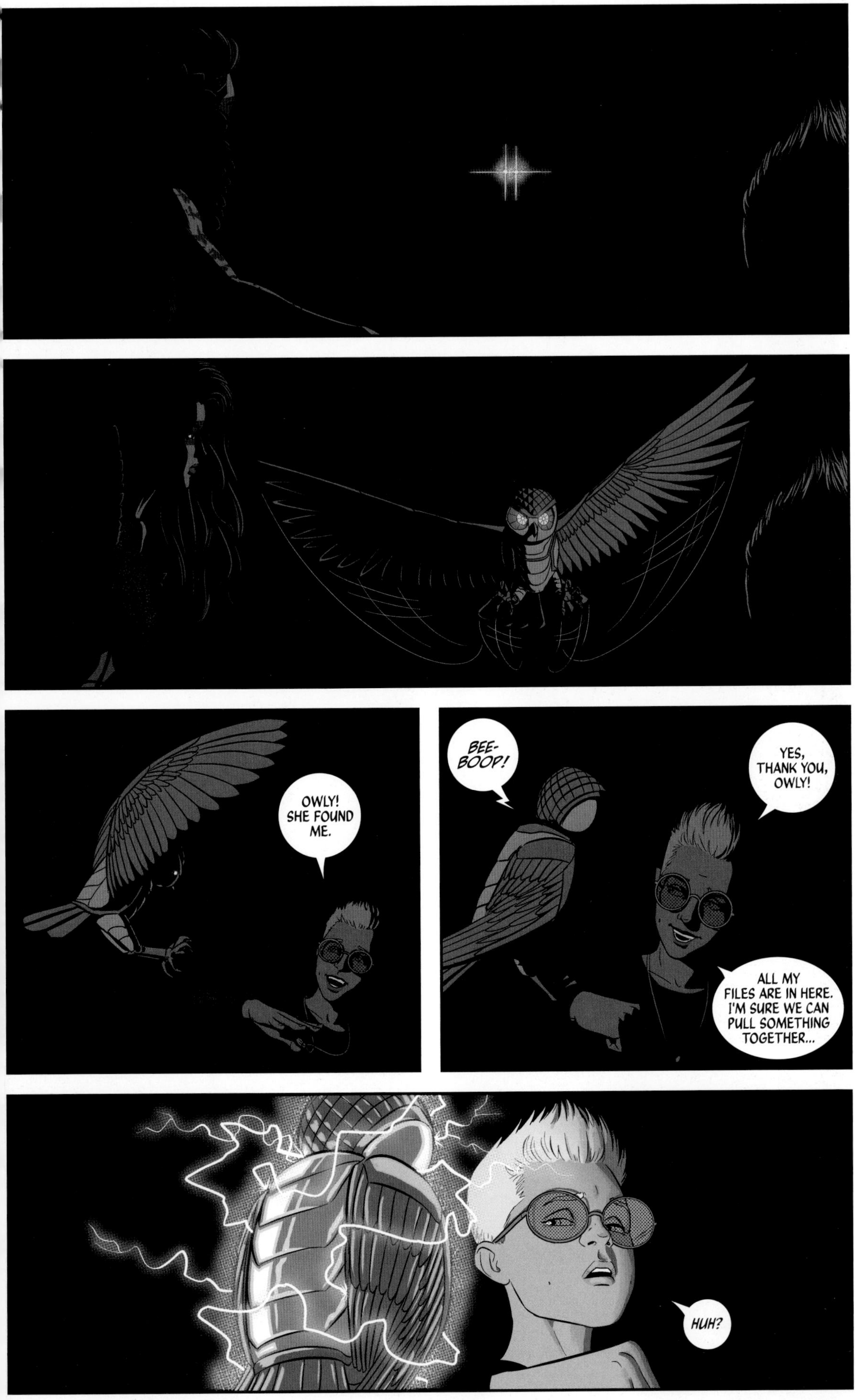
OWLY! SHE FOUND ME.
BEE-BOOP!
YES, THANK YOU, OWLY!
ALL MY FILES ARE IN HERE. I'M SURE WE CAN PULL SOMETHING TOGETHER...
HUH?

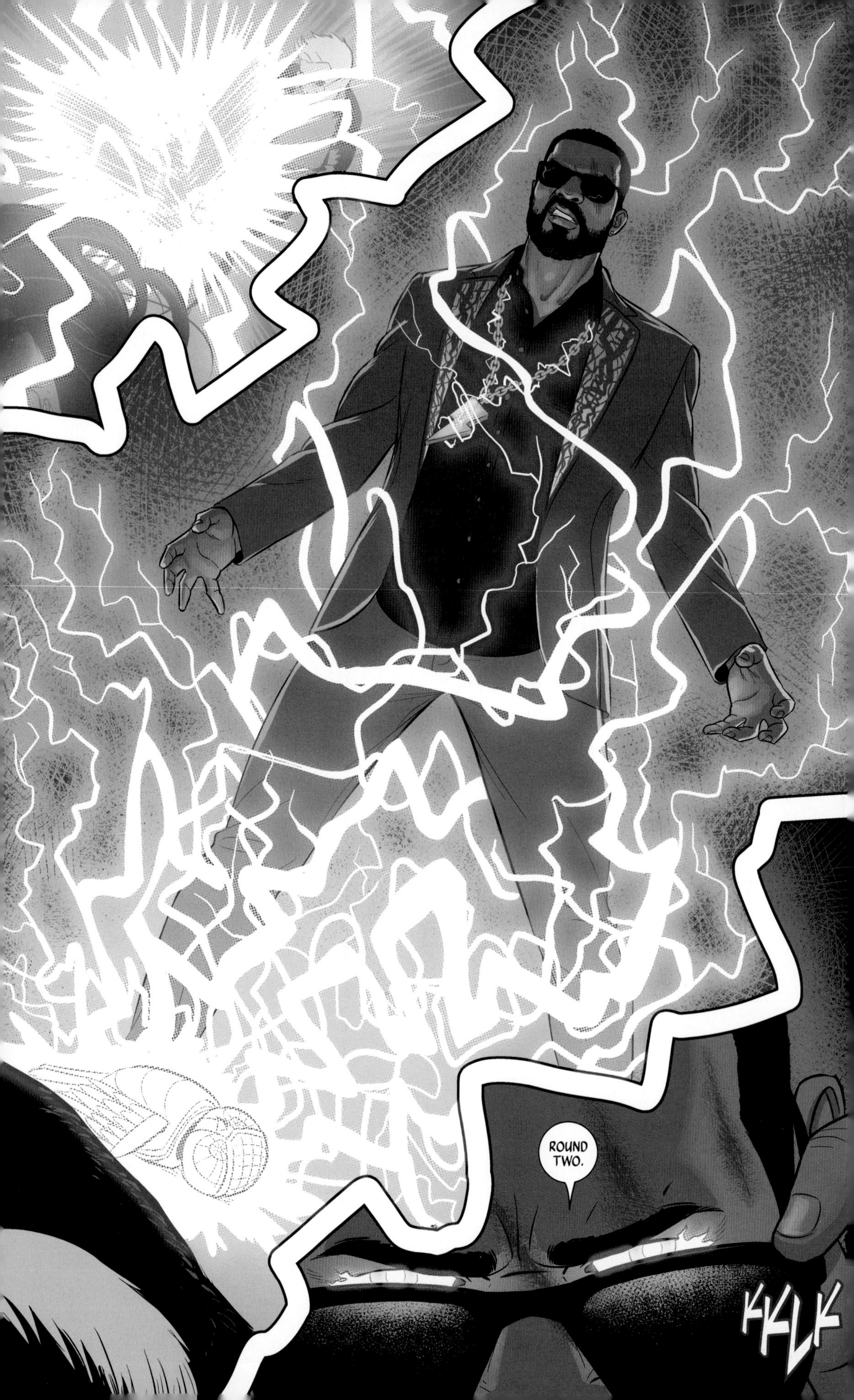
ROUND TWO.
KKLK

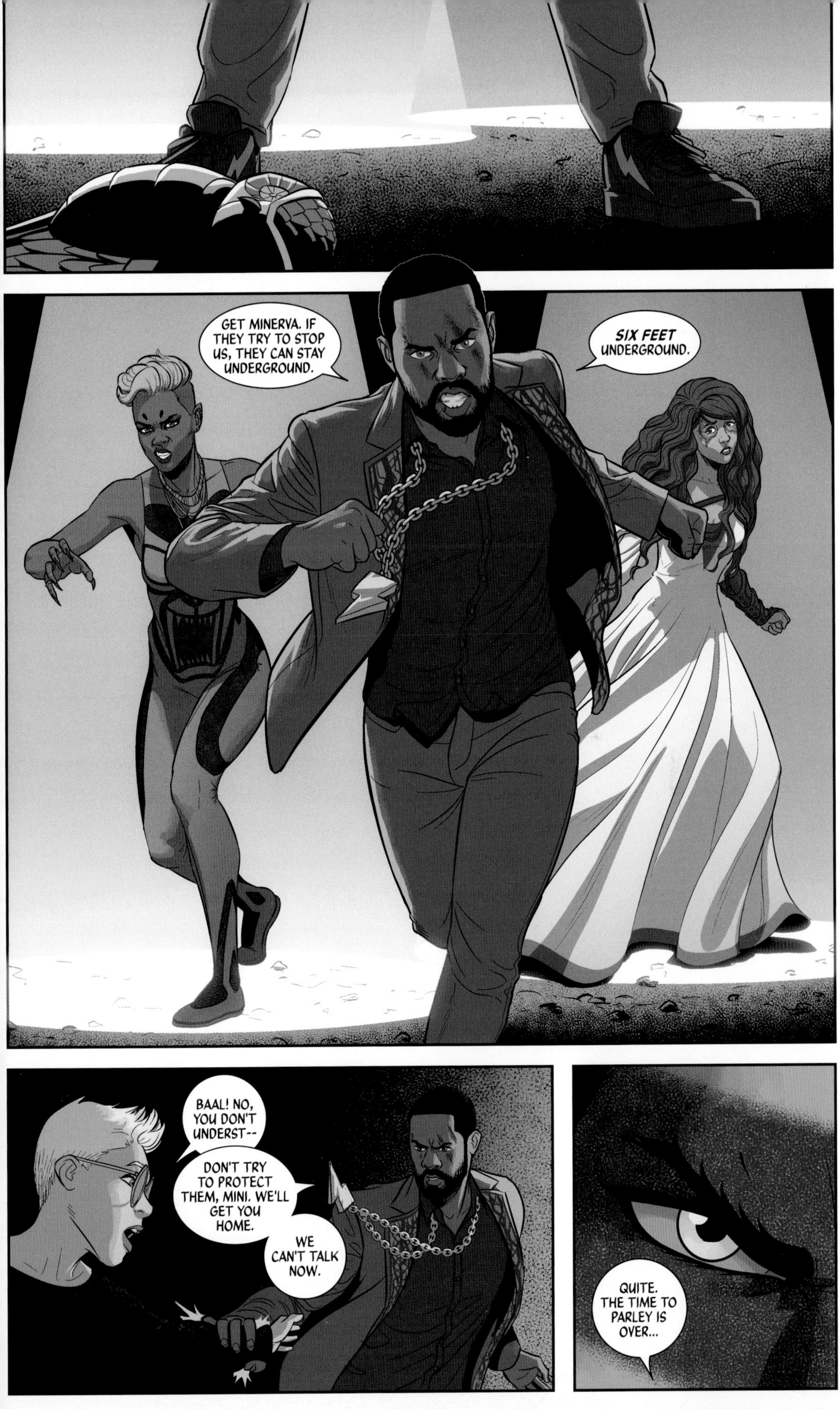
GET MINERVA. IF THEY TRY TO STOP US, THEY CAN STAY UNDERGROUND.
SIX FEET UNDERGROUND.
BAAL! NO, YOU DON'T UNDERST--
DON'T TRY TO PROTECT THEM, MINI. WE'LL GET YOU HOME.
WE CAN'T TALK NOW.
QUITE. THE TIME TO PARLEY IS OVER...

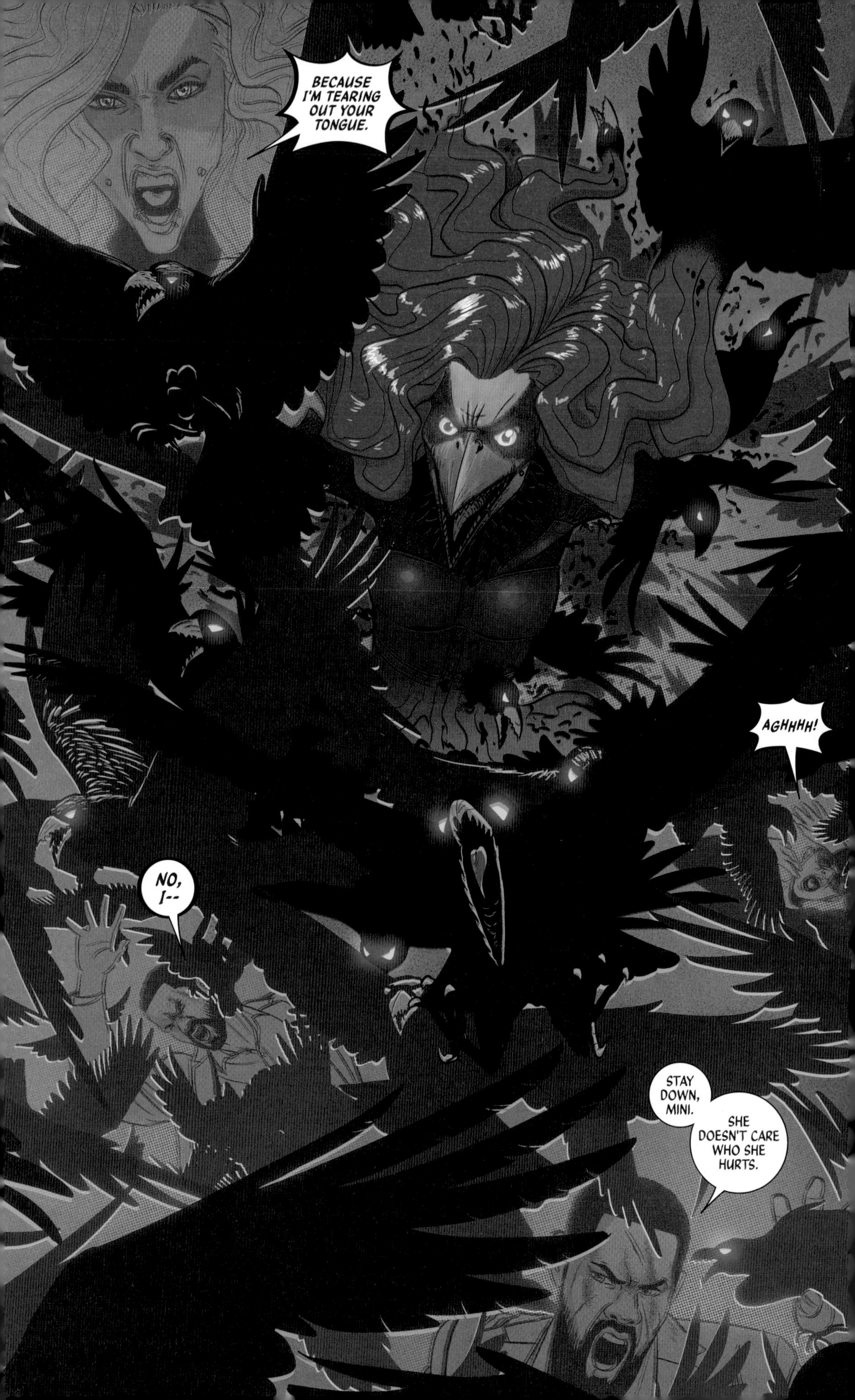
BECAUSE I'M TEARING OUT YOUR TONGUE.
AGHHHH!
NO, I--
STAY DOWN, MINI.
SHE DOESN'T CARE WHO SHE HURTS.

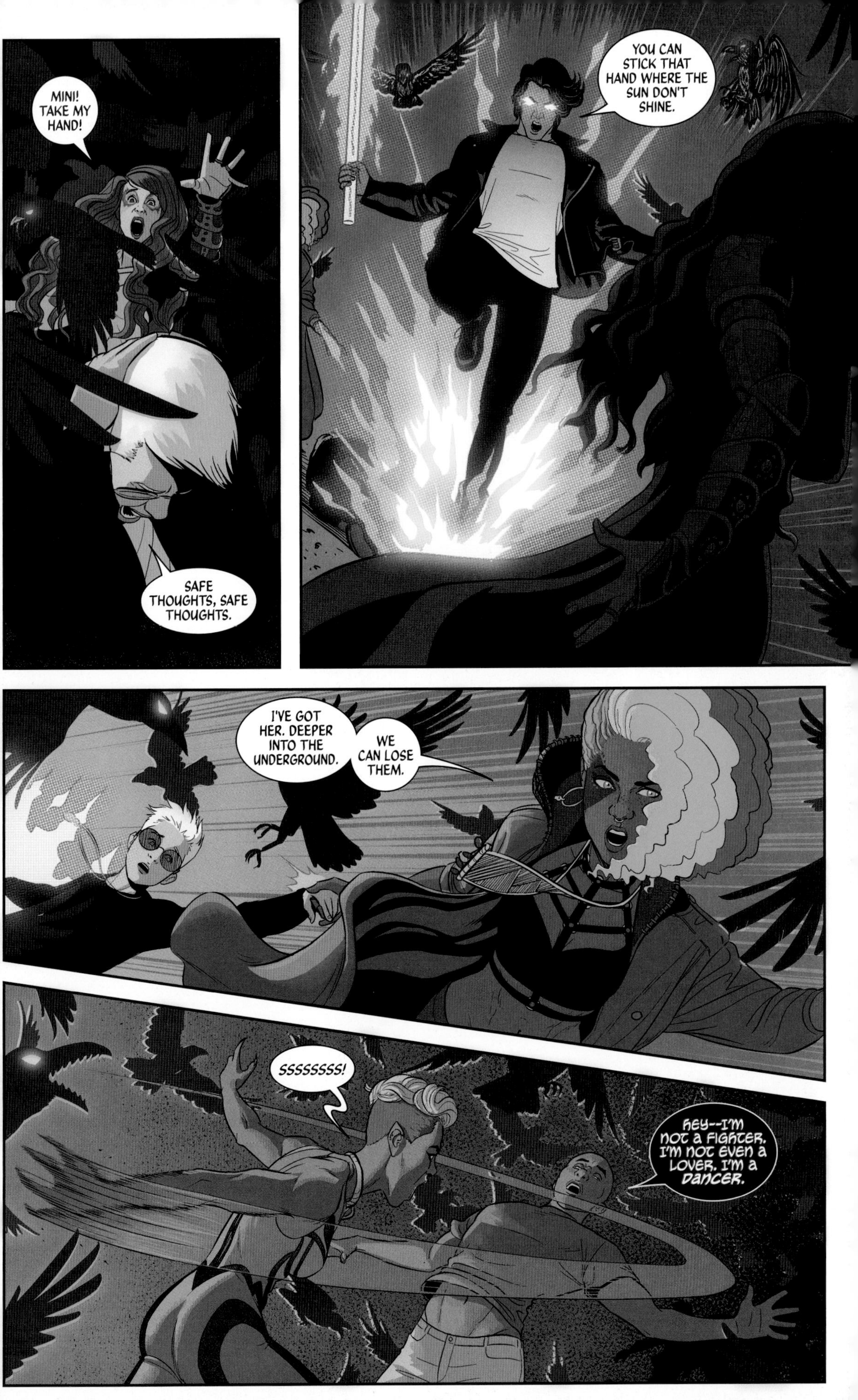

MINI! TAKE MY HAND!
SAFE THOUGHTS, SAFE THOUGHTS.
YOU CAN STICK THAT HAND WHERE THE SUN DON'T SHINE.
I'VE GOT HER. DEEPER INTO THE UNDERGROUND.
WE CAN LOSE THEM.
SSSSSSSS!
HEY--I'M NOT A FIGHTER. I'M NOT EVEN A LOVER. I'M A DANCER.

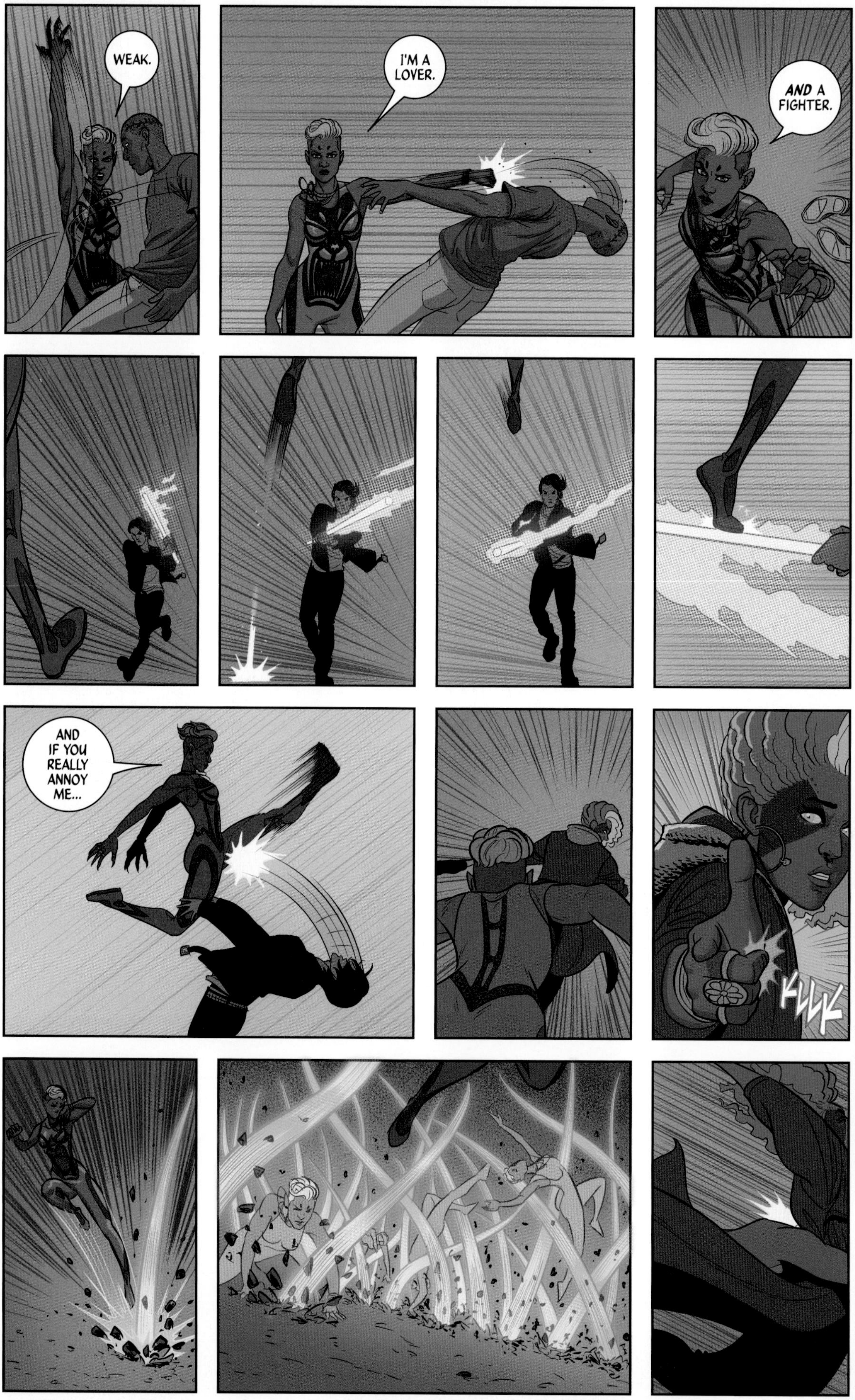
WEAK.
I'M A LOVER.
AND A FIGHTER.
AND IF YOU REALLY ANNOY ME...
KLLK

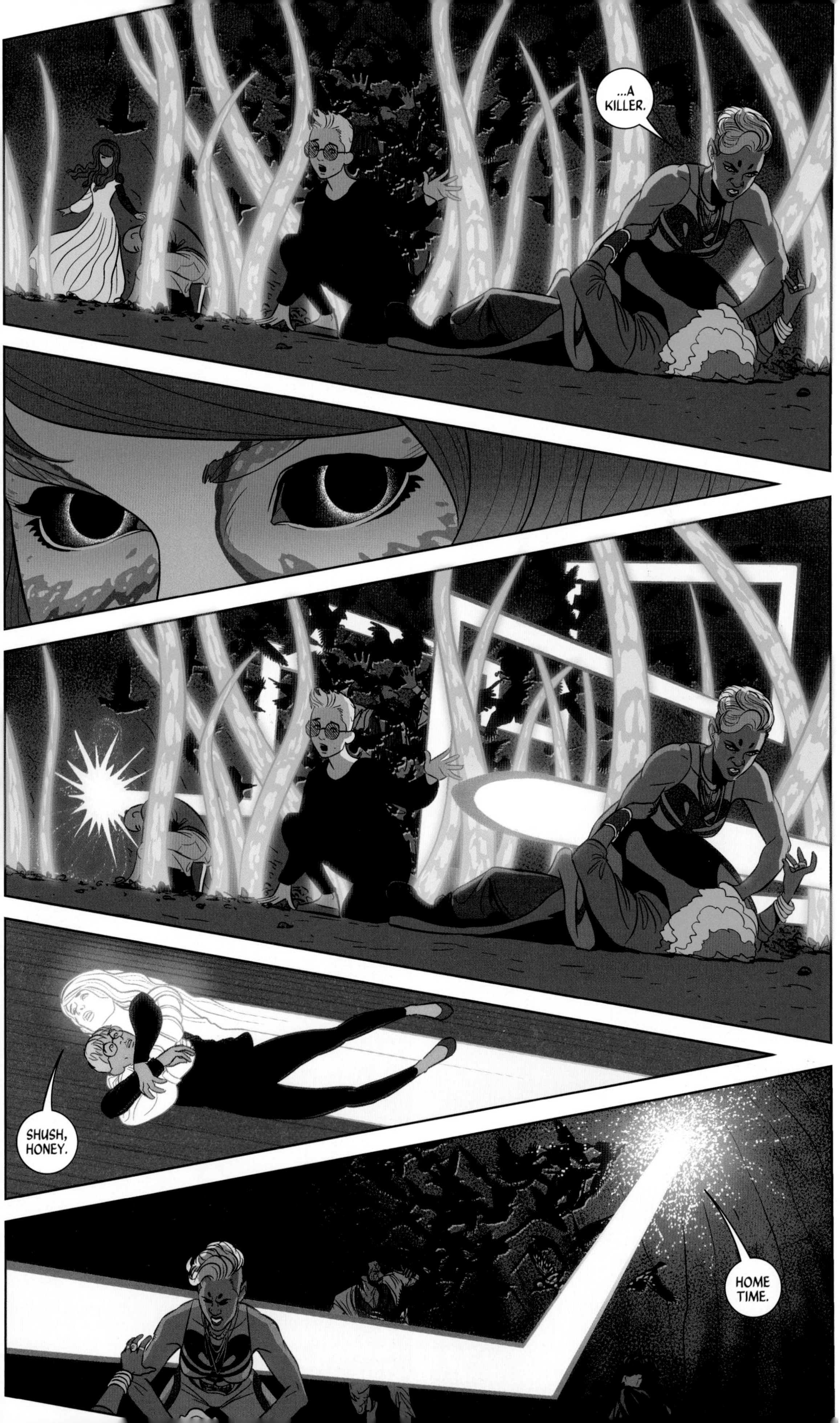
...A KILLER.
SHUSH, HONEY.
HOME TIME.

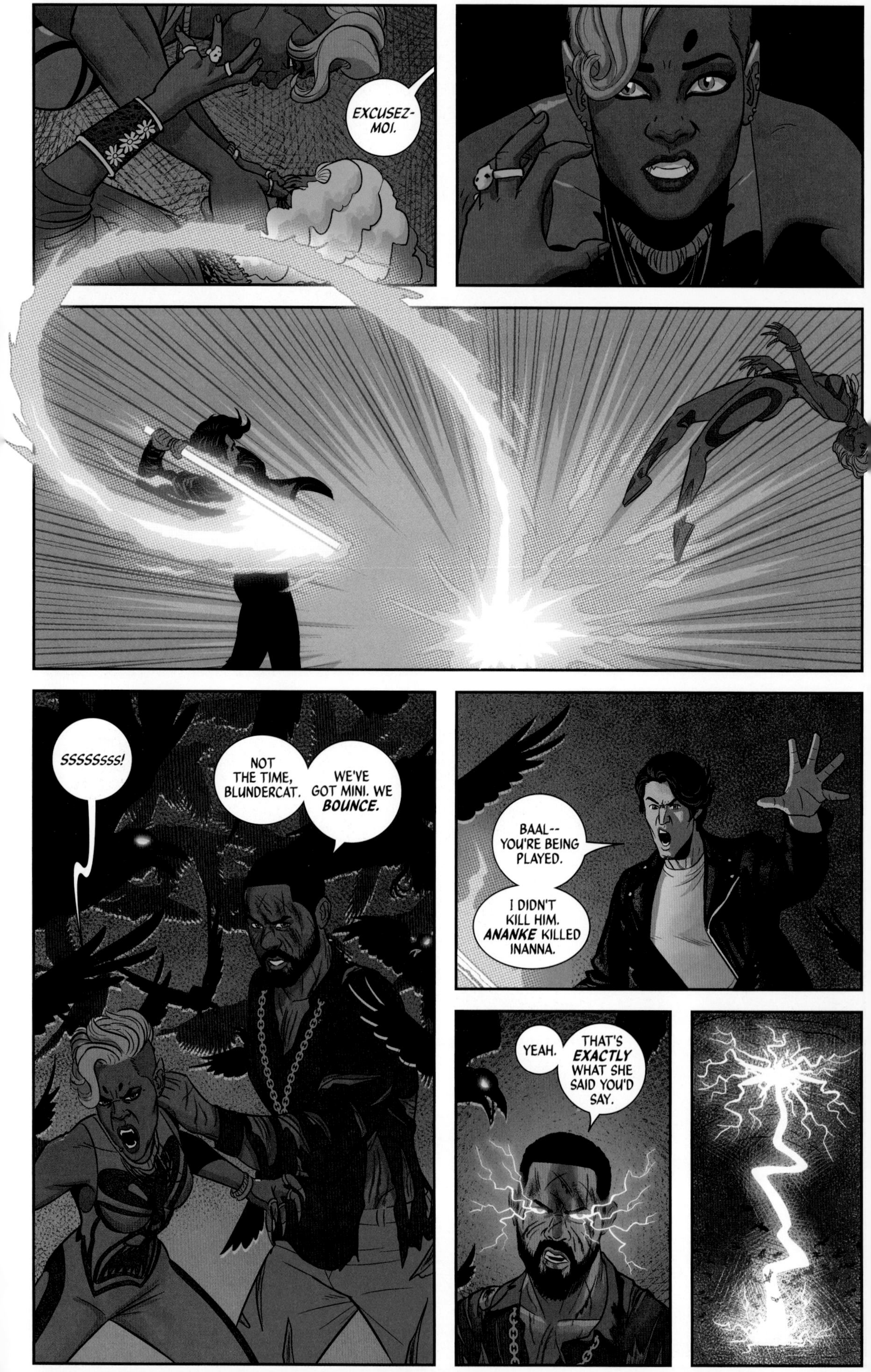
EXCUSEZ-MOI.
SSSSSSSS!
NOT THE TIME, BLUNDERCAT.
WE'VE GOT MINI. WE BOUNCE.
BAAL-- YOU'RE BEING PLAYED.
I DIDN'T KILL HIM. ANANKE KILLED INANNA.
YEAH.
THAT'S EXACTLY WHAT SHE SAID YOU'D SAY.

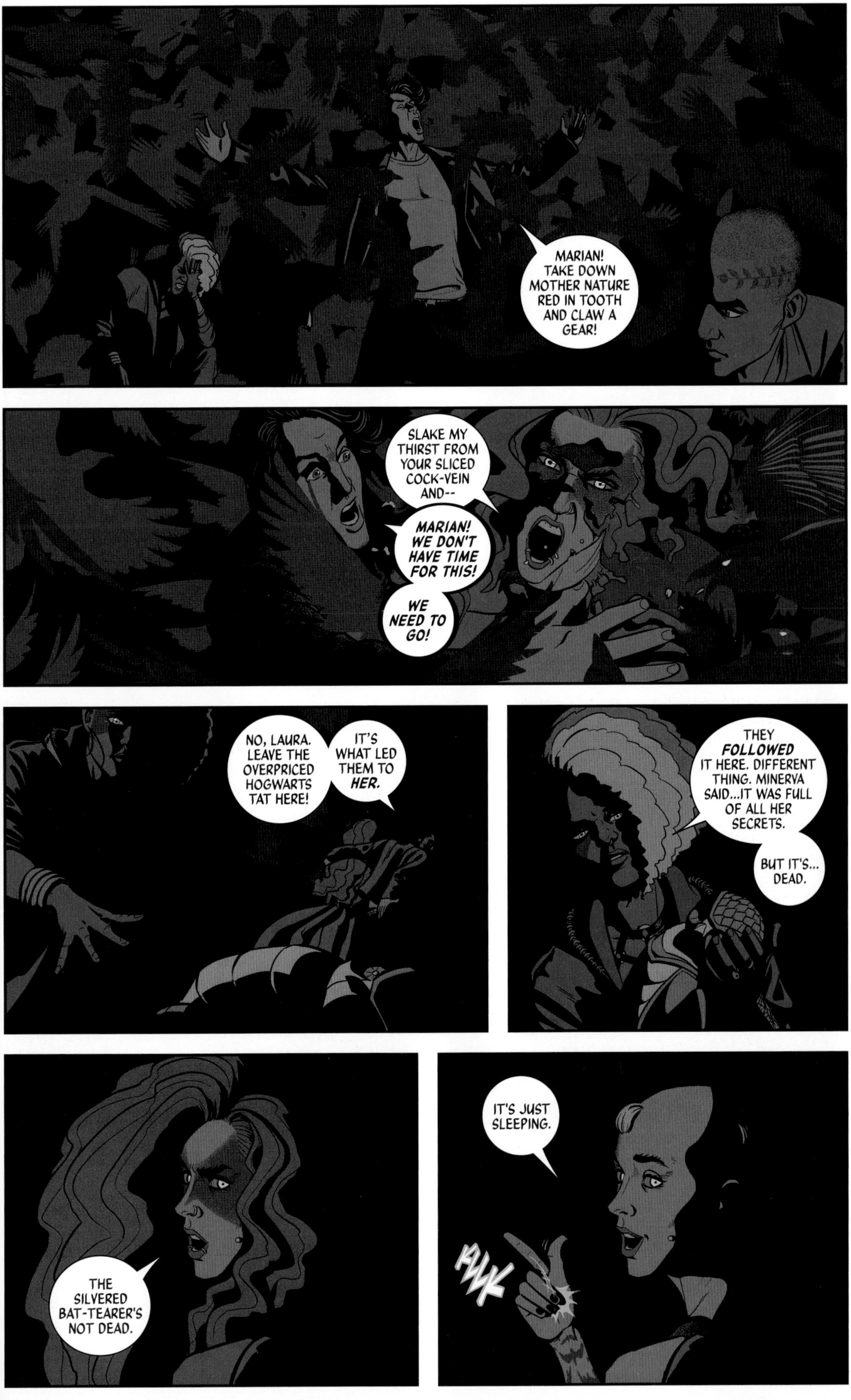
MARIAN! TAKE DOWN MOTHER NATURE RED IN TOOTH AND CLAW A GEAR!
SLAKE MY THIRST FROM YOUR SLICED COCK-VEIN AND--
MARIAN! WE DON'T HAVE TIME FOR THIS!
WE NEED TO GO!
NO, LAURA. LEAVE THE OVERPRICED HOGWARTS TAT HERE!
IT'S WHAT LED THEM TO *HER.*
THEY ***FOLLOWED*** IT HERE. DIFFERENT THING. MINERVA SAID...IT WAS FULL OF ALL HER SECRETS.
BUT IT'S... DEAD.
THE SILVERED BAT-TEARER'S NOT DEAD.
IT'S JUST SLEEPING.

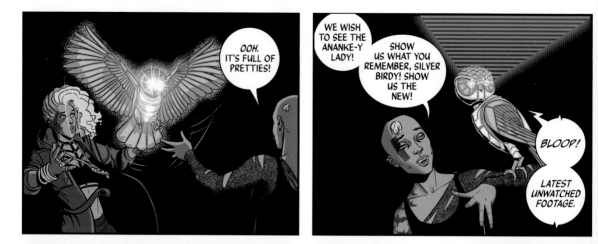

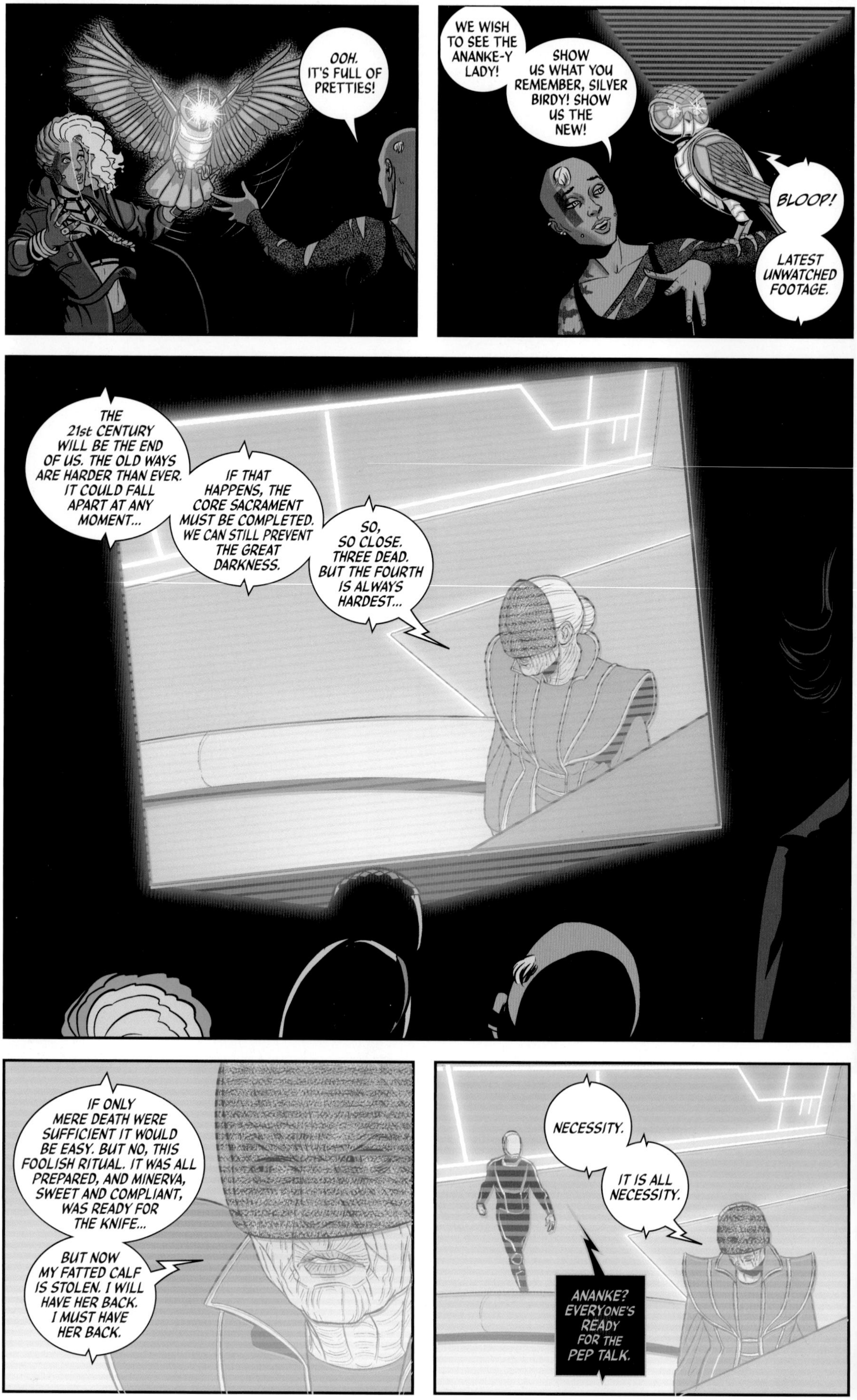

OOH. IT'S FULL OF PRETTIES!

WE WISH TO SEE THE ANANKE-Y LADY! SHOW US WHAT YOU REMEMBER, SILVER BIRDY! SHOW US THE NEW!

BLOOP!

LATEST UNWATCHED FOOTAGE.

THE 21st CENTURY WILL BE THE END OF US. THE OLD WAYS ARE HARDER THAN EVER. IT COULD FALL APART AT ANY MOMENT...

IF THAT HAPPENS, THE CORE SACRAMENT MUST BE COMPLETED. WE CAN STILL PREVENT THE GREAT DARKNESS.

SO, SO CLOSE. THREE DEAD. BUT THE FOURTH IS ALWAYS HARDEST...

IF ONLY MERE DEATH WERE SUFFICIENT IT WOULD BE EASY. BUT NO, THIS FOOLISH RITUAL. IT WAS ALL PREPARED, AND MINERVA, SWEET AND COMPLIANT, WAS READY FOR THE KNIFE...

BUT NOW MY FATTED CALF IS STOLEN. I WILL HAVE HER BACK. I MUST HAVE HER BACK.

NECESSITY.

IT IS ALL NECESSITY.

ANANKE? EVERYONE'S READY FOR THE PEP TALK.

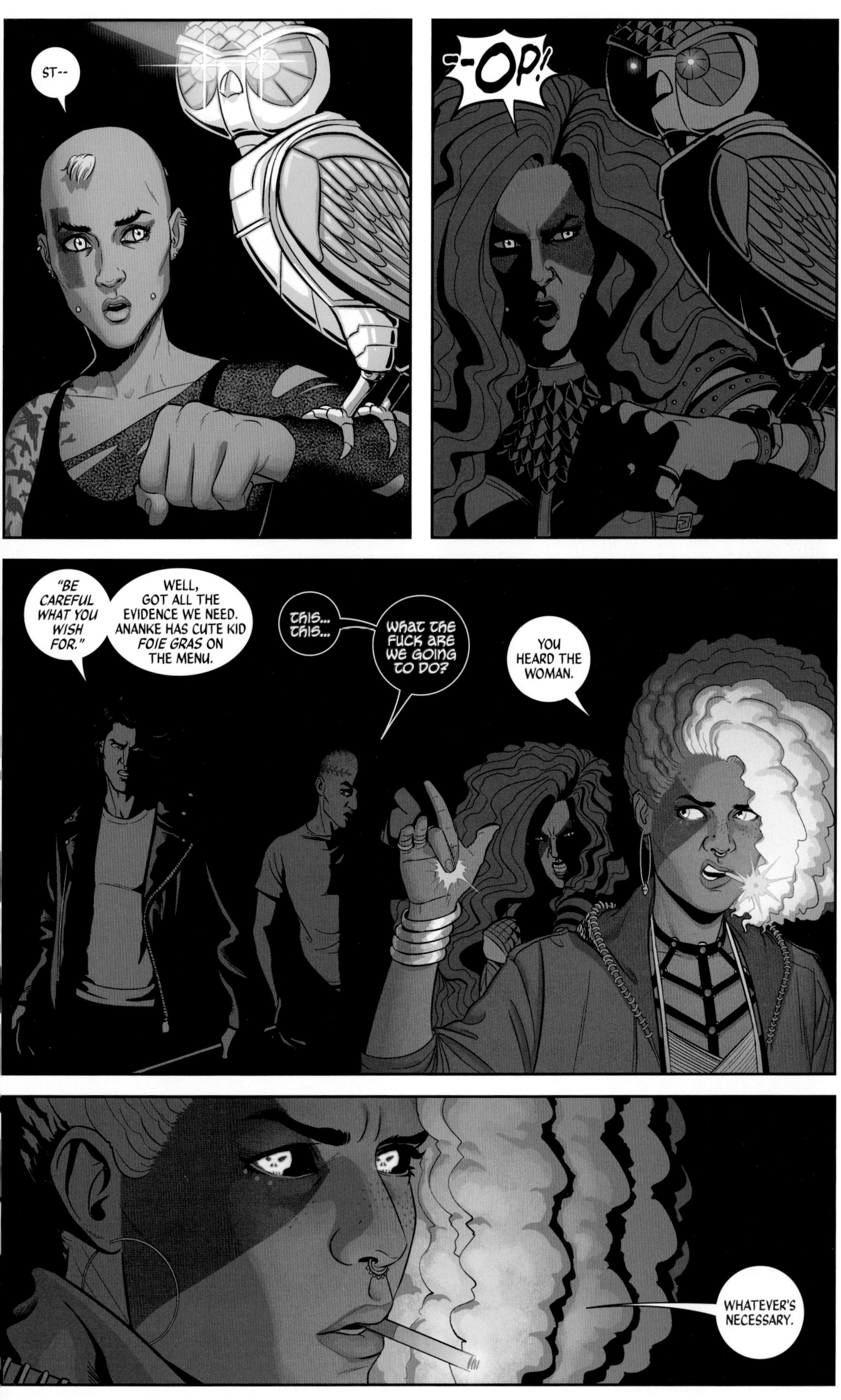
ST--
--OP!?
"BE CAREFUL WHAT YOU WISH FOR."
WELL, GOT ALL THE EVIDENCE WE NEED. ANANKE HAS CUTE KID FOIE GRAS ON THE MENU.
THIS... THIS...
WHAT THE FUCK ARE WE GOING TO DO?
YOU HEARD THE WOMAN.
WHATEVER'S NECESSARY.

KNOWING YOU
KNOW NOTHING

24 SEPTEMBER 2014

THE
WICKED
+
DIVINE
THE

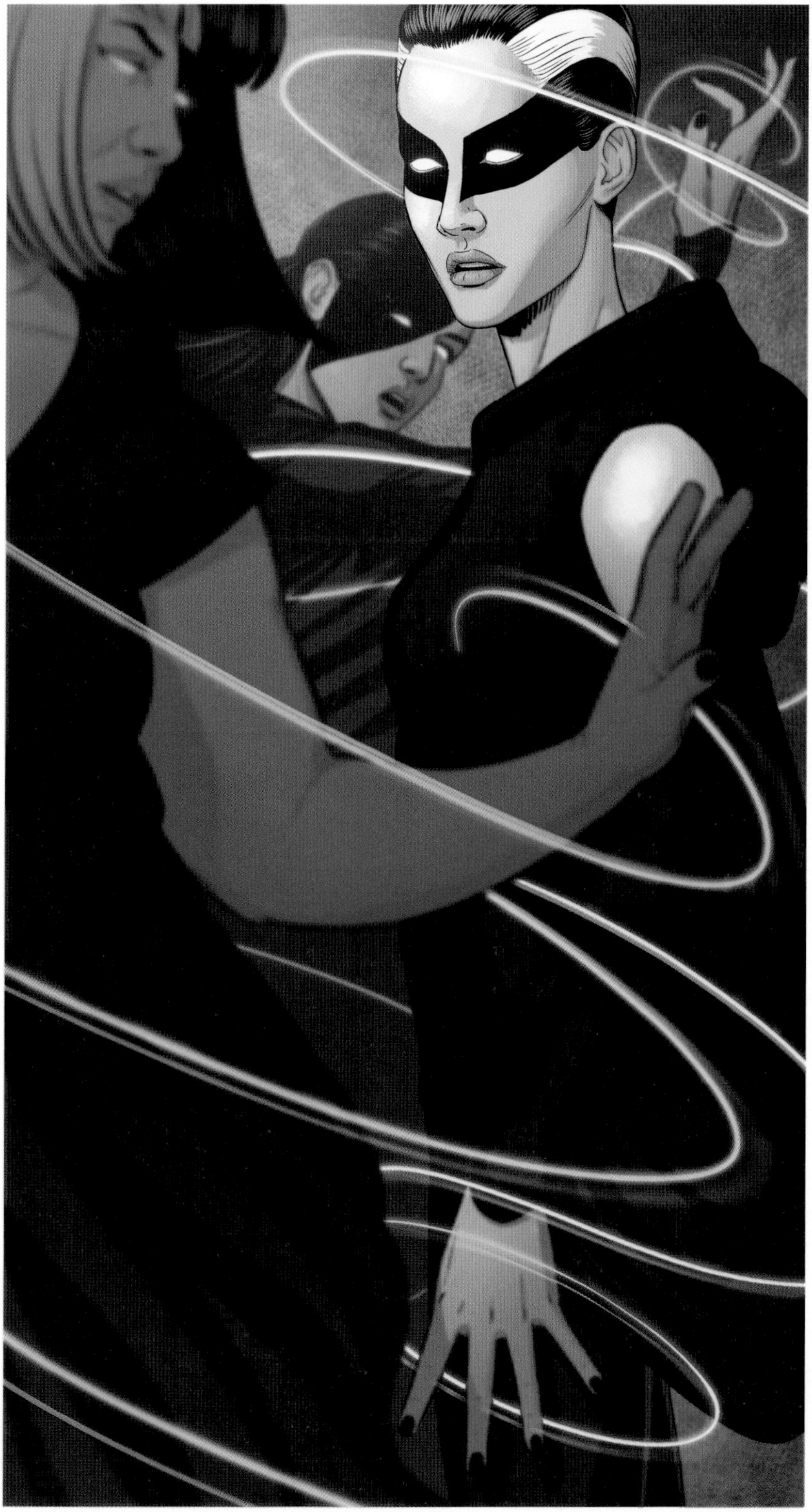

THE WICKED + THE DIVINE

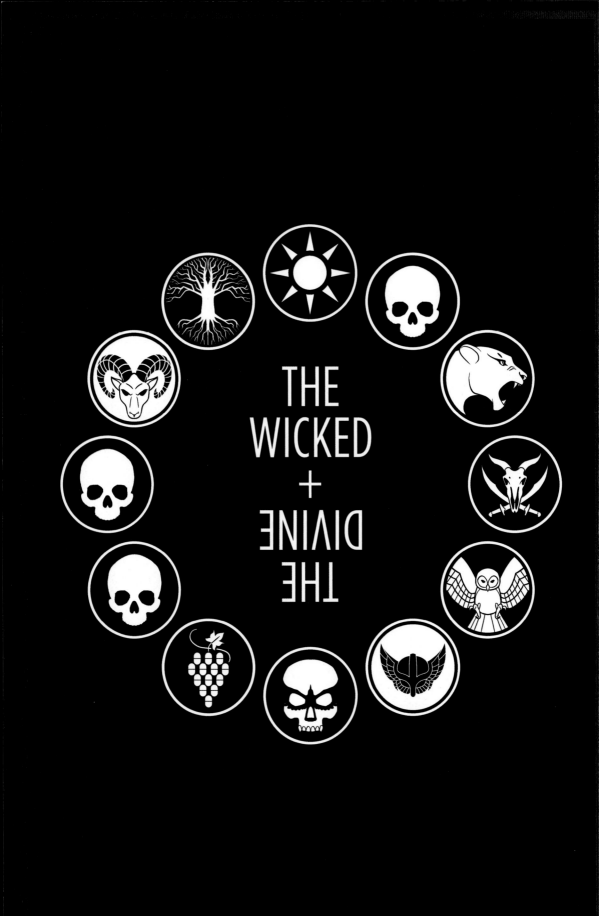

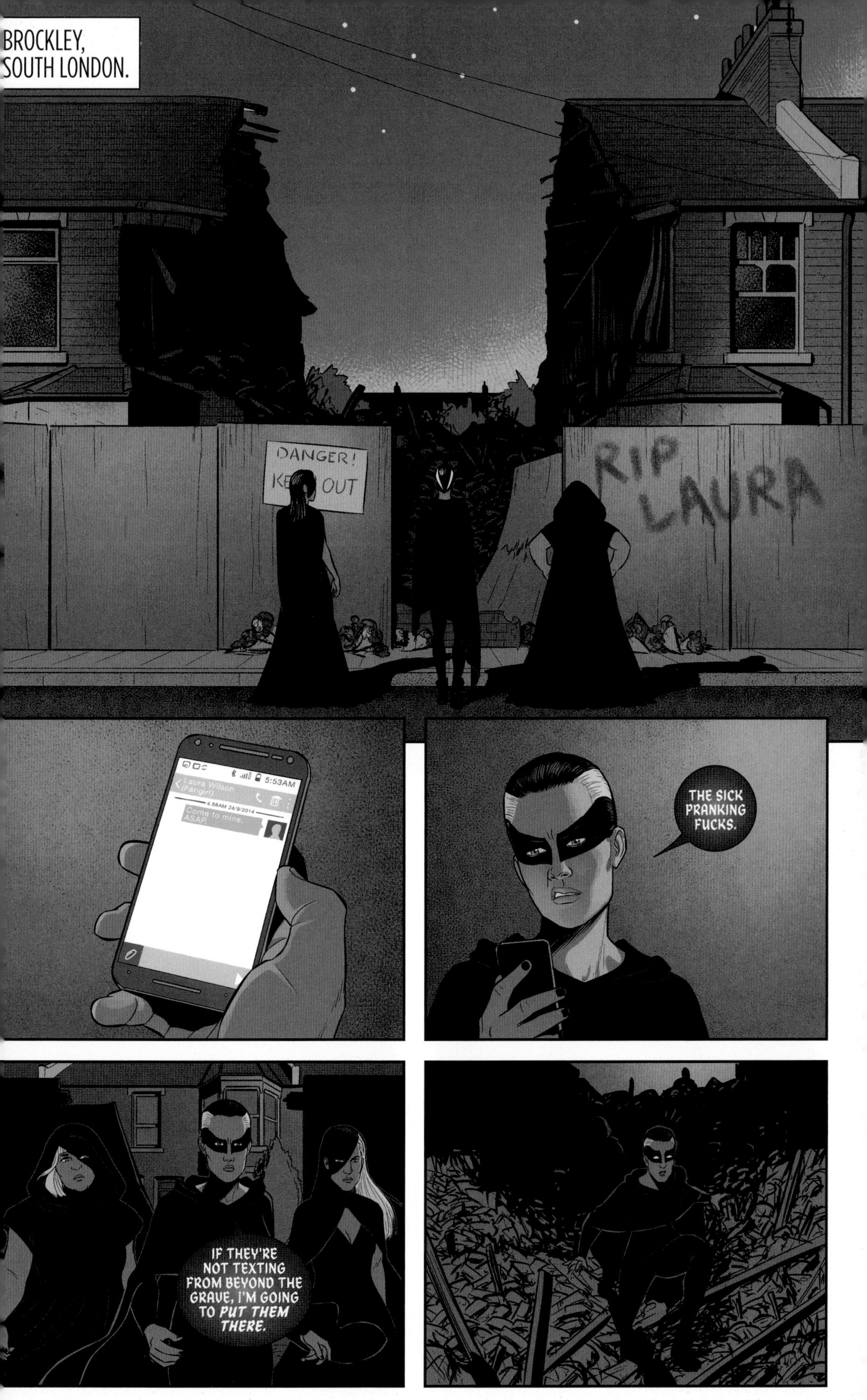
BROCKLEY, SOUTH LONDON.
DANGER! KE OUT
RIP LAURA
Laura Wilson (Fangirl)
5:53AM
4.58AM 24/9/2014
Come to mine. ASAP.
THE SICK PRANKING FUCKS.
IF THEY'RE NOT TEXTING FROM BEYOND THE GRAVE, I'M GOING TO *PUT THEM THERE.*

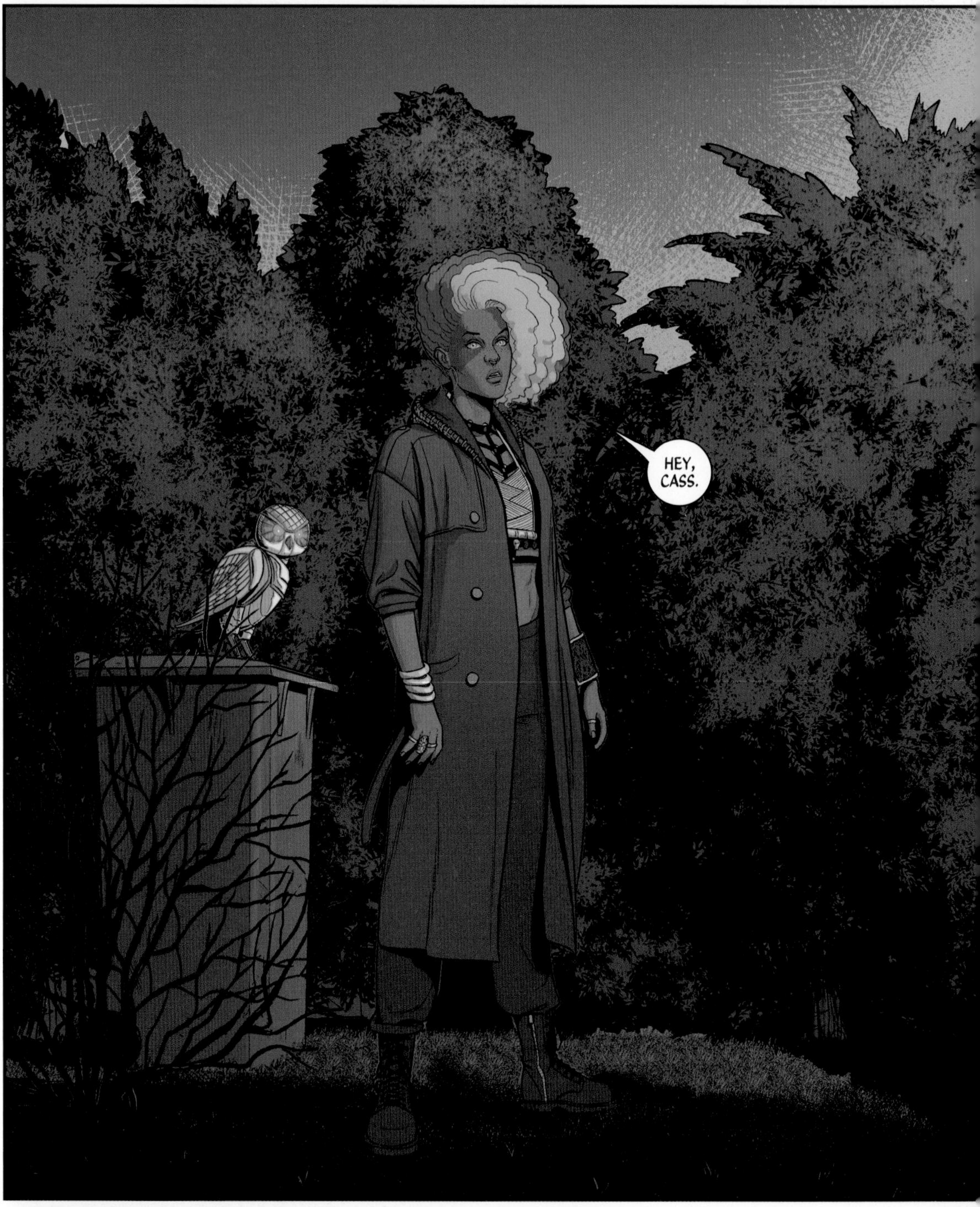
HEY,
CASS.

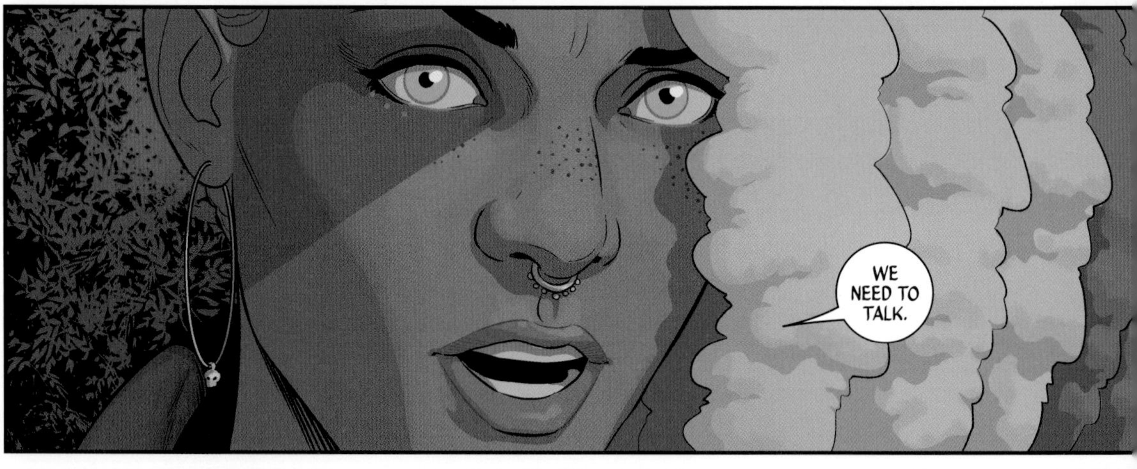
WE
NEED TO
TALK.

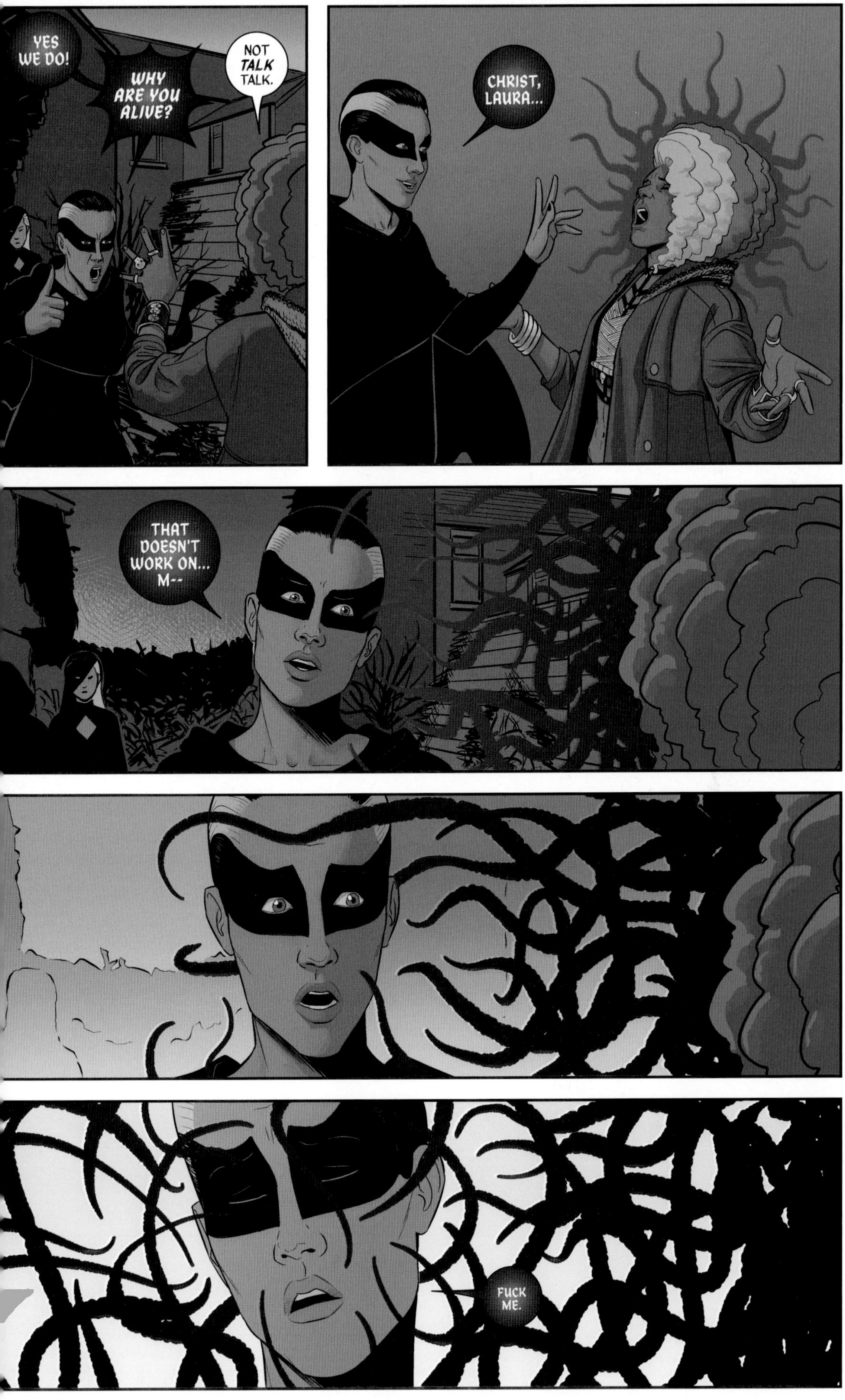
YES WE DO!
WHY ARE YOU ALIVE?
NOT TALK TALK.
CHRIST, LAURA...
THAT DOESN'T WORK ON... M--
FUCK ME.

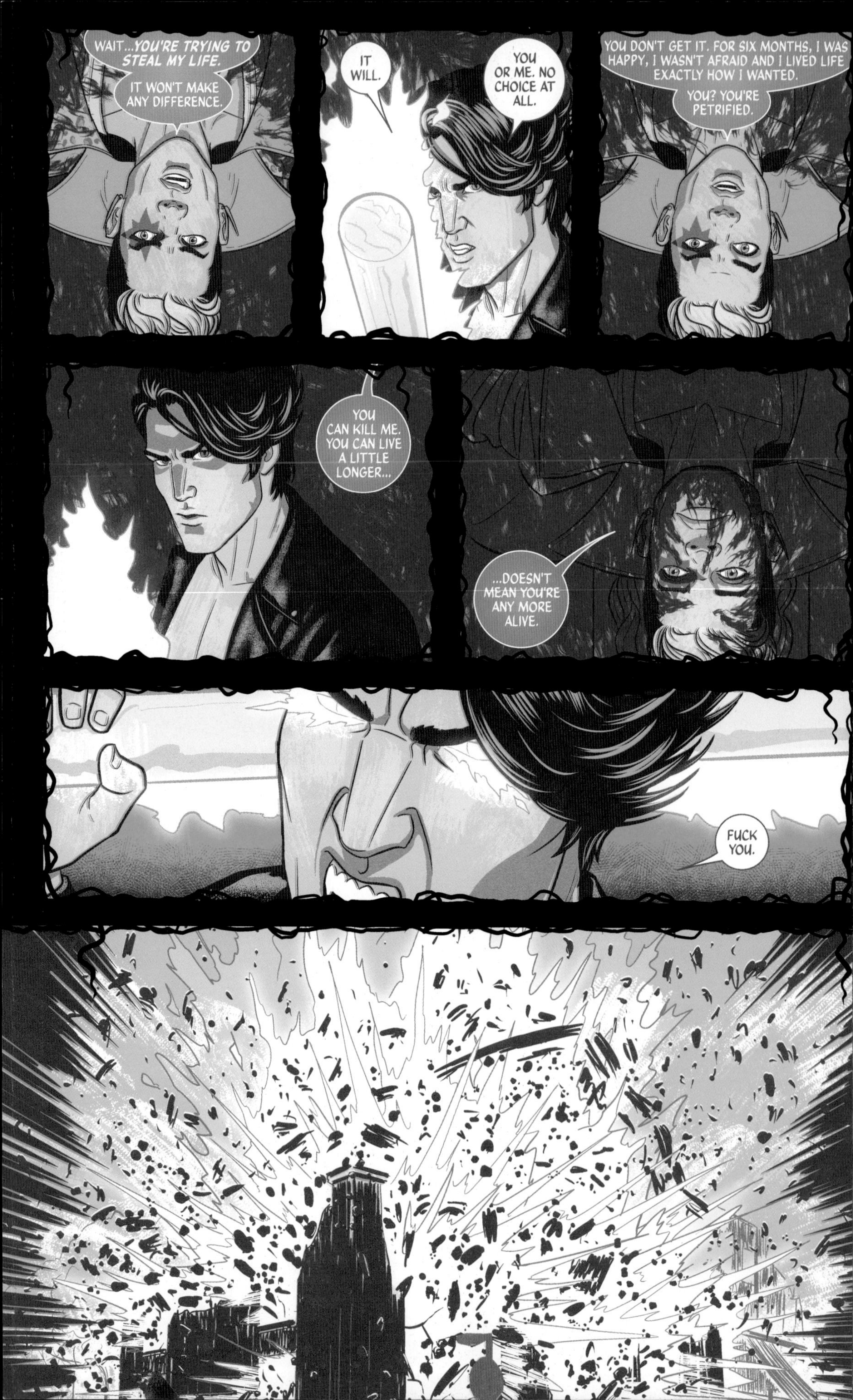
WAIT...YOU'RE TRYING TO STEAL MY LIFE.
IT WON'T MAKE ANY DIFFERENCE.
IT WILL.
YOU OR ME. NO CHOICE AT ALL.
YOU DON'T GET IT. FOR SIX MONTHS, I WAS HAPPY, I WASN'T AFRAID AND I LIVED LIFE EXACTLY HOW I WANTED.
YOU? YOU'RE PETRIFIED.
YOU CAN KILL ME. YOU CAN LIVE A LITTLE LONGER...
...DOESN'T MEAN YOU'RE ANY MORE ALIVE.
FUCK YOU.

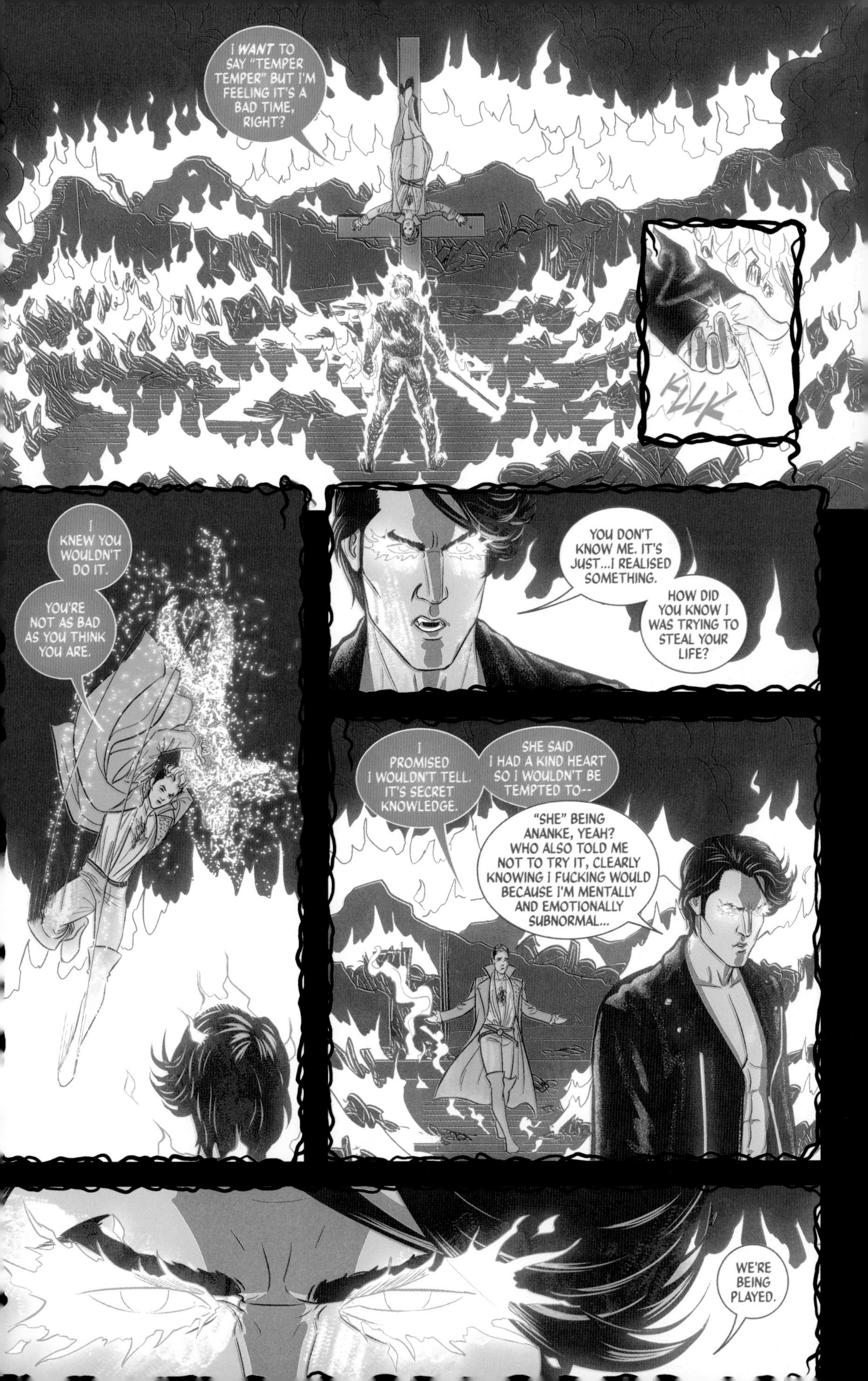
I WANT TO SAY "TEMPER TEMPER" BUT I'M FEELING IT'S A BAD TIME, RIGHT?
KLLK
I KNEW YOU WOULDN'T DO IT.
YOU'RE NOT AS BAD AS YOU THINK YOU ARE.
YOU DON'T KNOW ME. IT'S JUST...I REALISED SOMETHING.
HOW DID YOU KNOW I WAS TRYING TO STEAL YOUR LIFE?
I PROMISED I WOULDN'T TELL. IT'S SECRET KNOWLEDGE.
SHE SAID I HAD A KIND HEART SO I WOULDN'T BE TEMPTED TO--
"SHE" BEING ANANKE, YEAH? WHO ALSO TOLD ME NOT TO TRY IT, CLEARLY KNOWING I FUCKING WOULD BECAUSE I'M MENTALLY AND EMOTIONALLY SUBNORMAL...
WE'RE BEING PLAYED.

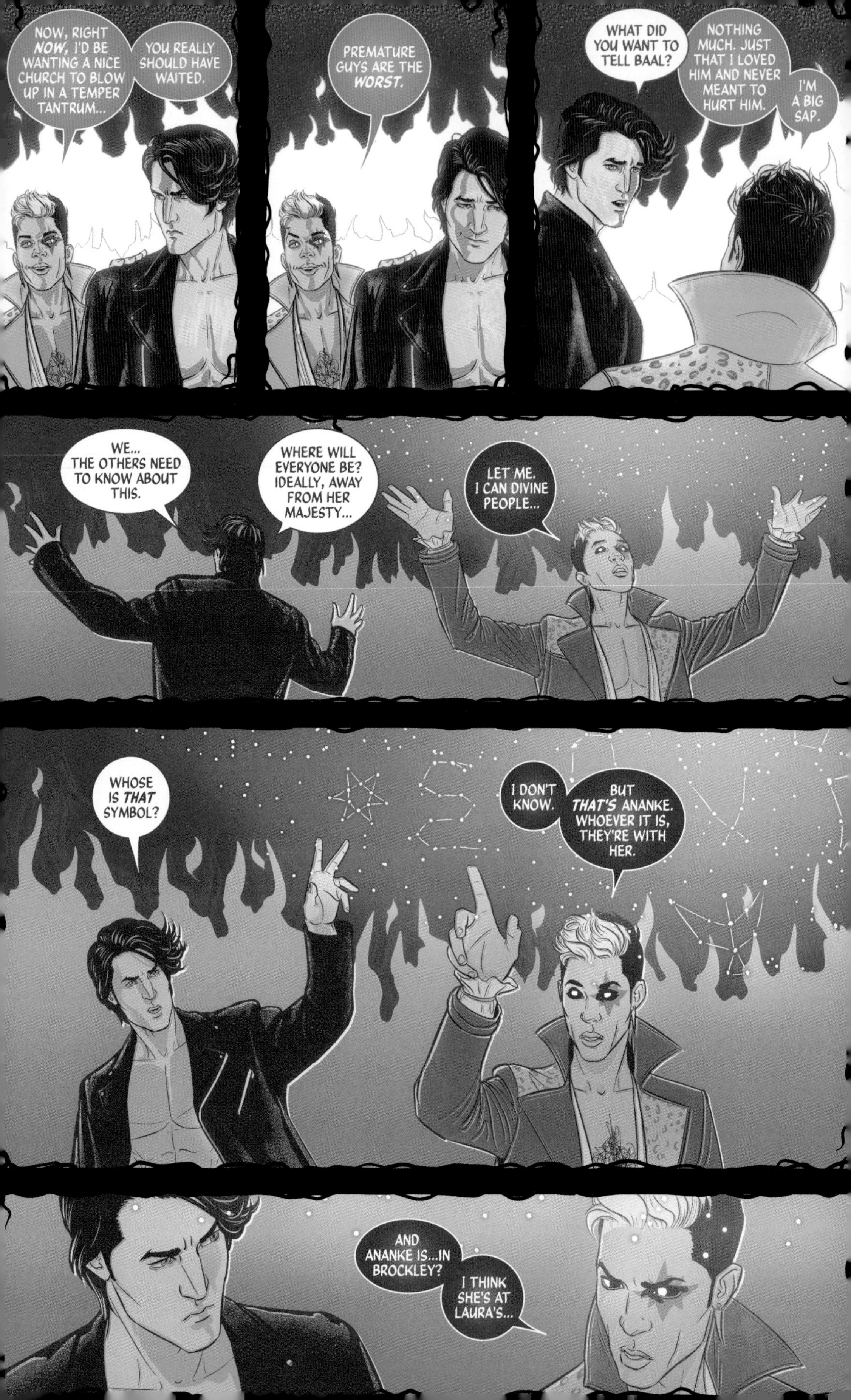
NOW, RIGHT *NOW*, I'D BE WANTING A NICE CHURCH TO BLOW UP IN A TEMPER TANTRUM...
YOU REALLY SHOULD HAVE WAITED.
PREMATURE GUYS ARE THE *WORST*.
WHAT DID YOU WANT TO TELL BAAL?
NOTHING MUCH. JUST THAT I LOVED HIM AND NEVER MEANT TO HURT HIM.
I'M A BIG SAP.
WE... THE OTHERS NEED TO KNOW ABOUT THIS.
WHERE WILL EVERYONE BE? IDEALLY, AWAY FROM HER MAJESTY...
LET ME. I CAN DIVINE PEOPLE...
WHOSE IS *THAT* SYMBOL?
I DON'T KNOW.
BUT *THAT'S* ANANKE. WHOEVER IT IS, THEY'RE WITH HER.
AND ANANKE IS...IN BROCKLEY?
I THINK SHE'S AT LAURA'S...

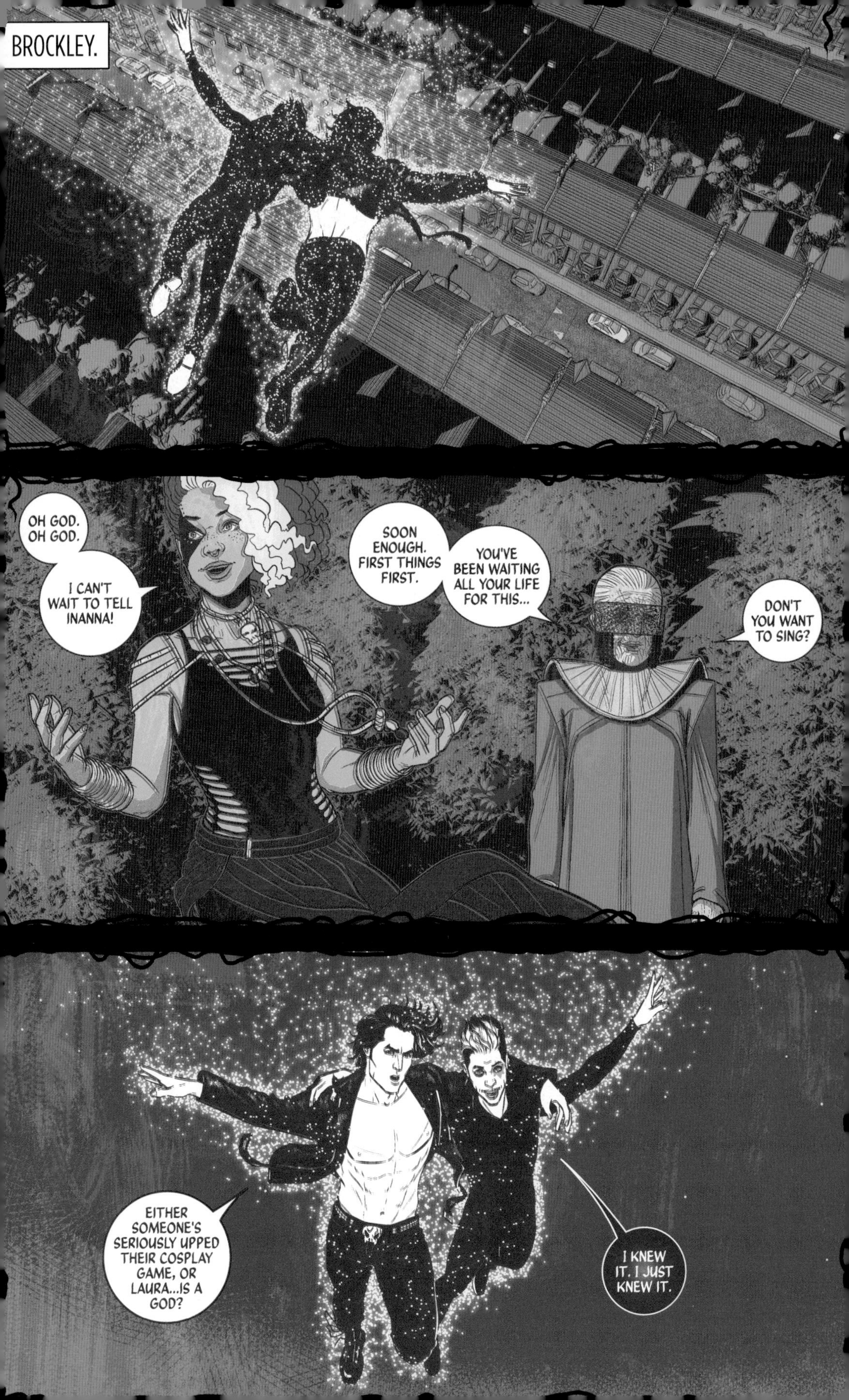
BROCKLEY.
OH GOD. OH GOD.
I CAN'T WAIT TO TELL INANNA!
SOON ENOUGH. FIRST THINGS FIRST.
YOU'VE BEEN WAITING ALL YOUR LIFE FOR THIS...
DON'T YOU WANT TO SING?
EITHER SOMEONE'S SERIOUSLY UPPED THEIR COSPLAY GAME, OR LAURA...IS A GOD?
I KNEW IT. I JUST KNEW IT.

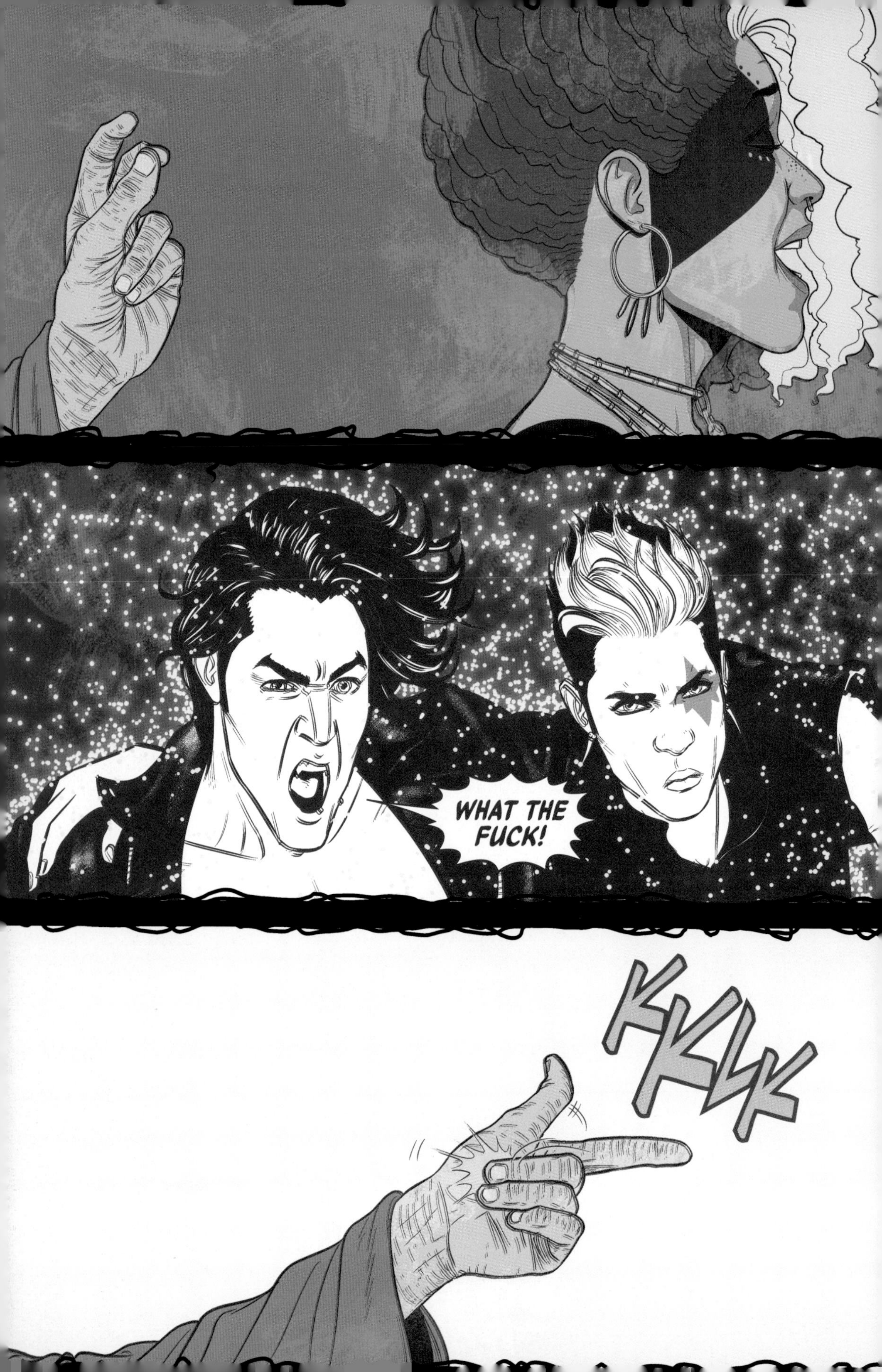
WHAT THE FUCK!
KKLK

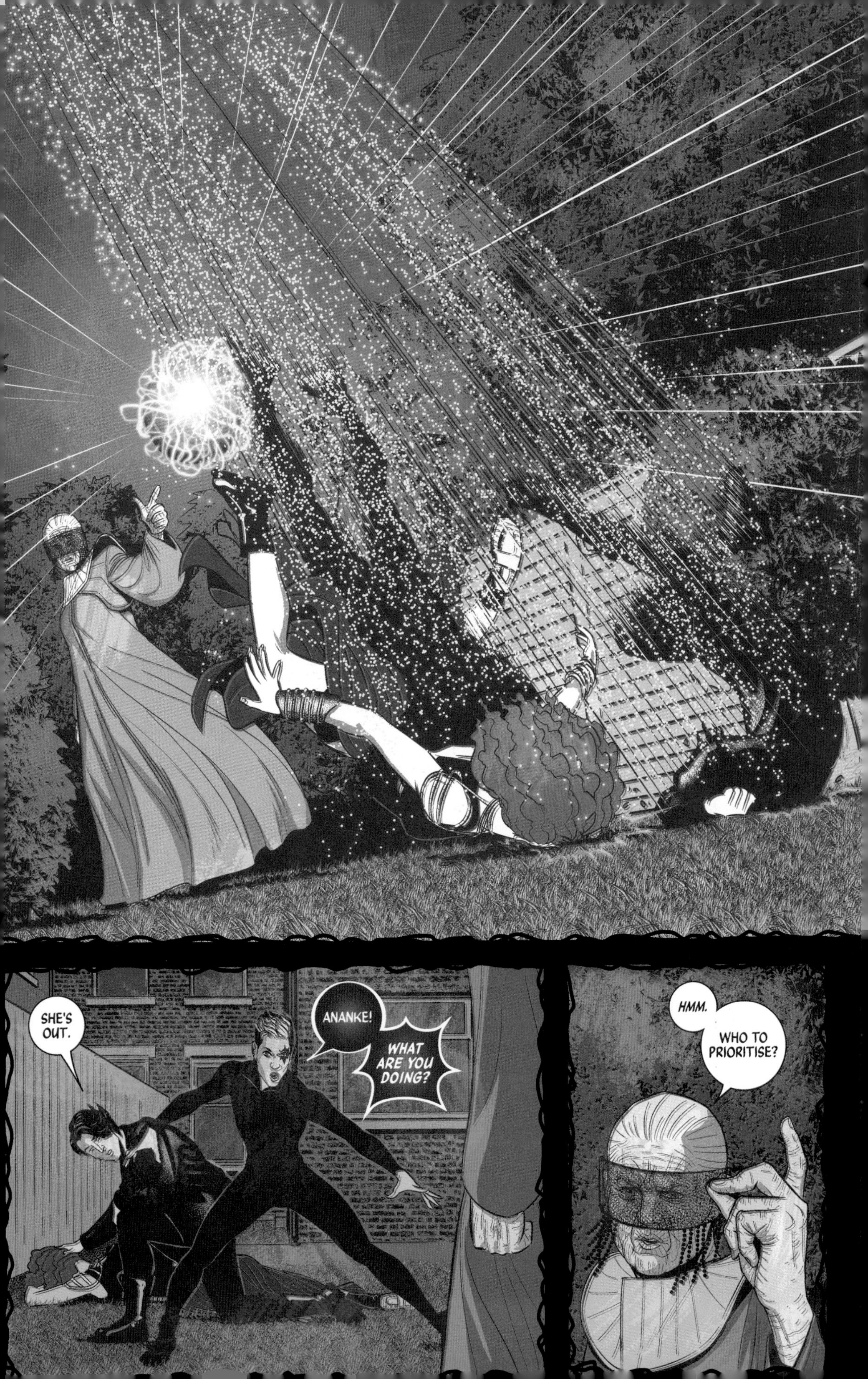
SHE'S OUT.
ANANKE!
WHAT ARE YOU DOING?
HMM.
WHO TO PRIORITISE?

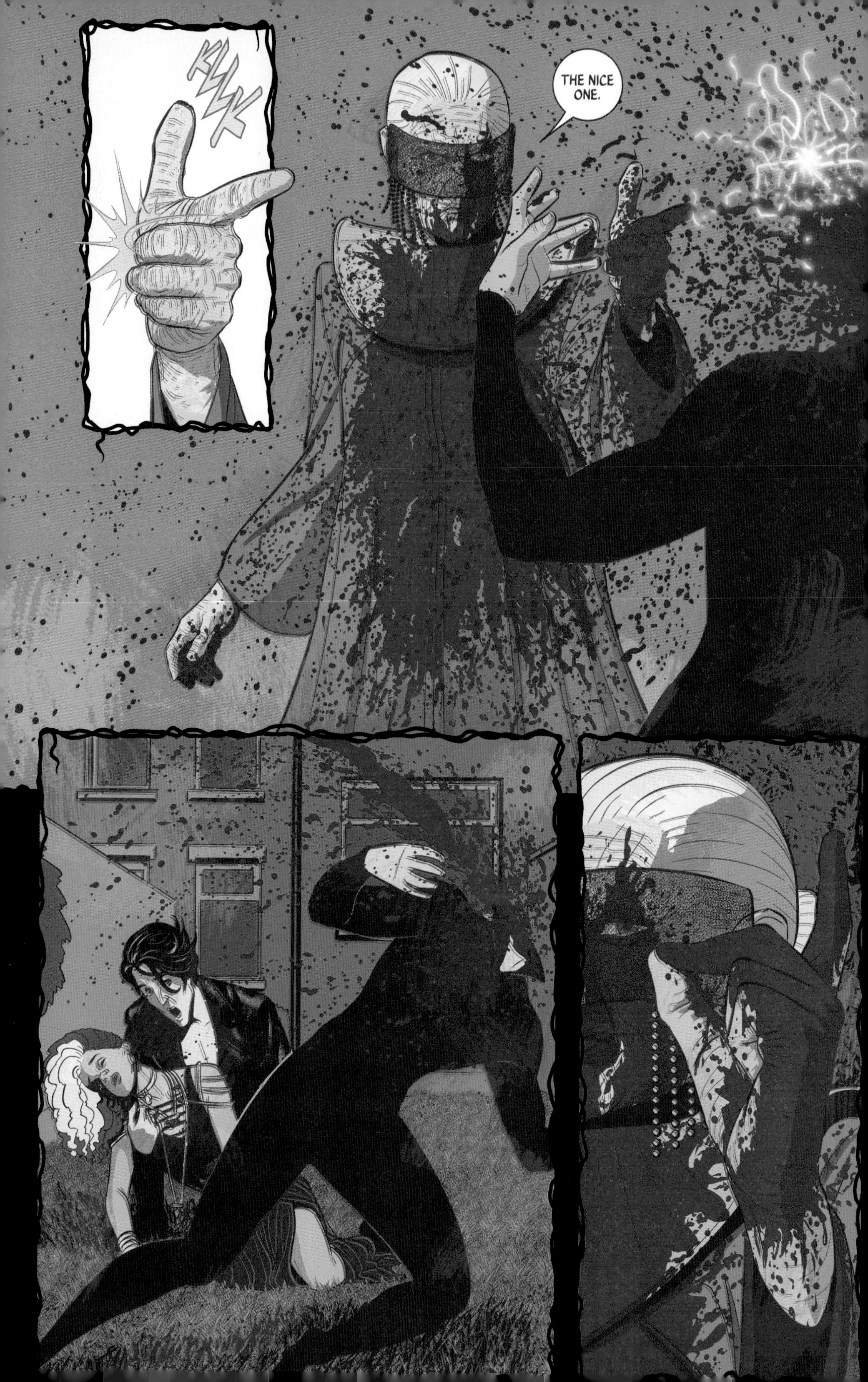
KLIK
THE NICE ONE.

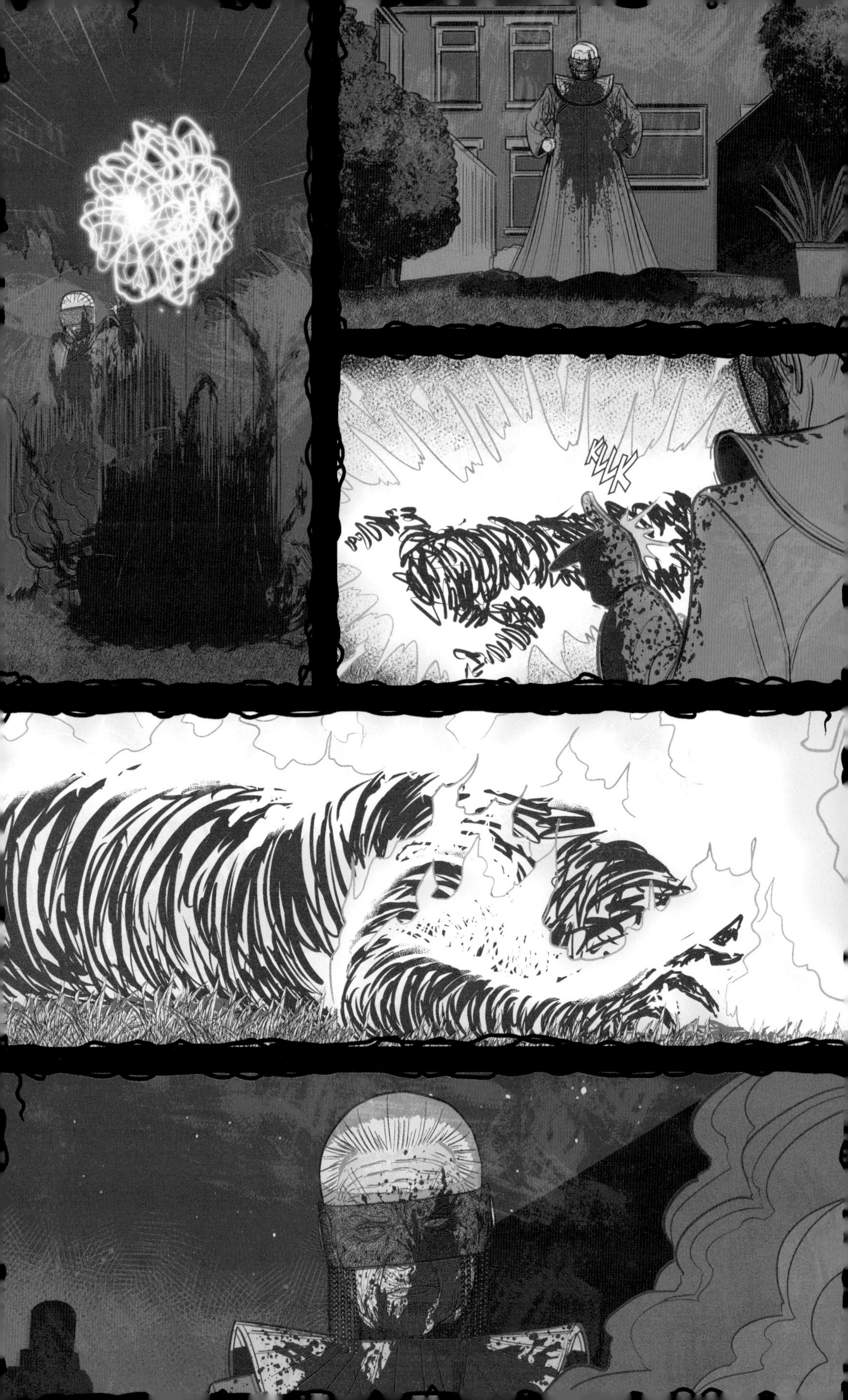
KLLK

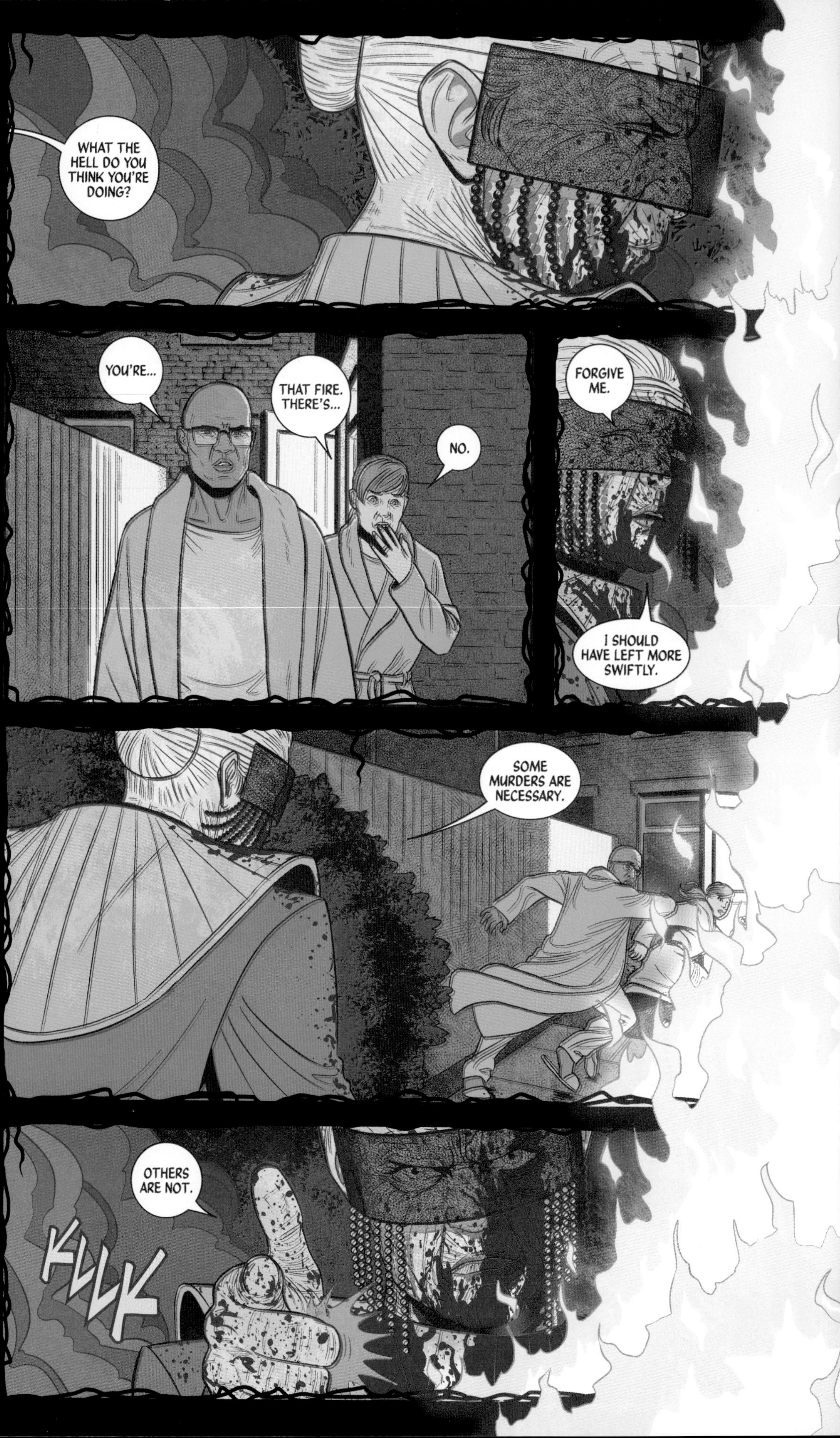
WHAT THE HELL DO YOU THINK YOU'RE DOING?
YOU'RE...
THAT FIRE. THERE'S...
NO.
FORGIVE ME.
I SHOULD HAVE LEFT MORE SWIFTLY.
SOME MURDERS ARE NECESSARY.
OTHERS ARE NOT.
KLLK

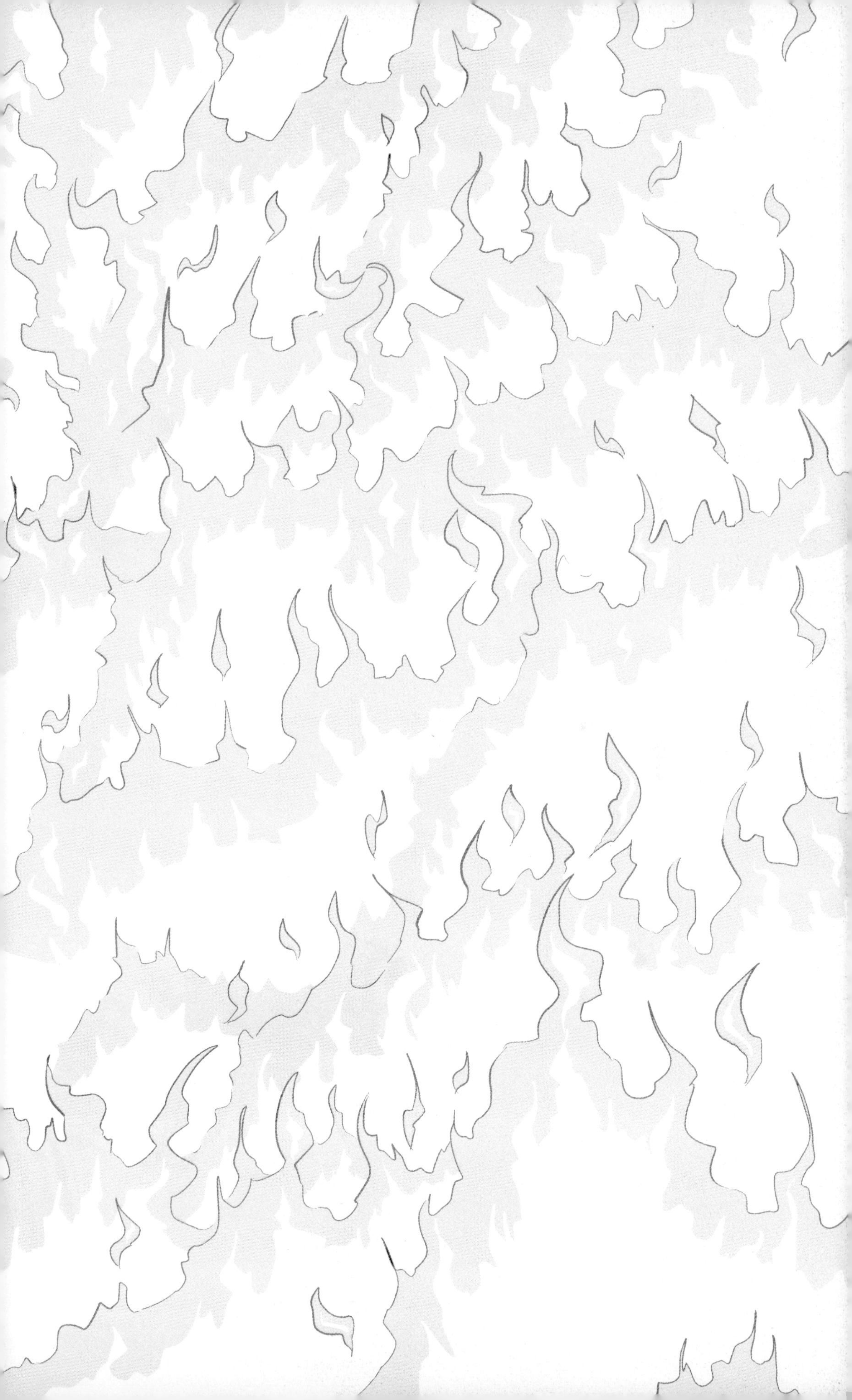

PERSEPHONE
IN HELL

AUGUST TO SEPTEMBER

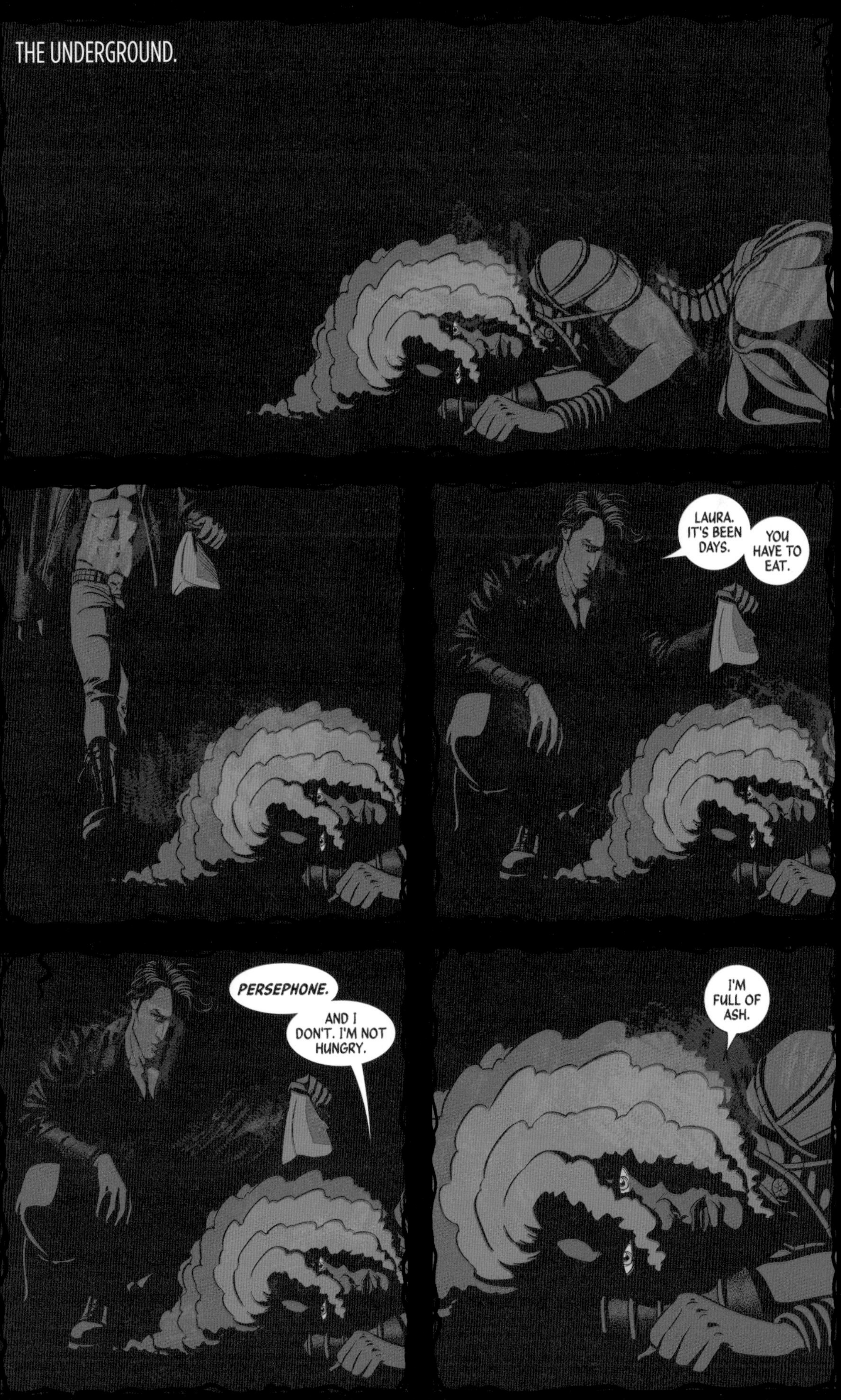
THE UNDERGROUND.
LAURA. IT'S BEEN DAYS.
YOU HAVE TO EAT.
PERSEPHONE.
AND I DON'T. I'M NOT HUNGRY.
I'M FULL OF ASH.

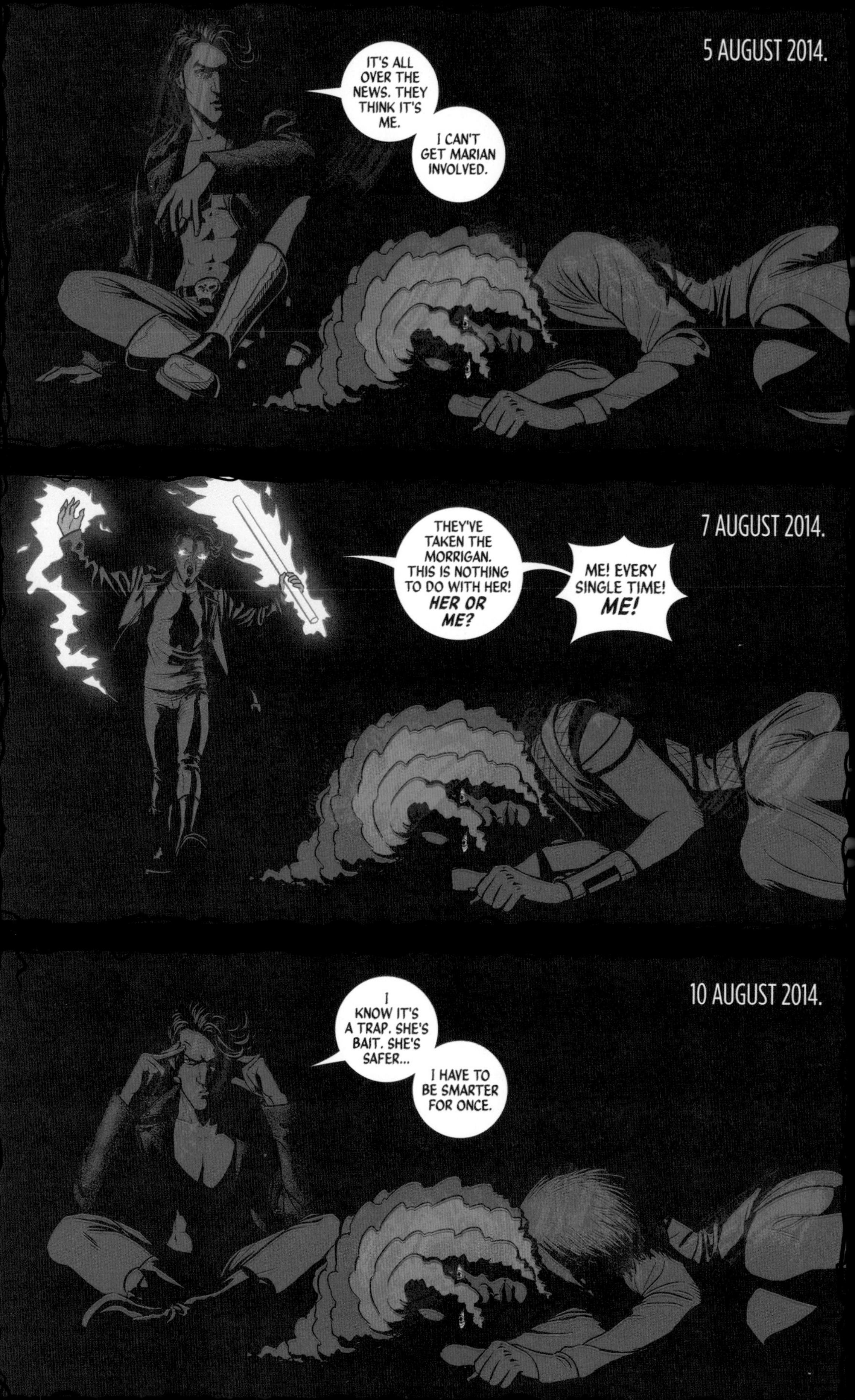
5 AUGUST 2014.
IT'S ALL OVER THE NEWS. THEY THINK IT'S ME.
I CAN'T GET MARIAN INVOLVED.
7 AUGUST 2014.
THEY'VE TAKEN THE MORRIGAN. THIS IS NOTHING TO DO WITH HER! HER OR ME?
ME! EVERY SINGLE TIME! ME!
10 AUGUST 2014.
I KNOW IT'S A TRAP. SHE'S BAIT. SHE'S SAFER...
I HAVE TO BE SMARTER FOR ONCE.

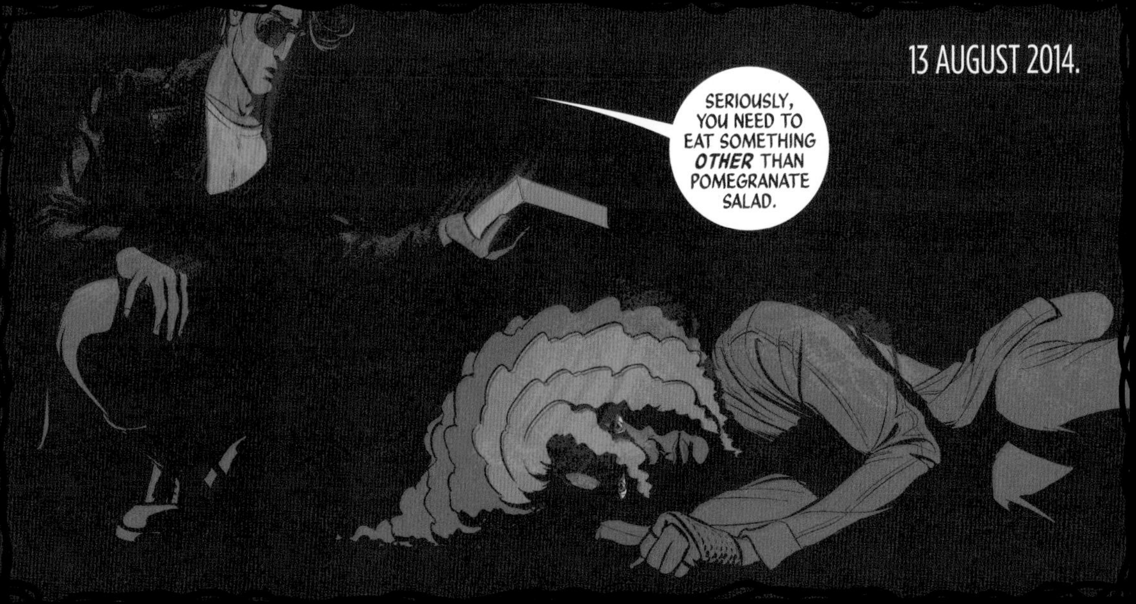
13 AUGUST 2014.
SERIOUSLY, YOU NEED TO EAT SOMETHING *OTHER* THAN POMEGRANATE SALAD.

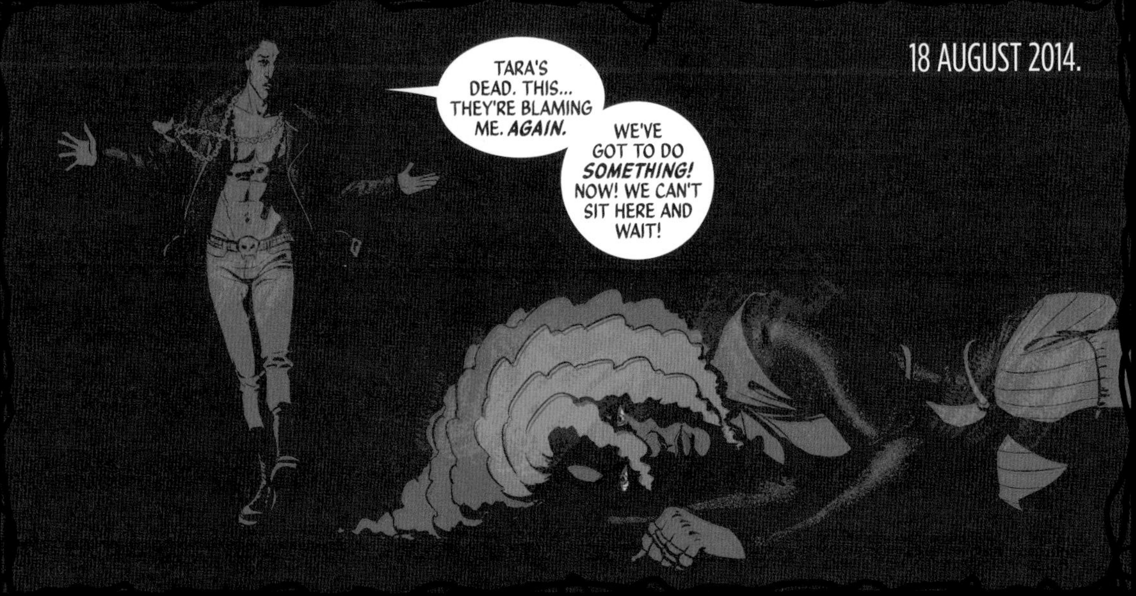
18 AUGUST 2014.
TARA'S DEAD. THIS... THEY'RE BLAMING ME. *AGAIN.*
WE'VE GOT TO DO *SOMETHING!* NOW! WE CAN'T SIT HERE AND WAIT!

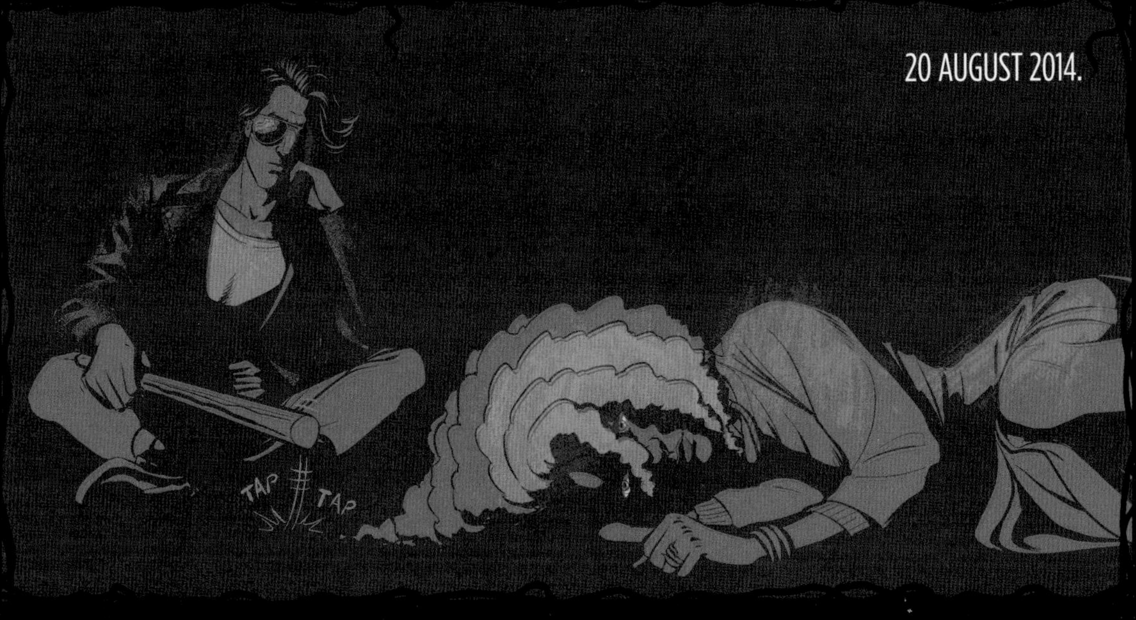
20 AUGUST 2014.
TAP
TAP

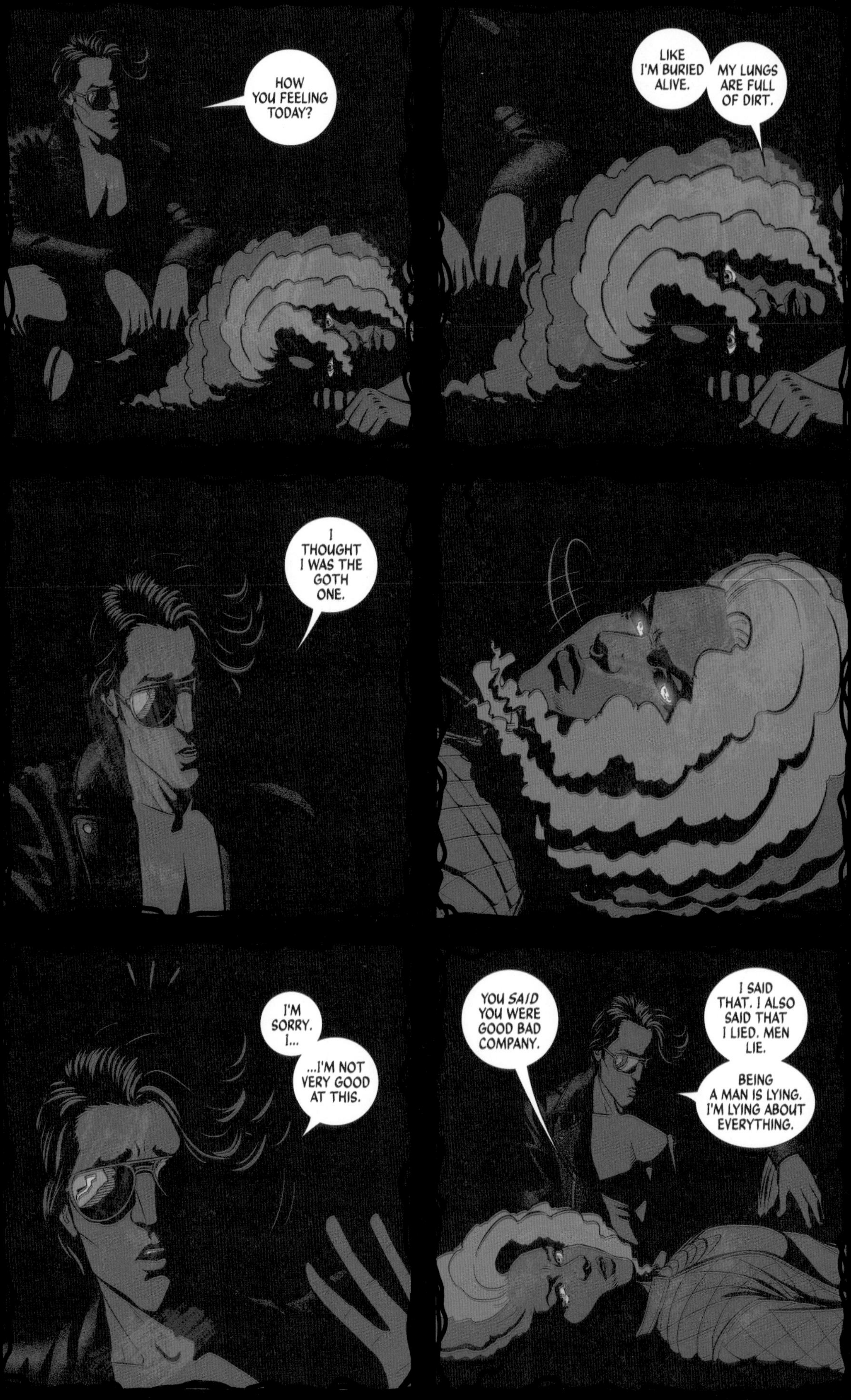
HOW YOU FEELING TODAY?
LIKE I'M BURIED ALIVE.
MY LUNGS ARE FULL OF DIRT.
I THOUGHT I WAS THE GOTH ONE.
I'M SORRY. I...
...I'M NOT VERY GOOD AT THIS.
YOU *SAID* YOU WERE GOOD BAD COMPANY.
I SAID THAT. I ALSO SAID THAT I LIED. MEN LIE.
BEING A MAN IS LYING. I'M LYING ABOUT EVERYTHING.

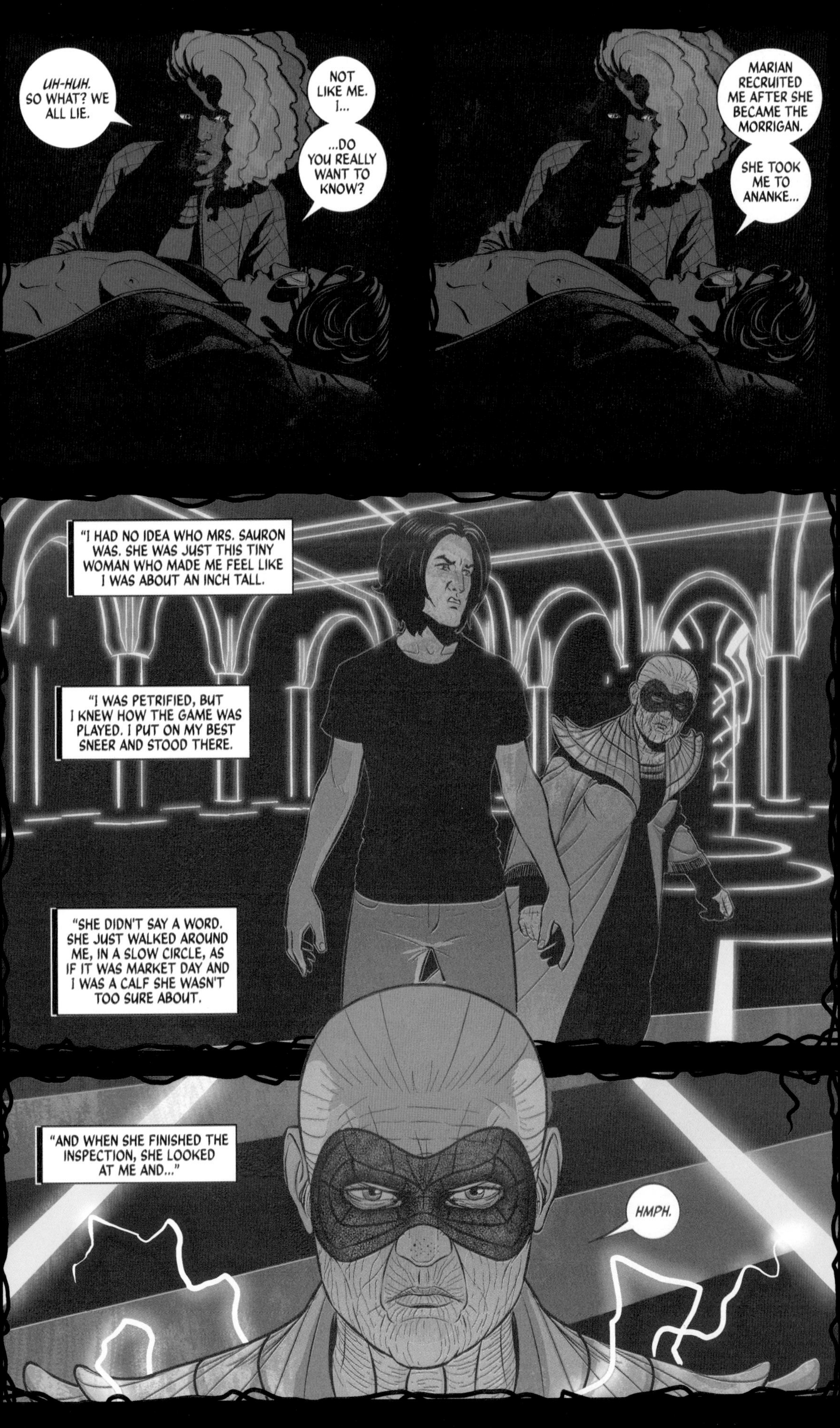
UH-HUH. SO WHAT? WE ALL LIE.
NOT LIKE ME. I...
...DO YOU REALLY WANT TO KNOW?
MARIAN RECRUITED ME AFTER SHE BECAME THE MORRIGAN.
SHE TOOK ME TO ANANKE...
"I HAD NO IDEA WHO MRS. SAURON WAS. SHE WAS JUST THIS TINY WOMAN WHO MADE ME FEEL LIKE I WAS ABOUT AN INCH TALL.
"I WAS PETRIFIED, BUT I KNEW HOW THE GAME WAS PLAYED. I PUT ON MY BEST SNEER AND STOOD THERE.
"SHE DIDN'T SAY A WORD. SHE JUST WALKED AROUND ME, IN A SLOW CIRCLE, AS IF IT WAS MARKET DAY AND I WAS A CALF SHE WASN'T TOO SURE ABOUT.
"AND WHEN SHE FINISHED THE INSPECTION, SHE LOOKED AT ME AND..."
HMPH.

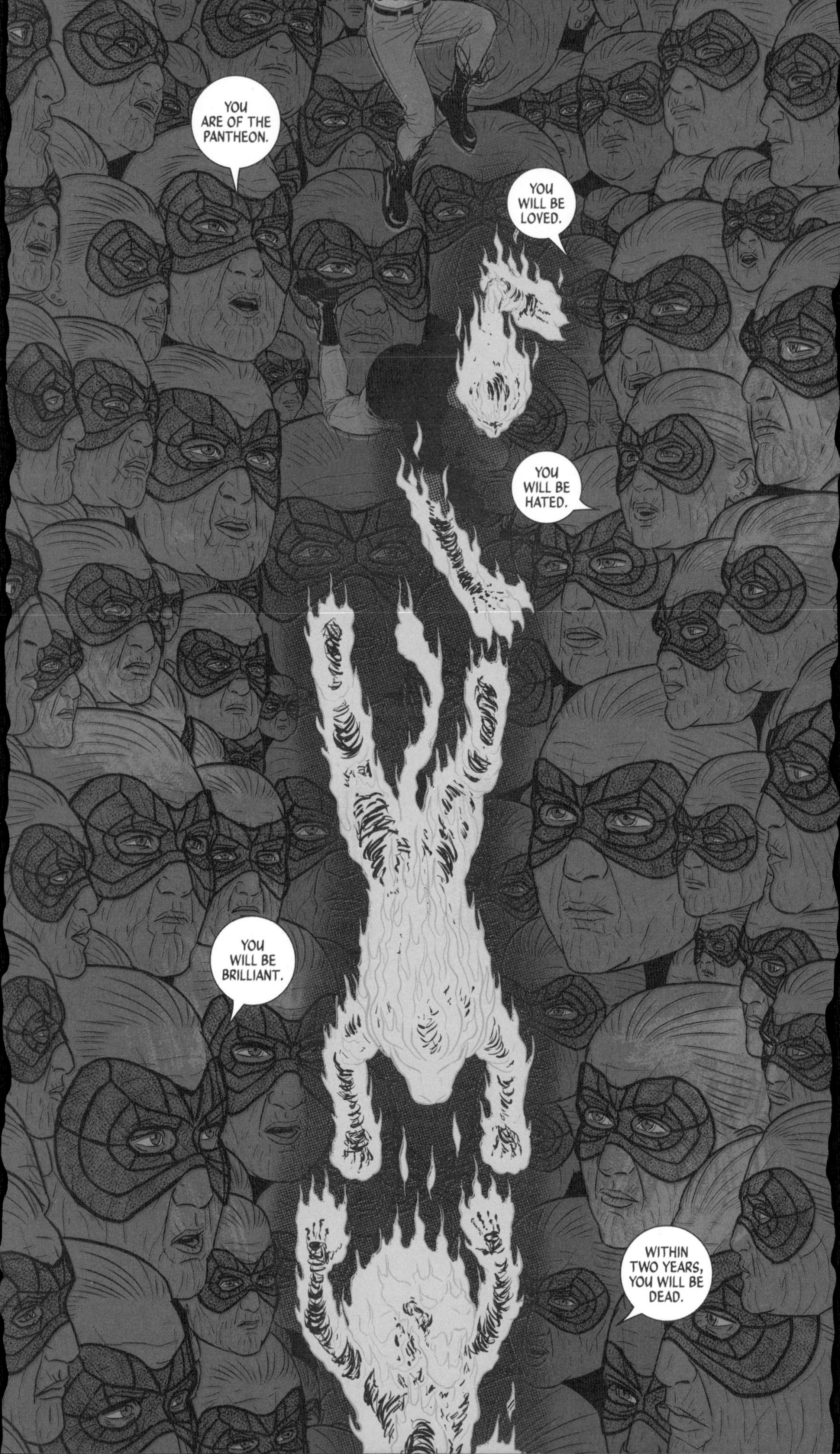
YOU ARE OF THE PANTHEON.
YOU WILL BE LOVED.
YOU WILL BE HATED.
YOU WILL BE BRILLIANT.
WITHIN TWO YEARS, YOU WILL BE DEAD.

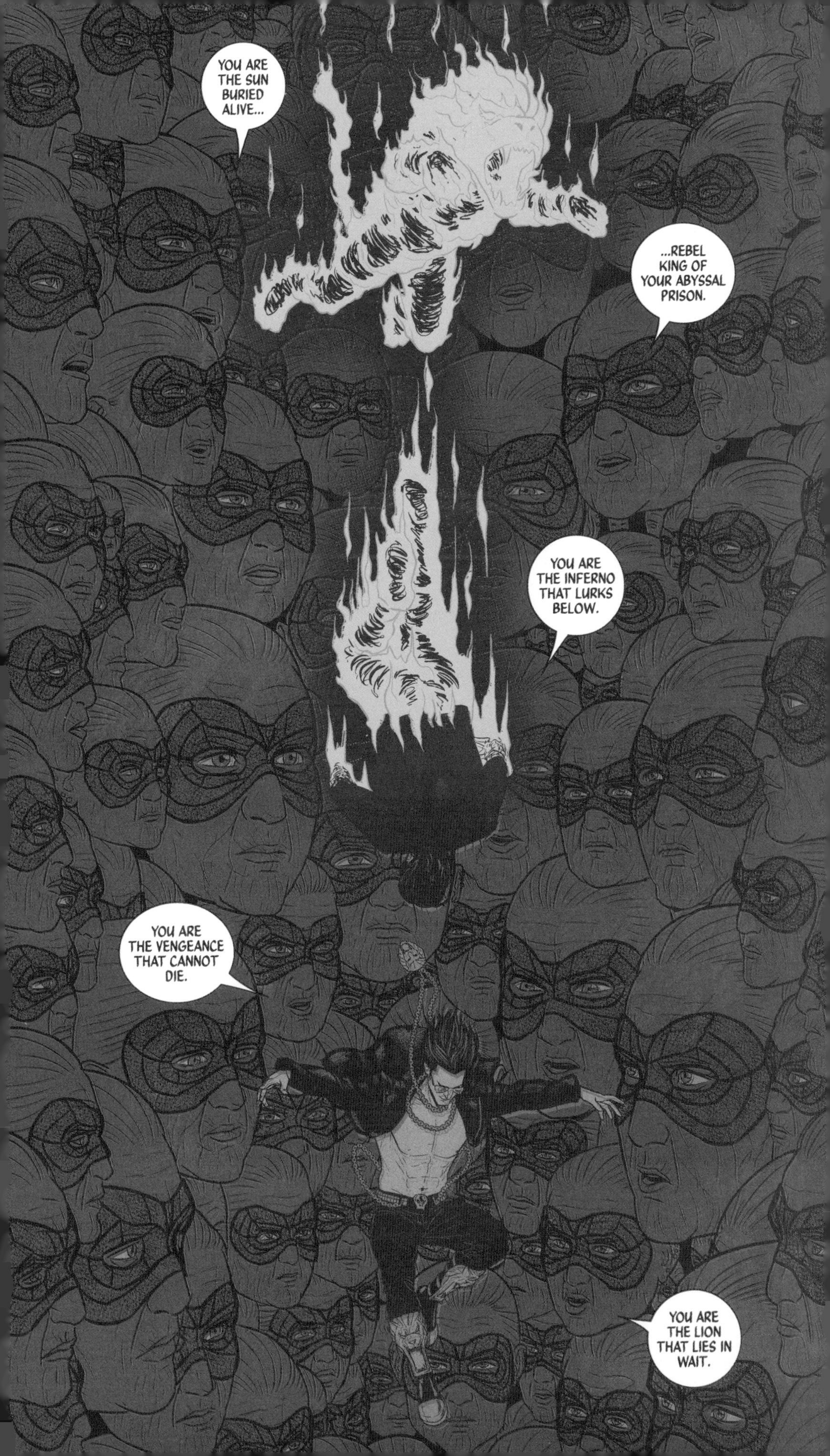
YOU ARE THE SUN BURIED ALIVE...
...REBEL KING OF YOUR ABYSSAL PRISON.
YOU ARE THE INFERNO THAT LURKS BELOW.
YOU ARE THE VENGEANCE THAT CANNOT DIE.
YOU ARE THE LION THAT LIES IN WAIT.

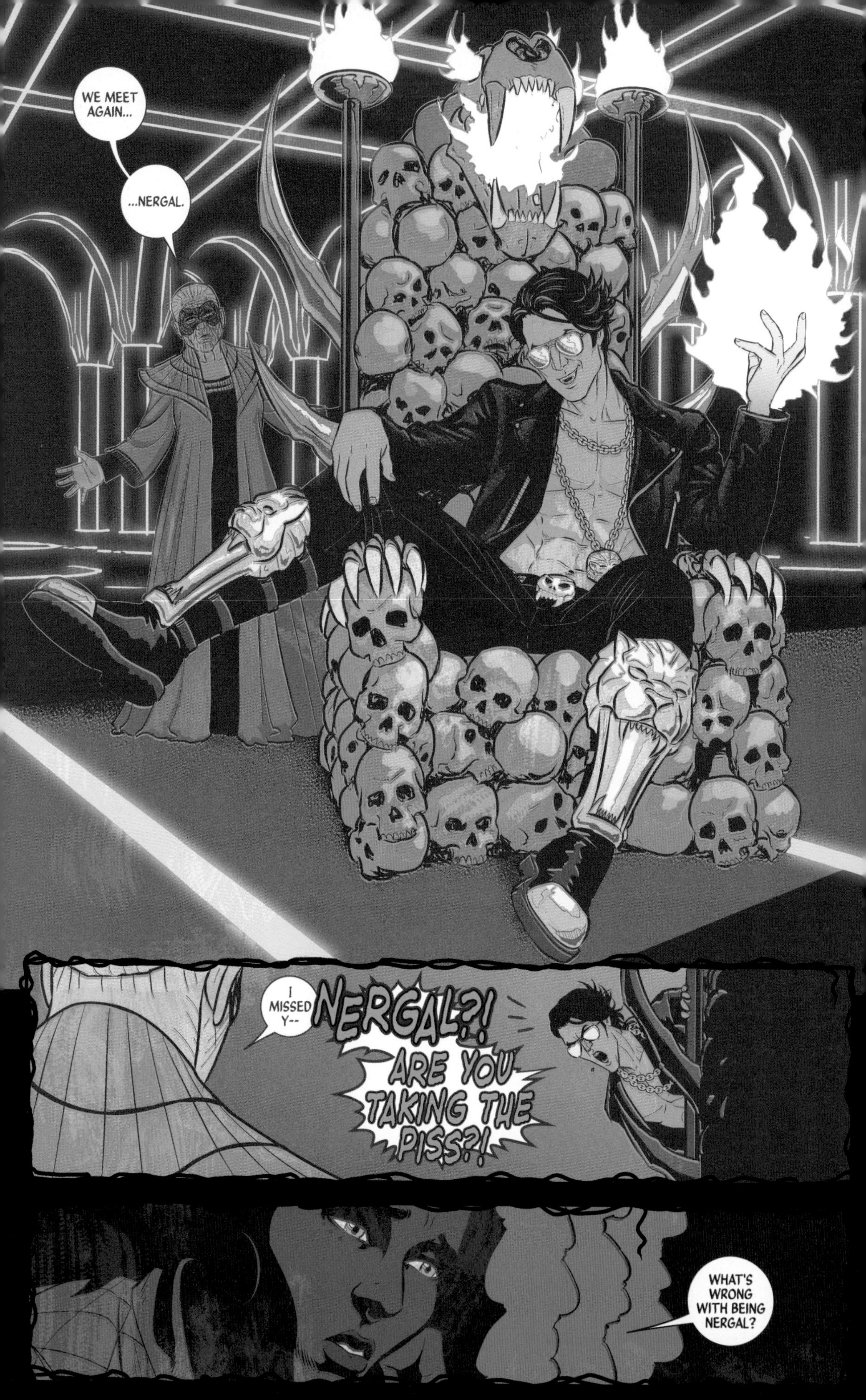
WE MEET AGAIN...
...NERGAL.
I MISSED Y--
NERGAL?! ARE YOU TAKING THE PISS?!
WHAT'S WRONG WITH BEING NERGAL?

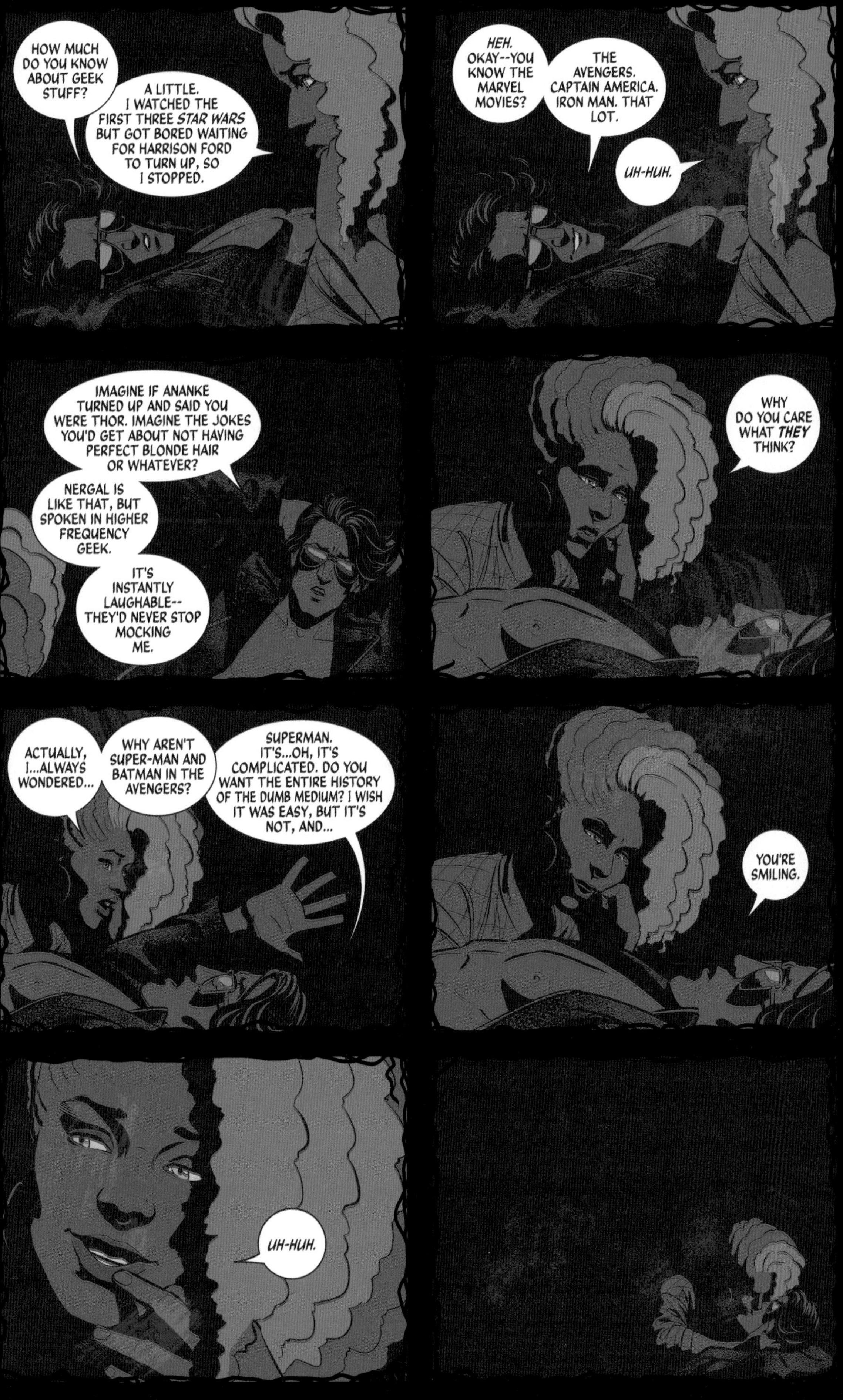
HOW MUCH DO YOU KNOW ABOUT GEEK STUFF?
A LITTLE. I WATCHED THE FIRST THREE *STAR WARS* BUT GOT BORED WAITING FOR HARRISON FORD TO TURN UP, SO I STOPPED.
HEH. OKAY--YOU KNOW THE MARVEL MOVIES?
THE AVENGERS. CAPTAIN AMERICA. IRON MAN. THAT LOT.
UH-HUH.
IMAGINE IF ANANKE TURNED UP AND SAID YOU WERE THOR. IMAGINE THE JOKES YOU'D GET ABOUT NOT HAVING PERFECT BLONDE HAIR OR WHATEVER?
NERGAL IS LIKE THAT, BUT SPOKEN IN HIGHER FREQUENCY GEEK.
IT'S INSTANTLY LAUGHABLE--THEY'D NEVER STOP MOCKING ME.
WHY DO YOU CARE WHAT ***THEY*** THINK?
ACTUALLY, I...ALWAYS WONDERED...
WHY AREN'T SUPER-MAN AND BATMAN IN THE AVENGERS?
SUPERMAN. IT'S...OH, IT'S COMPLICATED. DO YOU WANT THE ENTIRE HISTORY OF THE DUMB MEDIUM? I WISH IT WAS EASY, BUT IT'S NOT, AND...
YOU'RE SMILING.
UH-HUH.

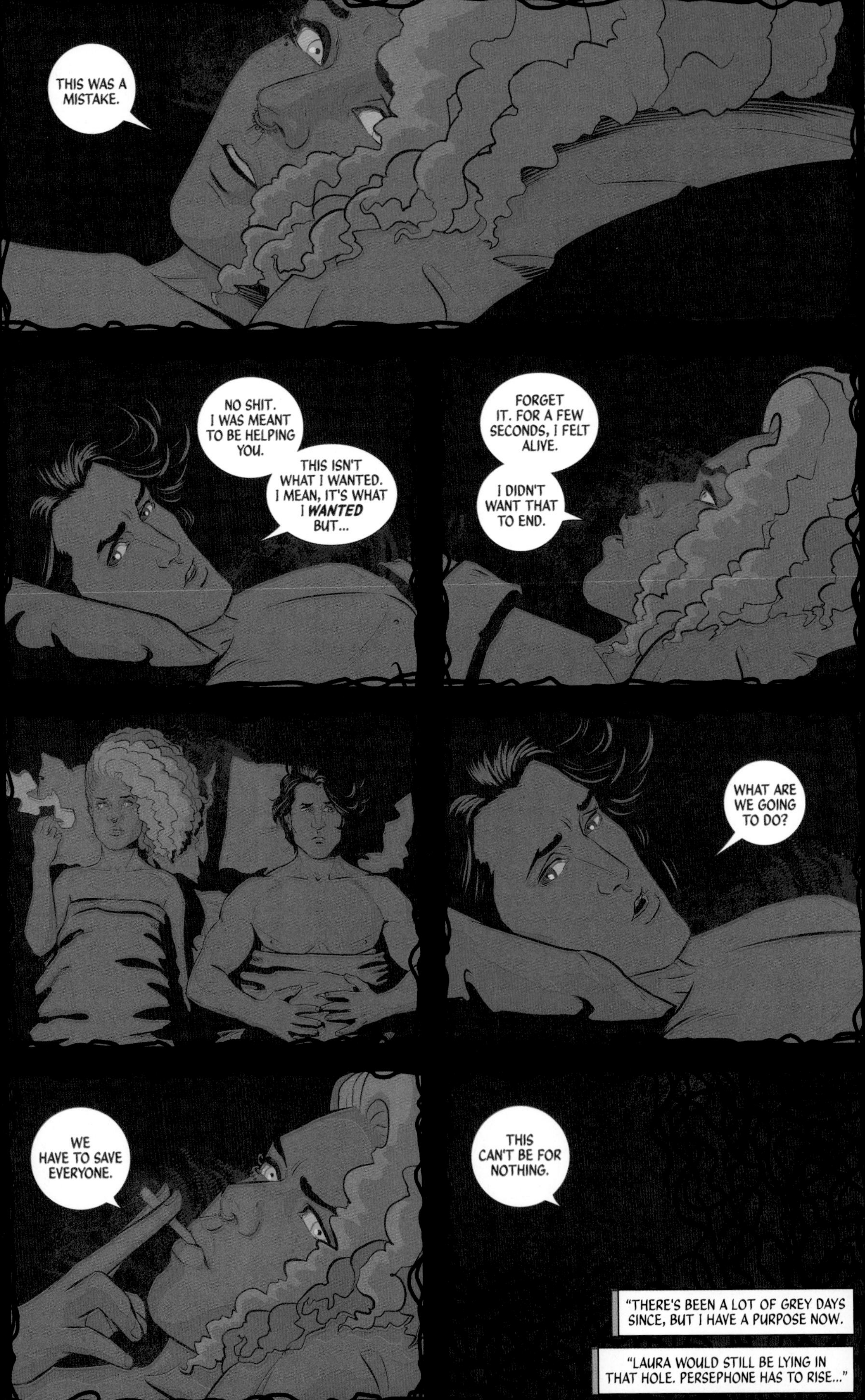
THIS WAS A MISTAKE.
NO SHIT. I WAS MEANT TO BE HELPING YOU.
THIS ISN'T WHAT I WANTED. I MEAN, IT'S WHAT I *WANTED* BUT...
FORGET IT. FOR A FEW SECONDS, I FELT ALIVE.
I DIDN'T WANT THAT TO END.
WHAT ARE WE GOING TO DO?
WE HAVE TO SAVE EVERYONE.
THIS CAN'T BE FOR NOTHING.
"THERE'S BEEN A LOT OF GREY DAYS SINCE, BUT I HAVE A PURPOSE NOW.
"LAURA WOULD STILL BE LYING IN THAT HOLE. PERSEPHONE HAS TO RISE..."

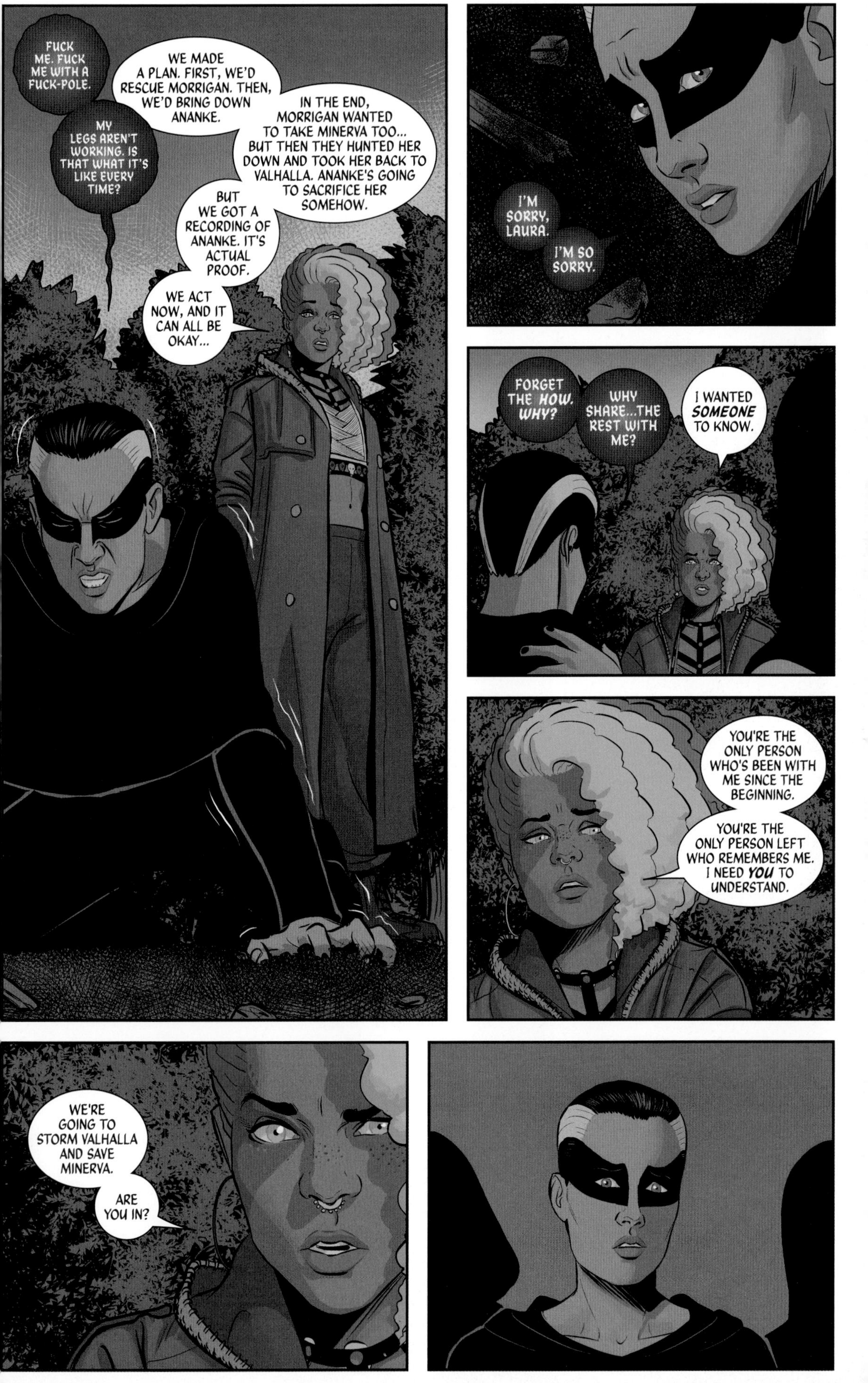
FUCK ME. FUCK ME WITH A FUCK-POLE.
MY LEGS AREN'T WORKING. IS THAT WHAT IT'S LIKE EVERY TIME?
WE MADE A PLAN. FIRST, WE'D RESCUE MORRIGAN. THEN, WE'D BRING DOWN ANANKE.
IN THE END, MORRIGAN WANTED TO TAKE MINERVA TOO... BUT THEN THEY HUNTED HER DOWN AND TOOK HER BACK TO VALHALLA. ANANKE'S GOING TO SACRIFICE HER SOMEHOW.
BUT WE GOT A RECORDING OF ANANKE. IT'S ACTUAL PROOF.
WE ACT NOW, AND IT CAN ALL BE OKAY...
I'M SORRY, LAURA.
I'M SO SORRY.
FORGET THE *HOW*. *WHY*?
WHY SHARE...THE REST WITH ME?
I WANTED ***SOMEONE*** TO KNOW.
YOU'RE THE ONLY PERSON WHO'S BEEN WITH ME SINCE THE BEGINNING.
YOU'RE THE ONLY PERSON LEFT WHO REMEMBERS ME. I NEED ***YOU*** TO UNDERSTAND.
WE'RE GOING TO STORM VALHALLA AND SAVE MINERVA.
ARE YOU IN?

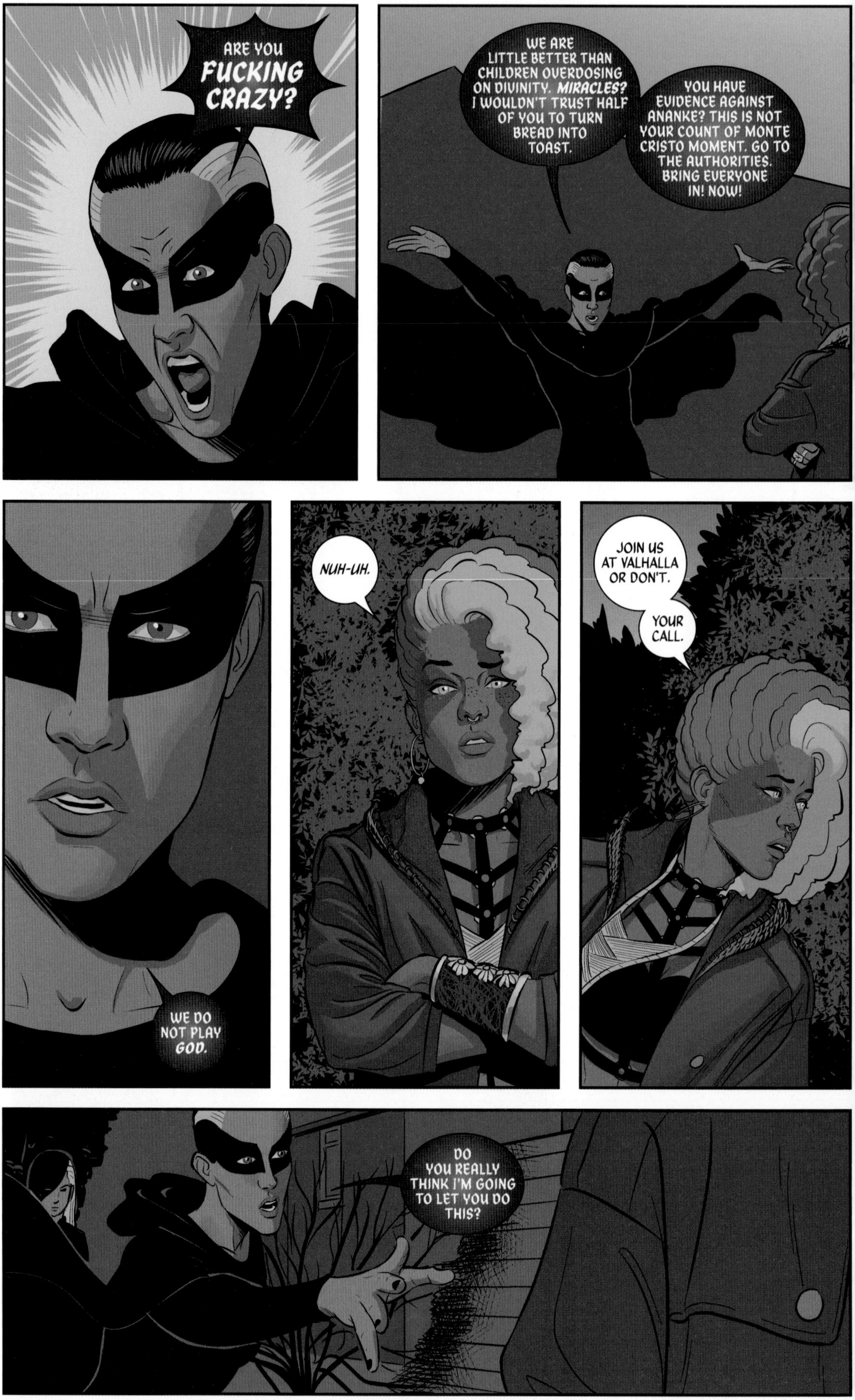
ARE YOU FUCKING CRAZY?
WE ARE LITTLE BETTER THAN CHILDREN OVERDOSING ON DIVINITY. MIRACLES? I WOULDN'T TRUST HALF OF YOU TO TURN BREAD INTO TOAST.
YOU HAVE EVIDENCE AGAINST ANANKE? THIS IS NOT YOUR COUNT OF MONTE CRISTO MOMENT. GO TO THE AUTHORITIES. BRING EVERYONE IN! NOW!
WE DO NOT PLAY GOD.
NUH-UH.
JOIN US AT VALHALLA OR DON'T.
YOUR CALL.
DO YOU REALLY THINK I'M GOING TO LET YOU DO THIS?

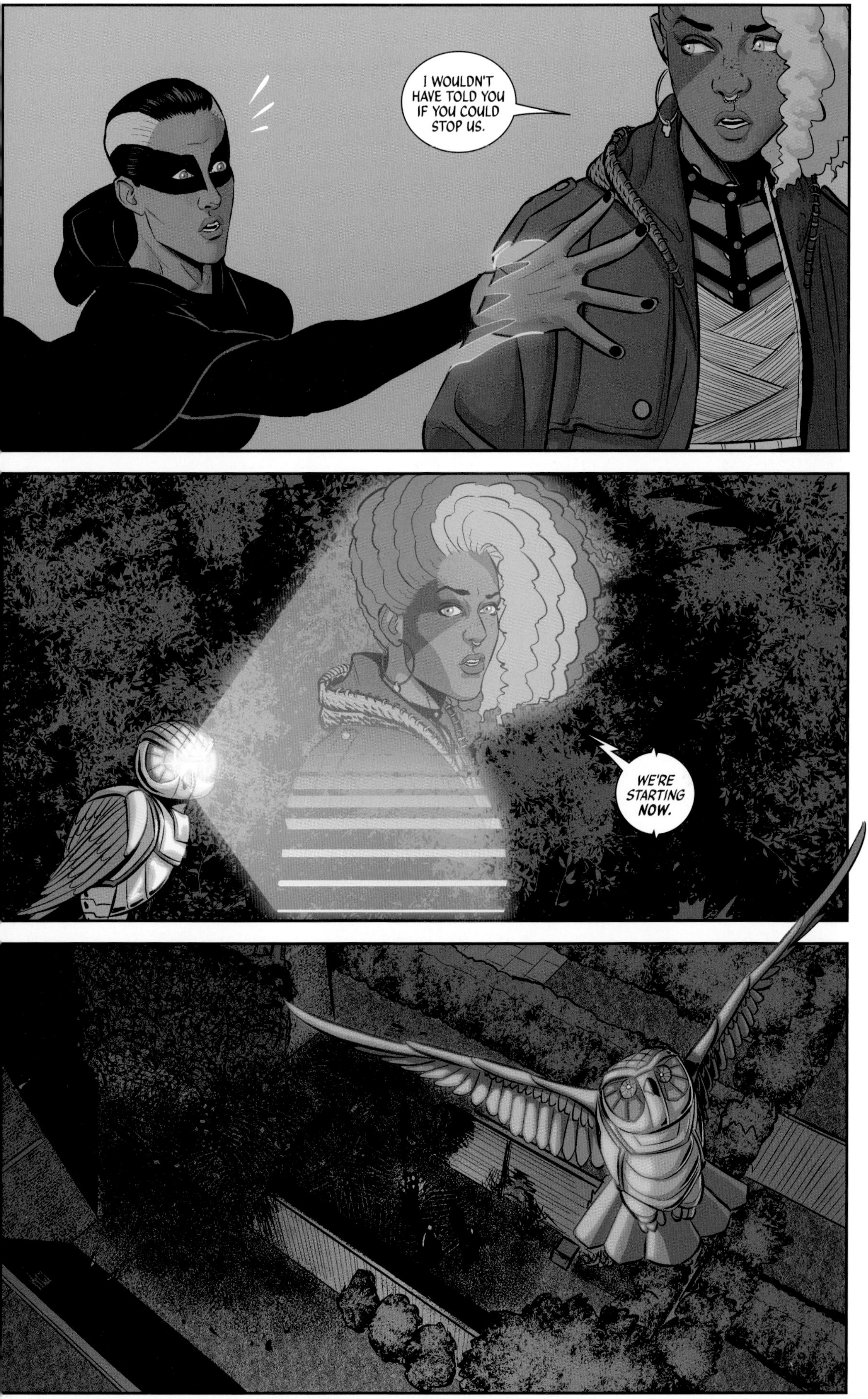
I WOULDN'T HAVE TOLD YOU IF YOU COULD STOP US.
WE'RE STARTING NOW.

THE MESS
WE'RE IN

24 SEPTEMBER 2014

THE
WICKED
+
THE
DIVINE

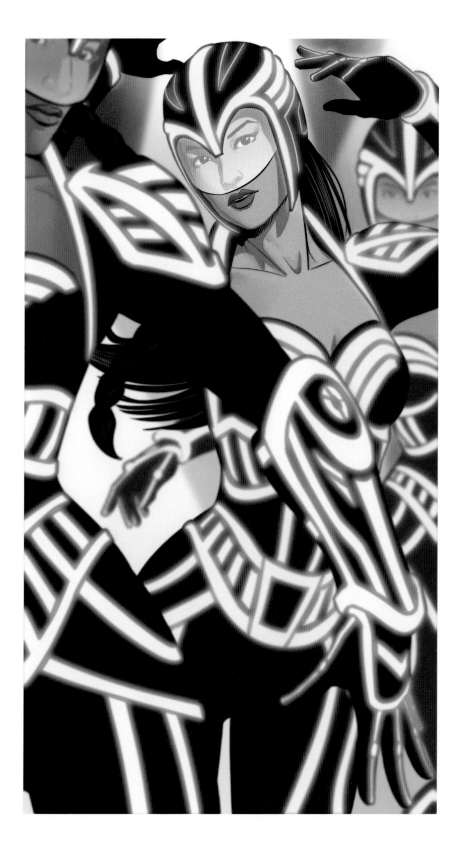

THE
WICKED
+
THE DIVINE

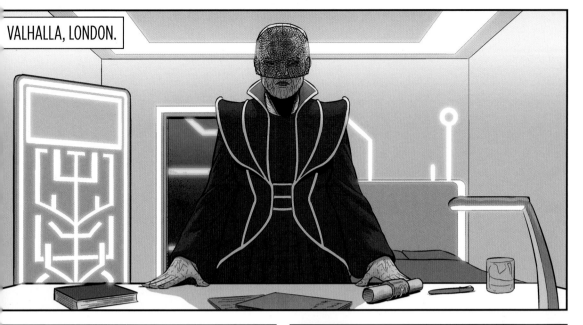

VALHALLA, LONDON.

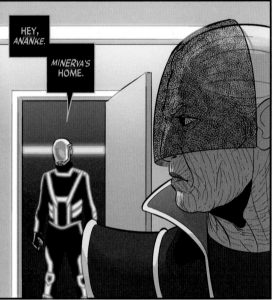

HEY, ANANKE.

MINERVA'S HOME.

IS THE MACHINE READY?

YES, BUT--

PREPARE IT.

WHY, YES, YOUR HIGHNESS.

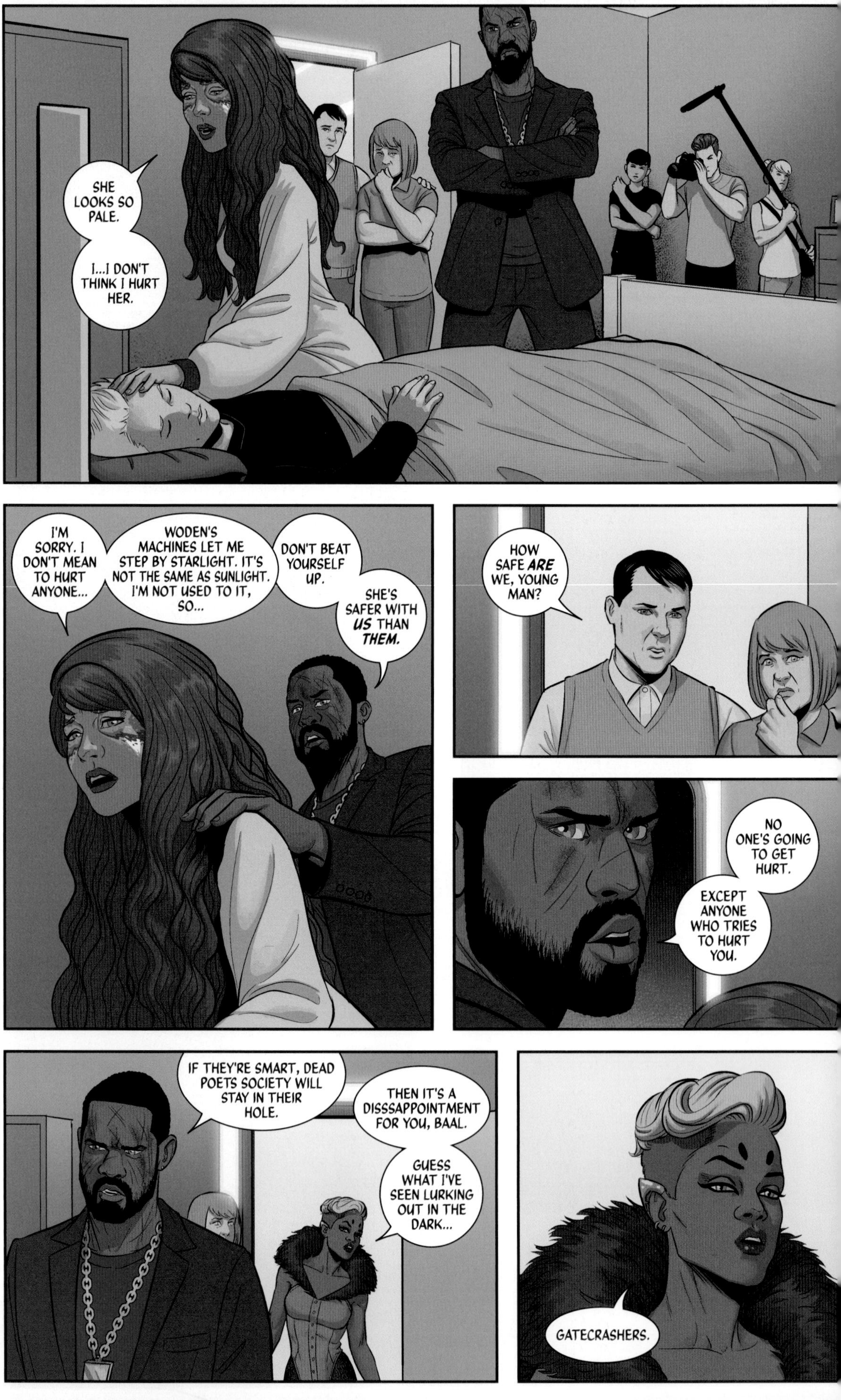
SHE LOOKS SO PALE.
I...I DON'T THINK I HURT HER.
I'M SORRY. I DON'T MEAN TO HURT ANYONE...
WODEN'S MACHINES LET ME STEP BY STARLIGHT. IT'S NOT THE SAME AS SUNLIGHT. I'M NOT USED TO IT, SO...
DON'T BEAT YOURSELF UP.
SHE'S SAFER WITH US THAN THEM.
HOW SAFE ARE WE, YOUNG MAN?
NO ONE'S GOING TO GET HURT.
EXCEPT ANYONE WHO TRIES TO HURT YOU.
IF THEY'RE SMART, DEAD POETS SOCIETY WILL STAY IN THEIR HOLE.
THEN IT'S A DISSSAPPOINTMENT FOR YOU, BAAL.
GUESS WHAT I'VE SEEN LURKING OUT IN THE DARK...
GATECRASHERS.

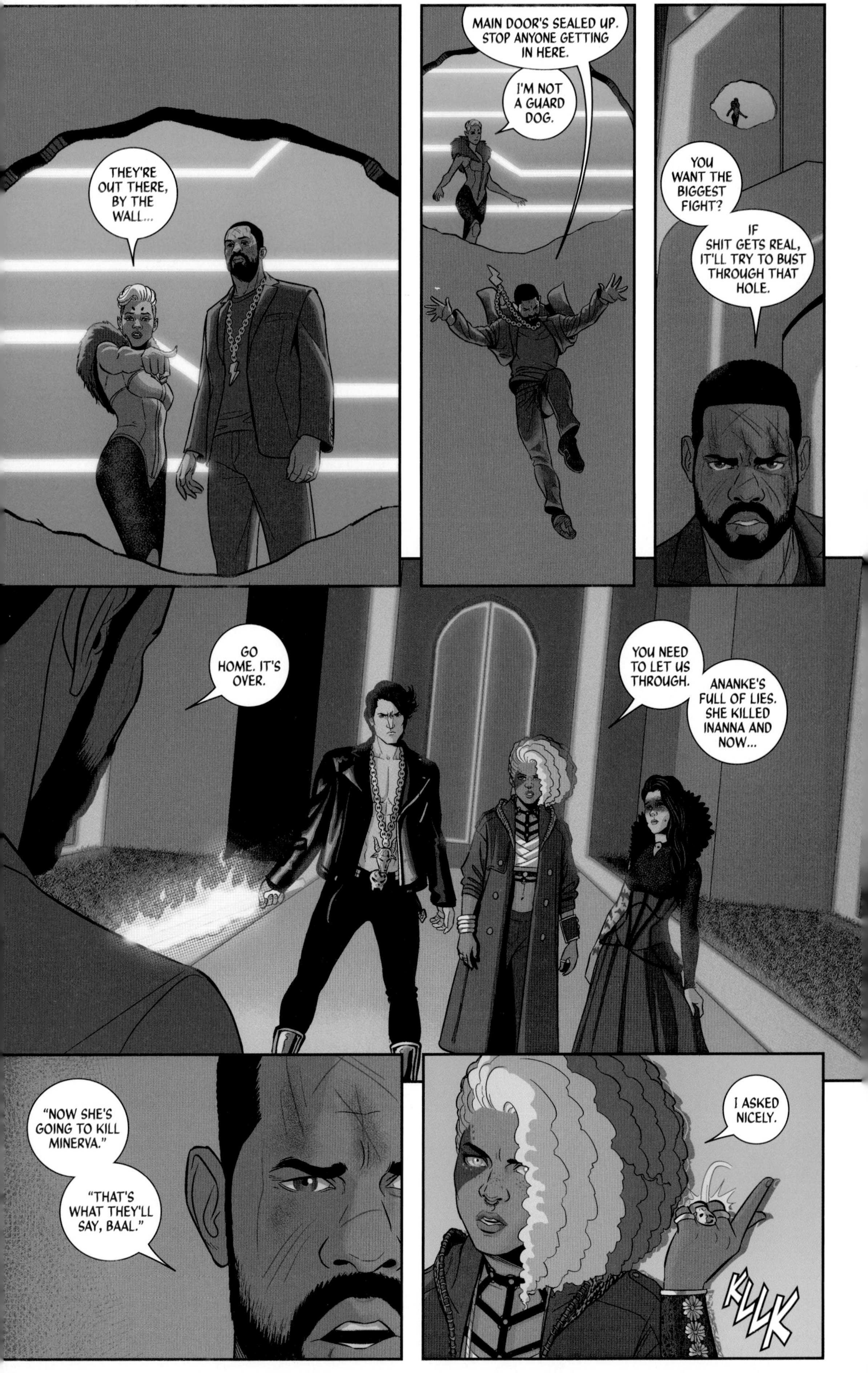
THEY'RE OUT THERE, BY THE WALL...
MAIN DOOR'S SEALED UP. STOP ANYONE GETTING IN HERE.
I'M NOT A GUARD DOG.
YOU WANT THE BIGGEST FIGHT?
IF SHIT GETS REAL, IT'LL TRY TO BUST THROUGH THAT HOLE.
GO HOME. IT'S OVER.
YOU NEED TO LET US THROUGH.
ANANKE'S FULL OF LIES. SHE KILLED INANNA AND NOW...
"NOW SHE'S GOING TO KILL MINERVA."
"THAT'S WHAT THEY'LL SAY, BAAL."
I ASKED NICELY.
KLLK

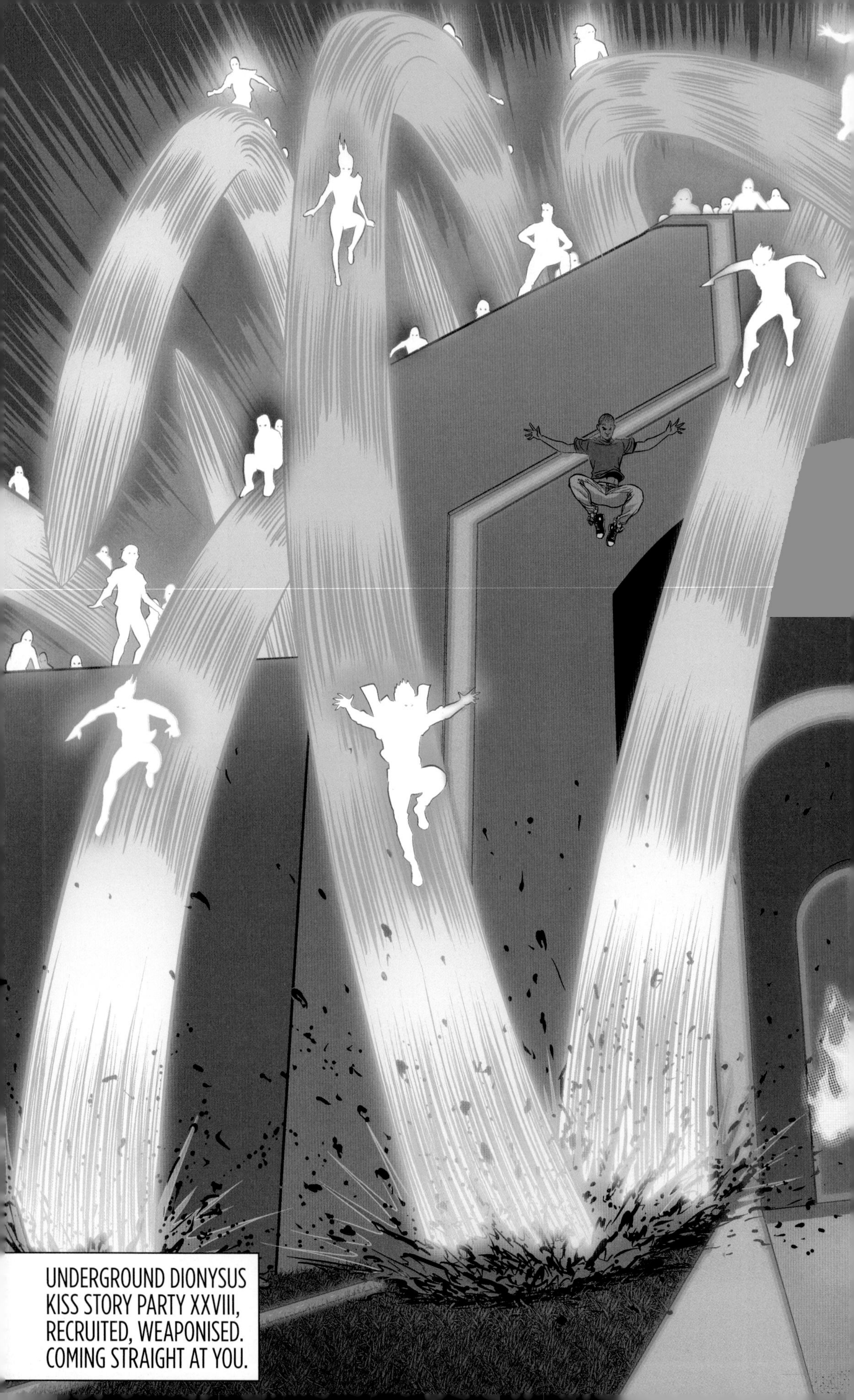
UNDERGROUND DIONYSUS KISS STORY PARTY XXVIII, RECRUITED, WEAPONISED. COMING STRAIGHT AT YOU.

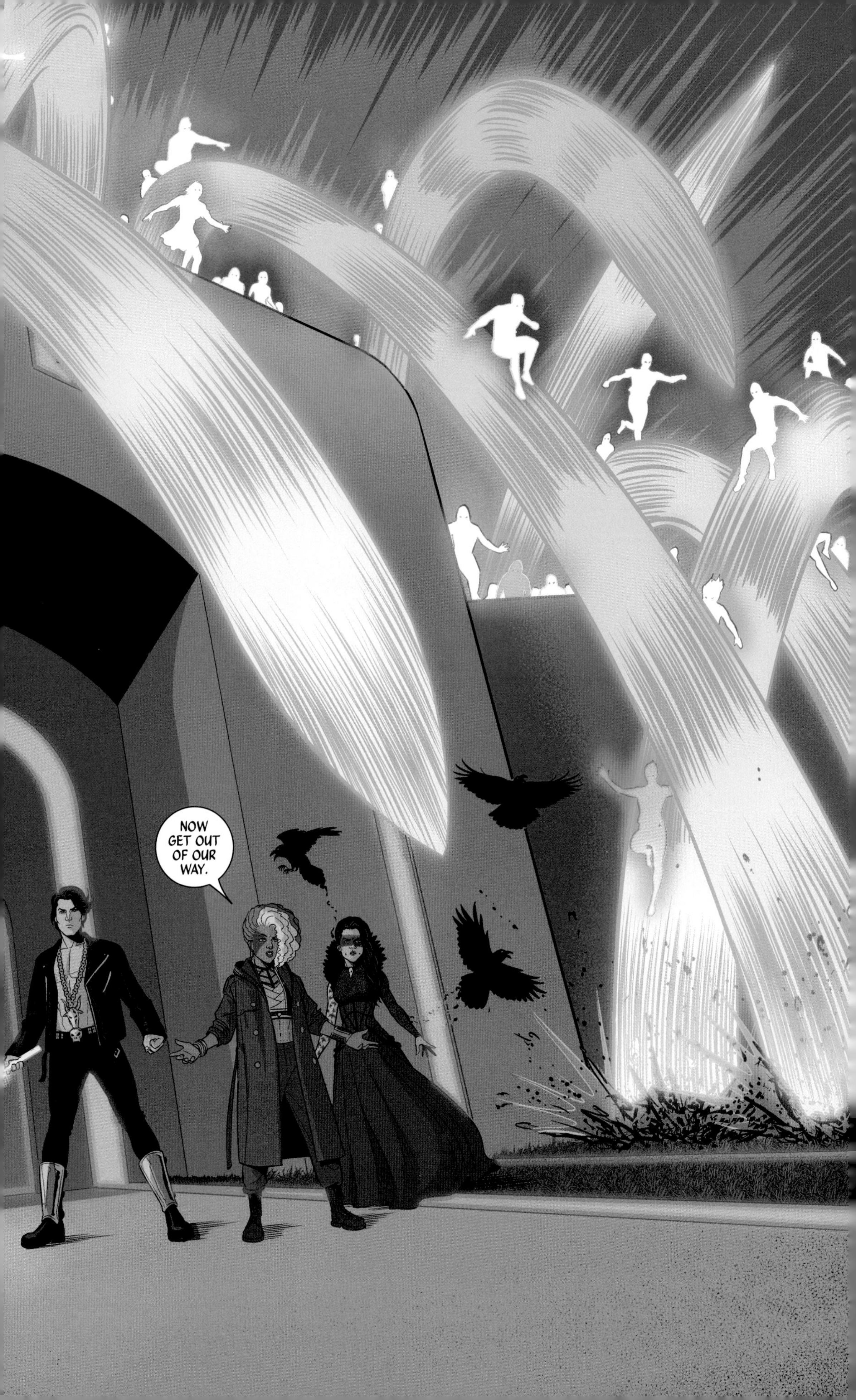
NOW GET OUT OF OUR WAY.

SHIT, BECOMING

24 SEPTEMBER 2014

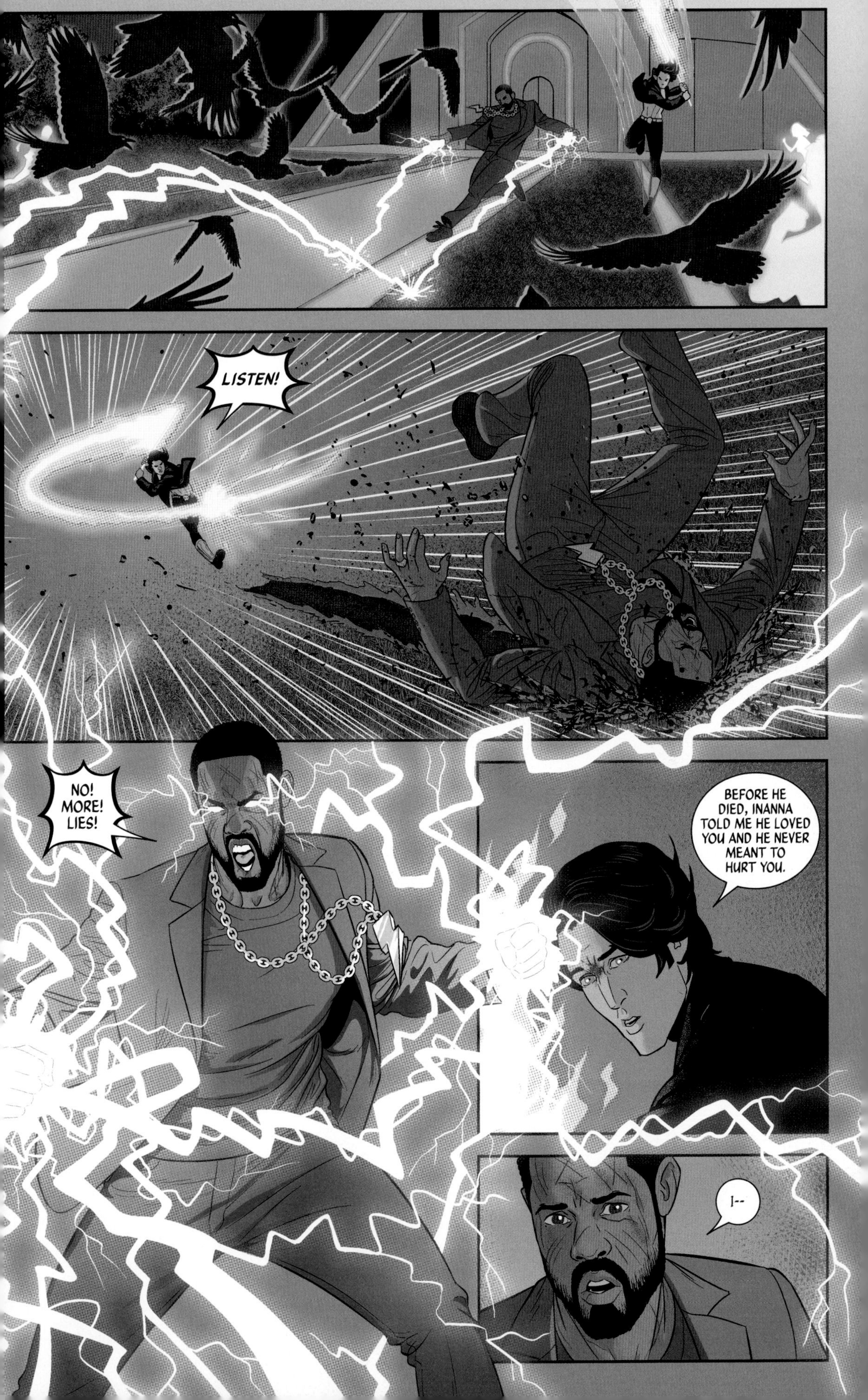
LISTEN!
NO! MORE! LIES!
BEFORE HE DIED, INANNA TOLD ME HE LOVED YOU AND HE NEVER MEANT TO HURT YOU.
I--

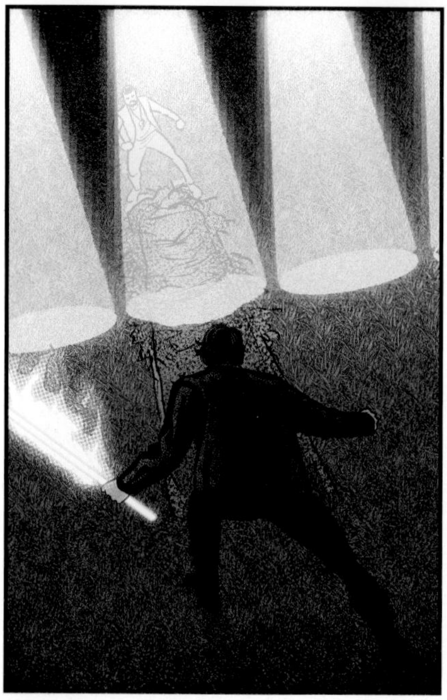

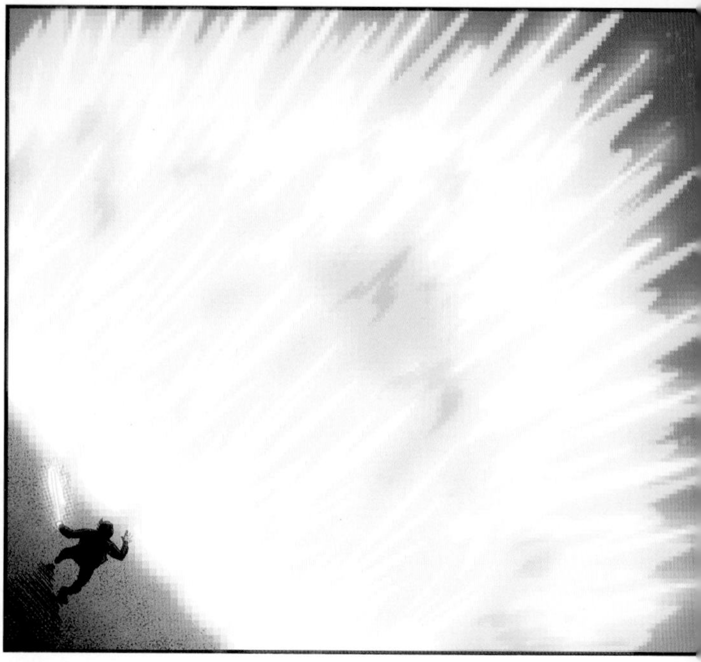

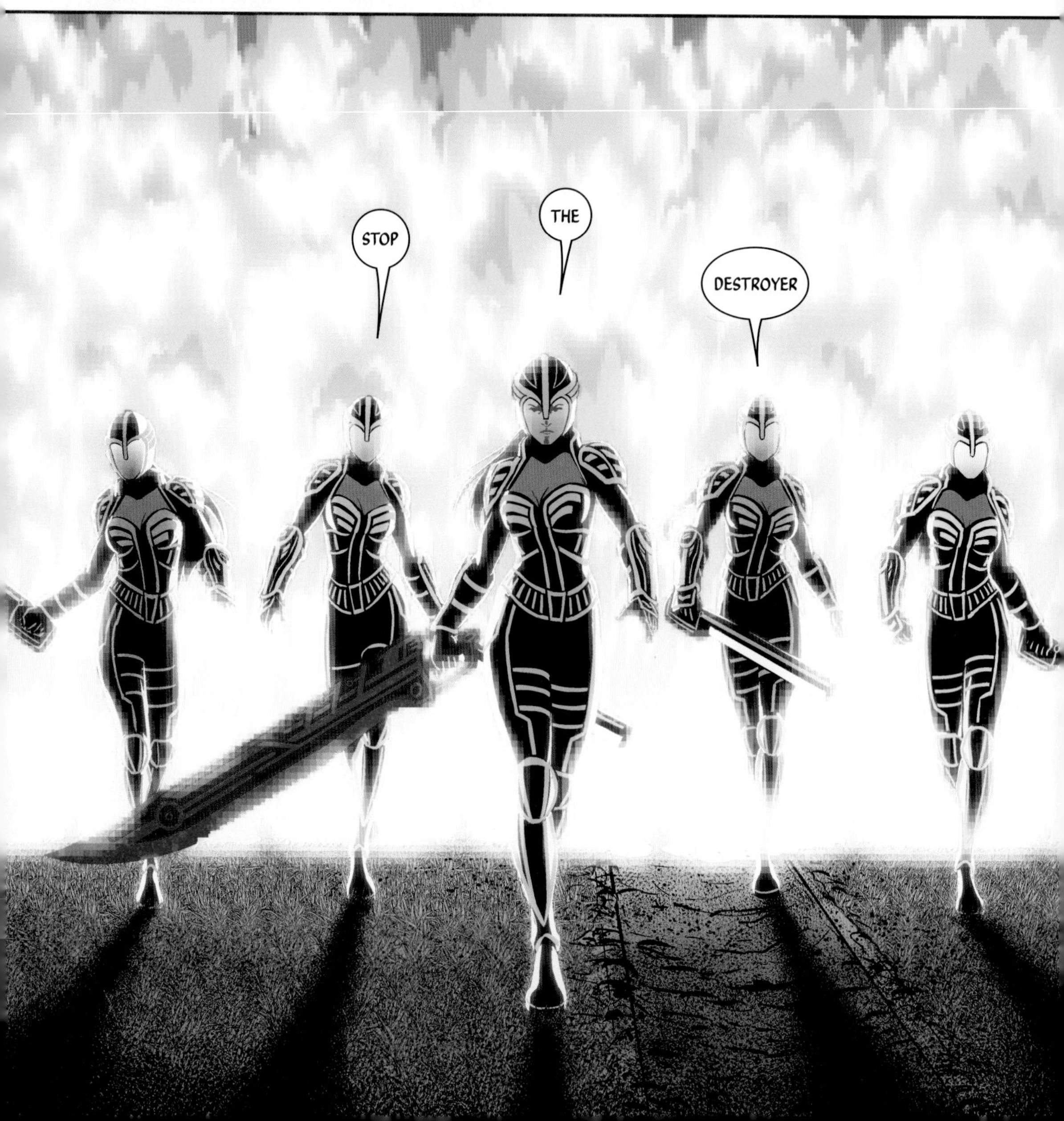
STOP
THE
DESTROYER

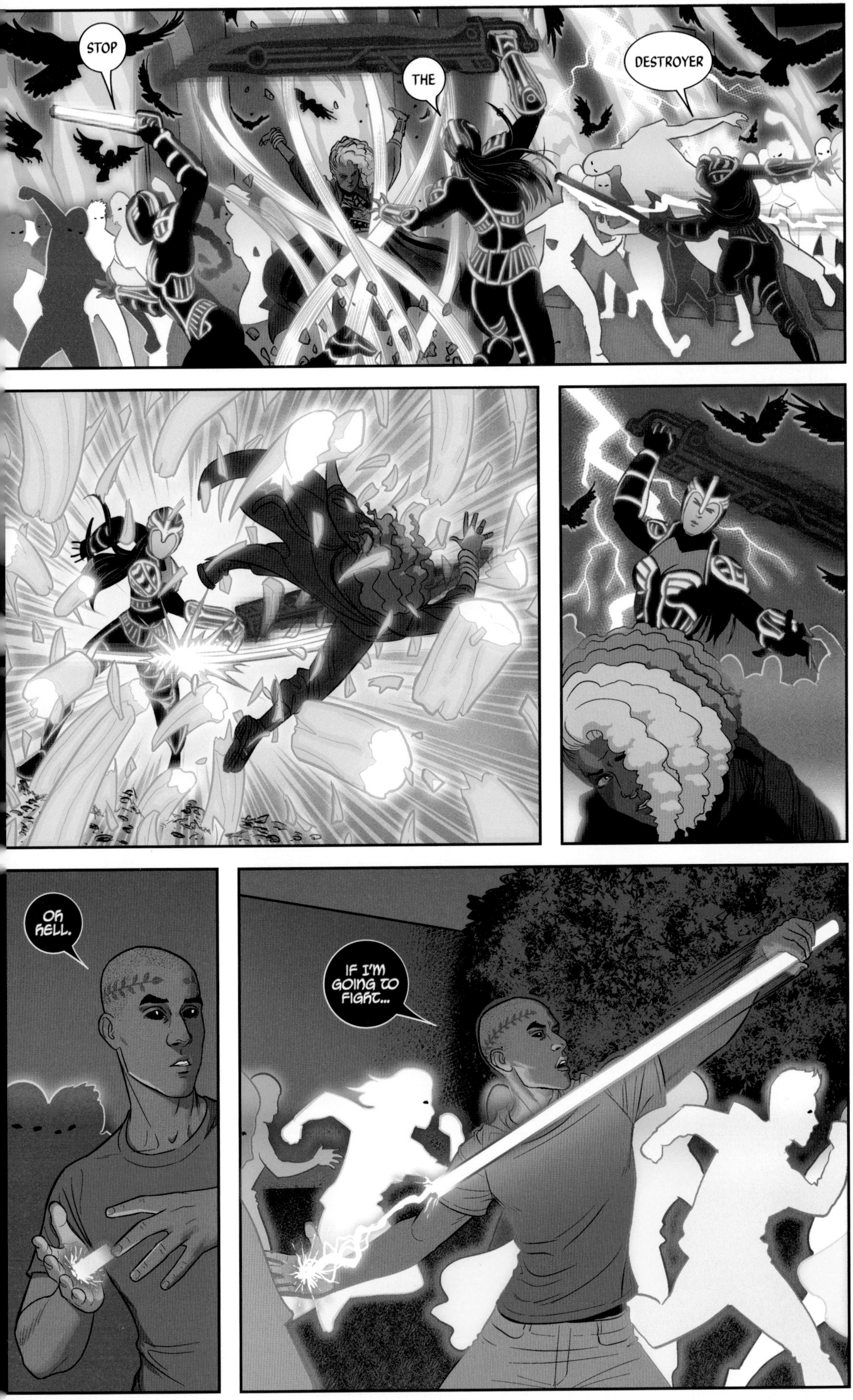
STOP
THE
DESTROYER
OH HELL.
IF I'M GOING TO FIGHT...

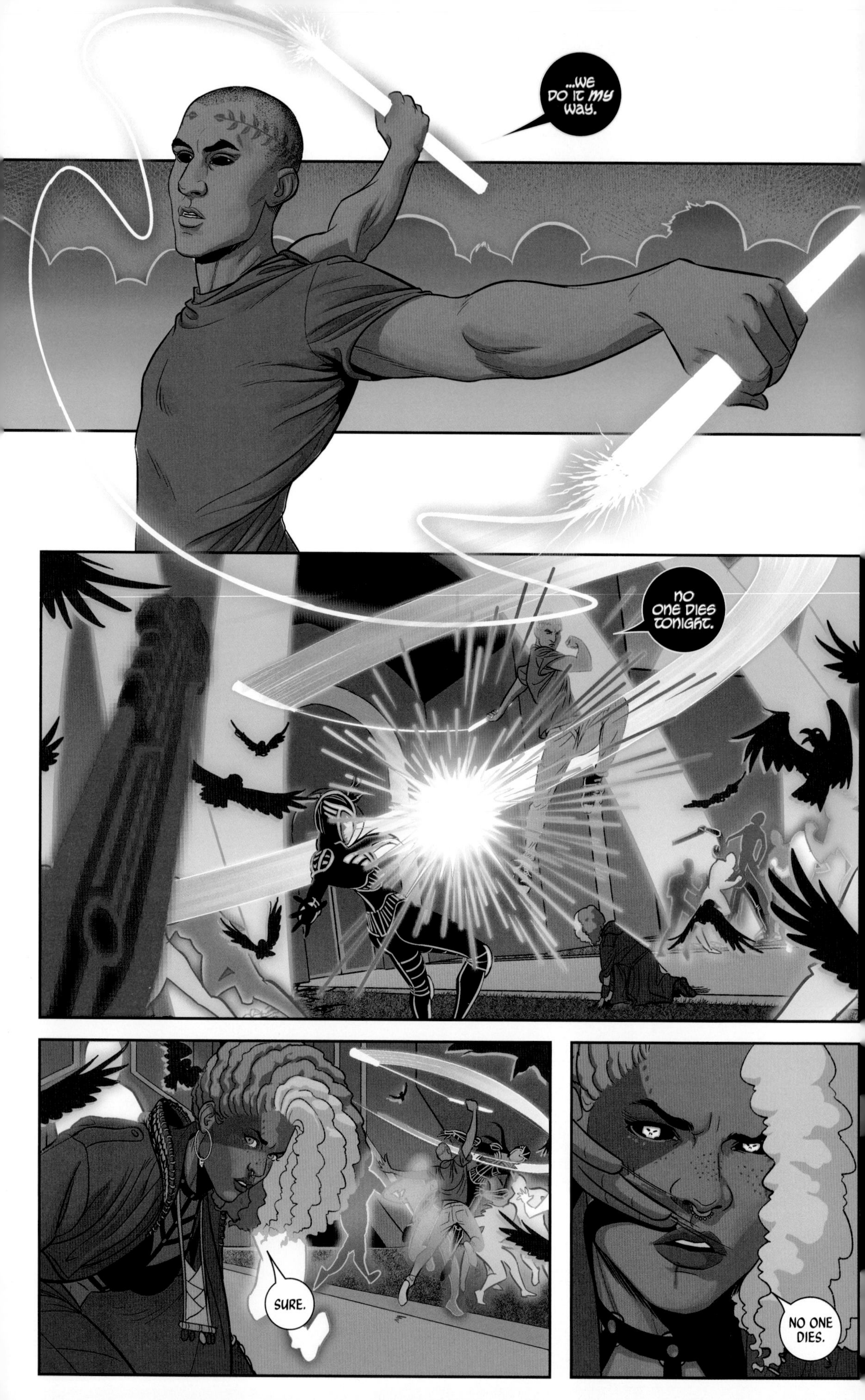
...WE DO IT MY WAY.
NO ONE DIES TONIGHT.
SURE.
NO ONE DIES.

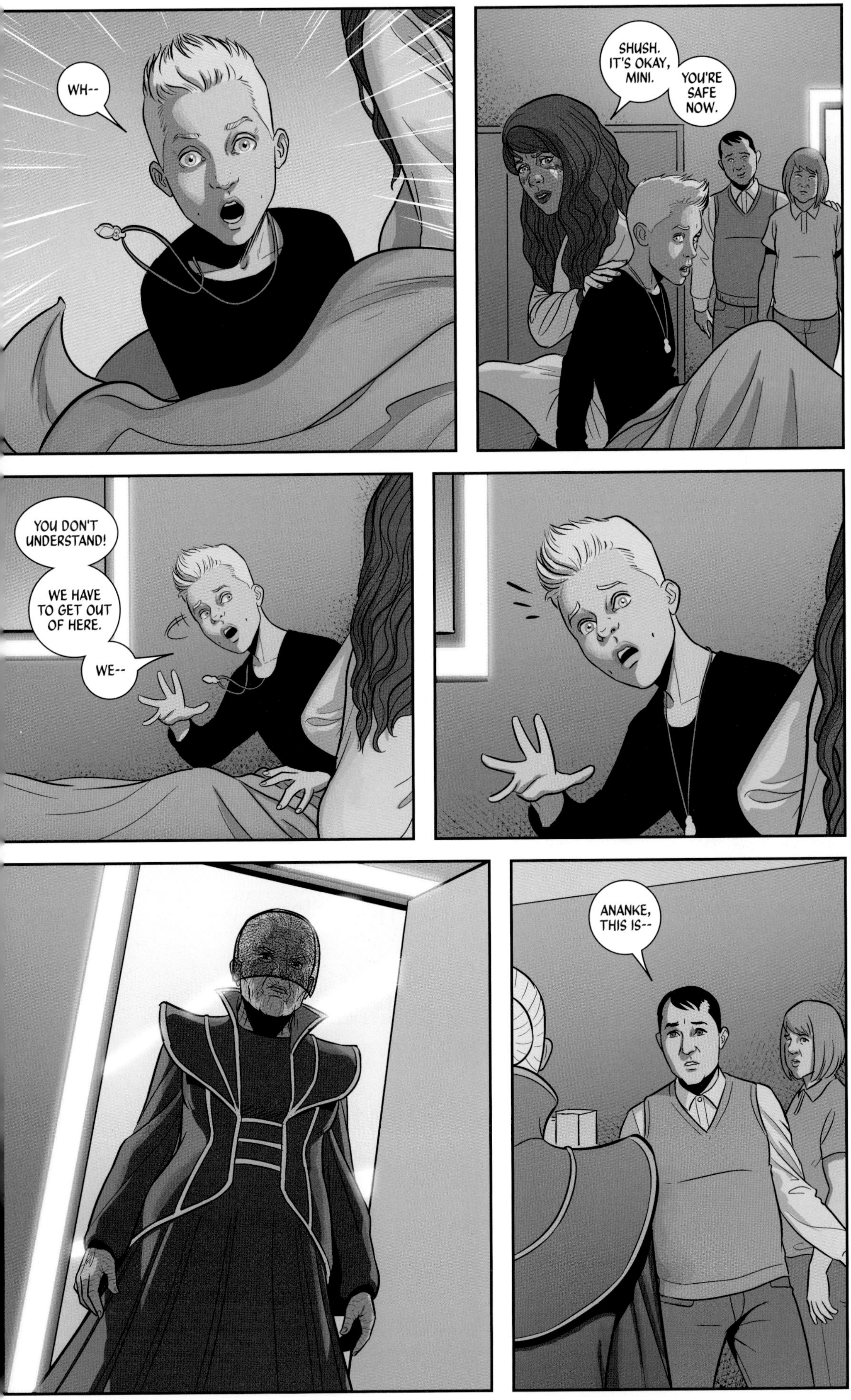
WH--
SHUSH. IT'S OKAY, MINI.
YOU'RE SAFE NOW.
YOU DON'T UNDERSTAND!
WE HAVE TO GET OUT OF HERE.
WE--
ANANKE, THIS IS--

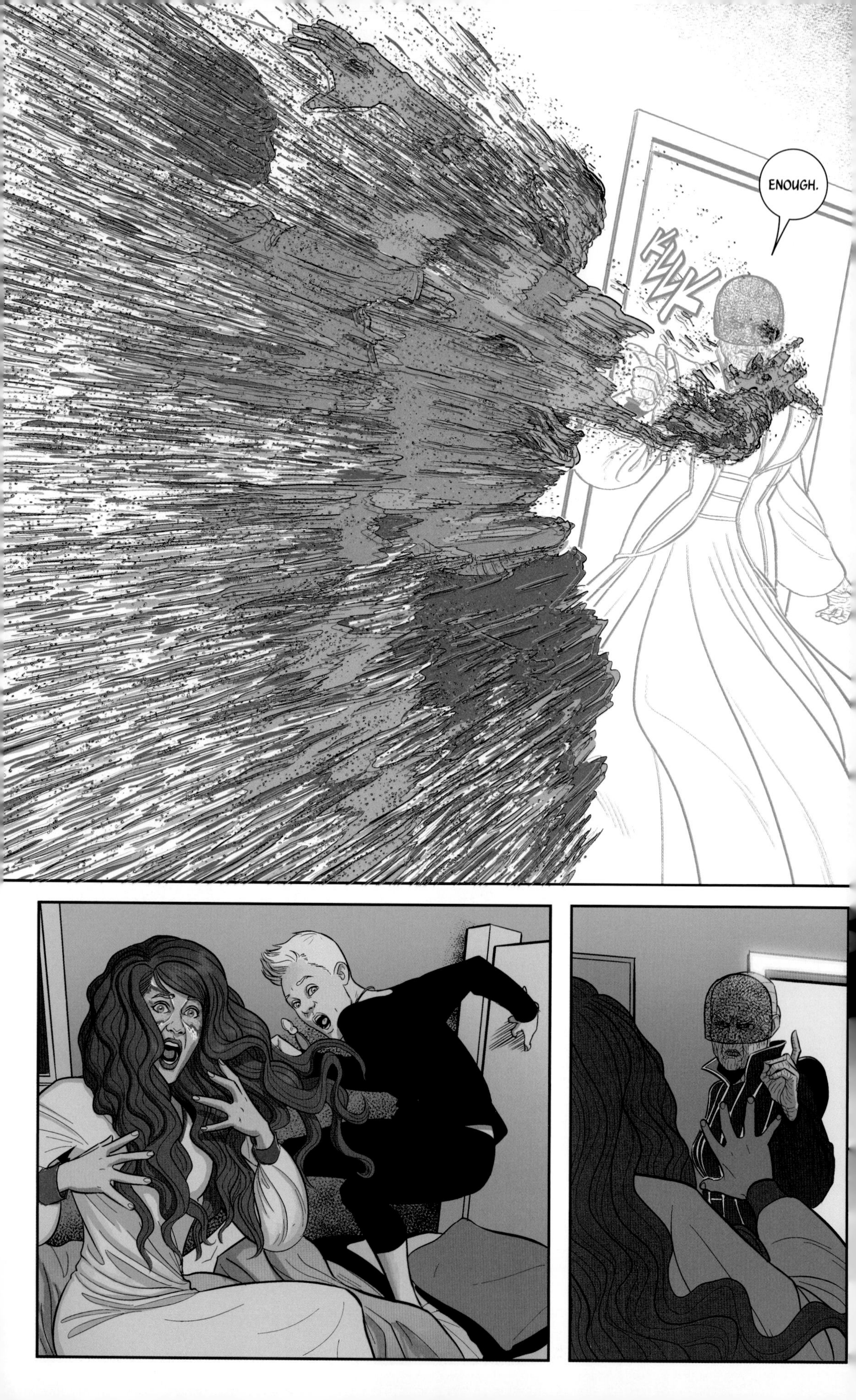
ENOUGH.

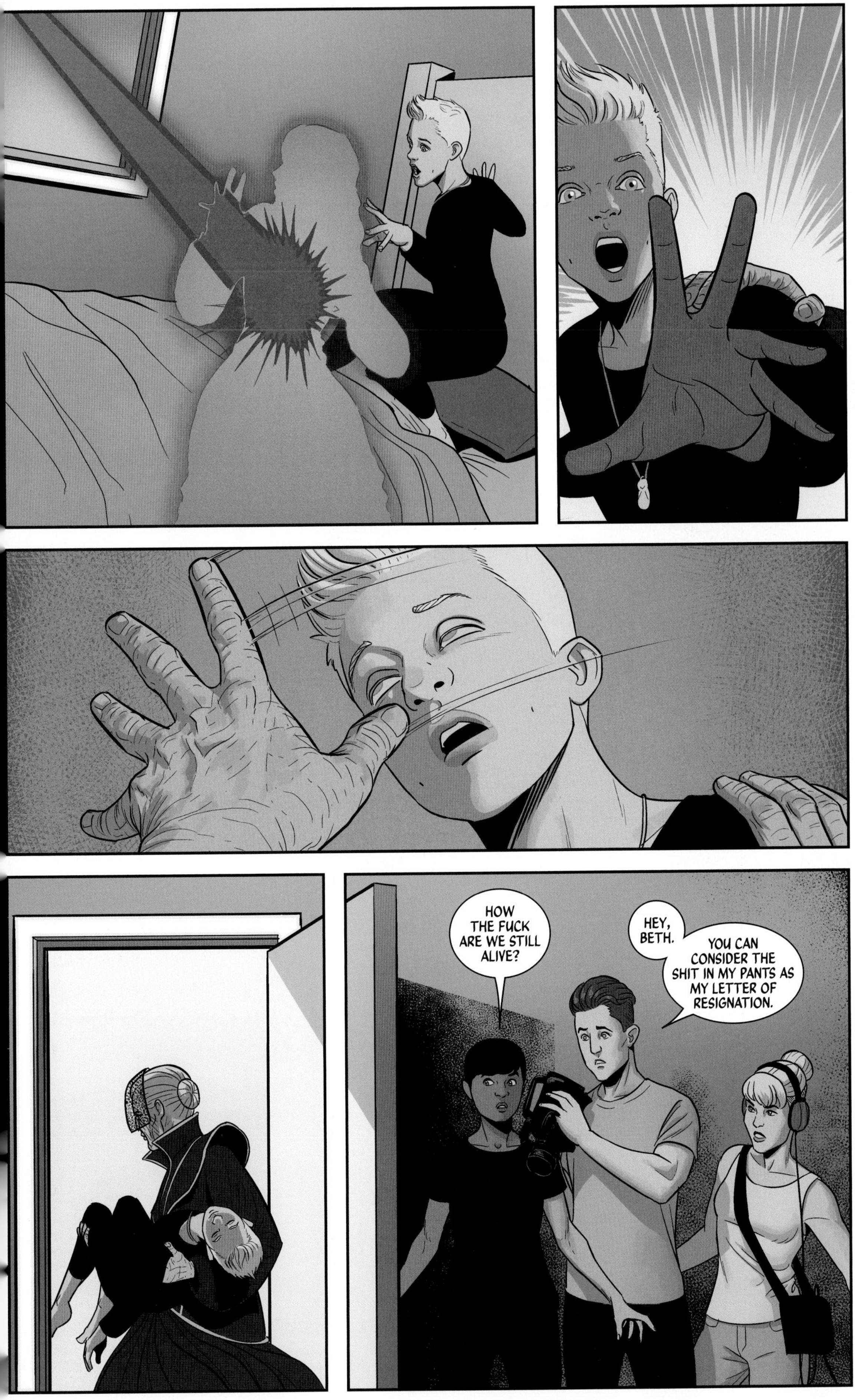
HOW THE FUCK ARE WE STILL ALIVE?
HEY, BETH.
YOU CAN CONSIDER THE SHIT IN MY PANTS AS MY LETTER OF RESIGNATION.

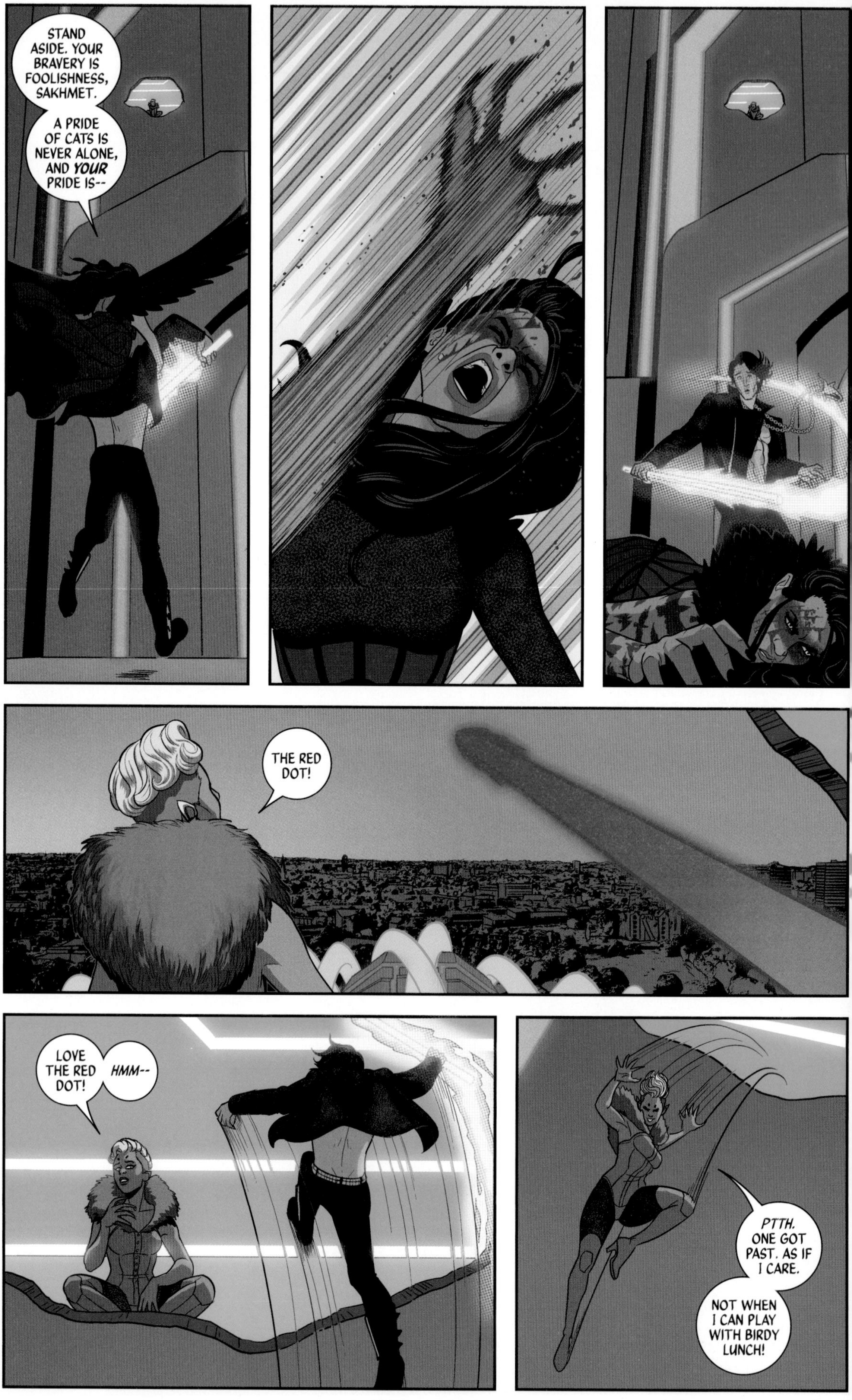
STAND ASIDE. YOUR BRAVERY IS FOOLISHNESS, SAKHMET.
A PRIDE OF CATS IS NEVER ALONE, AND *YOUR* PRIDE IS--
THE RED DOT!
LOVE THE RED DOT!
HMM--
PTTH. ONE GOT PAST. AS IF I CARE.
NOT WHEN I CAN PLAY WITH BIRDY LUNCH!

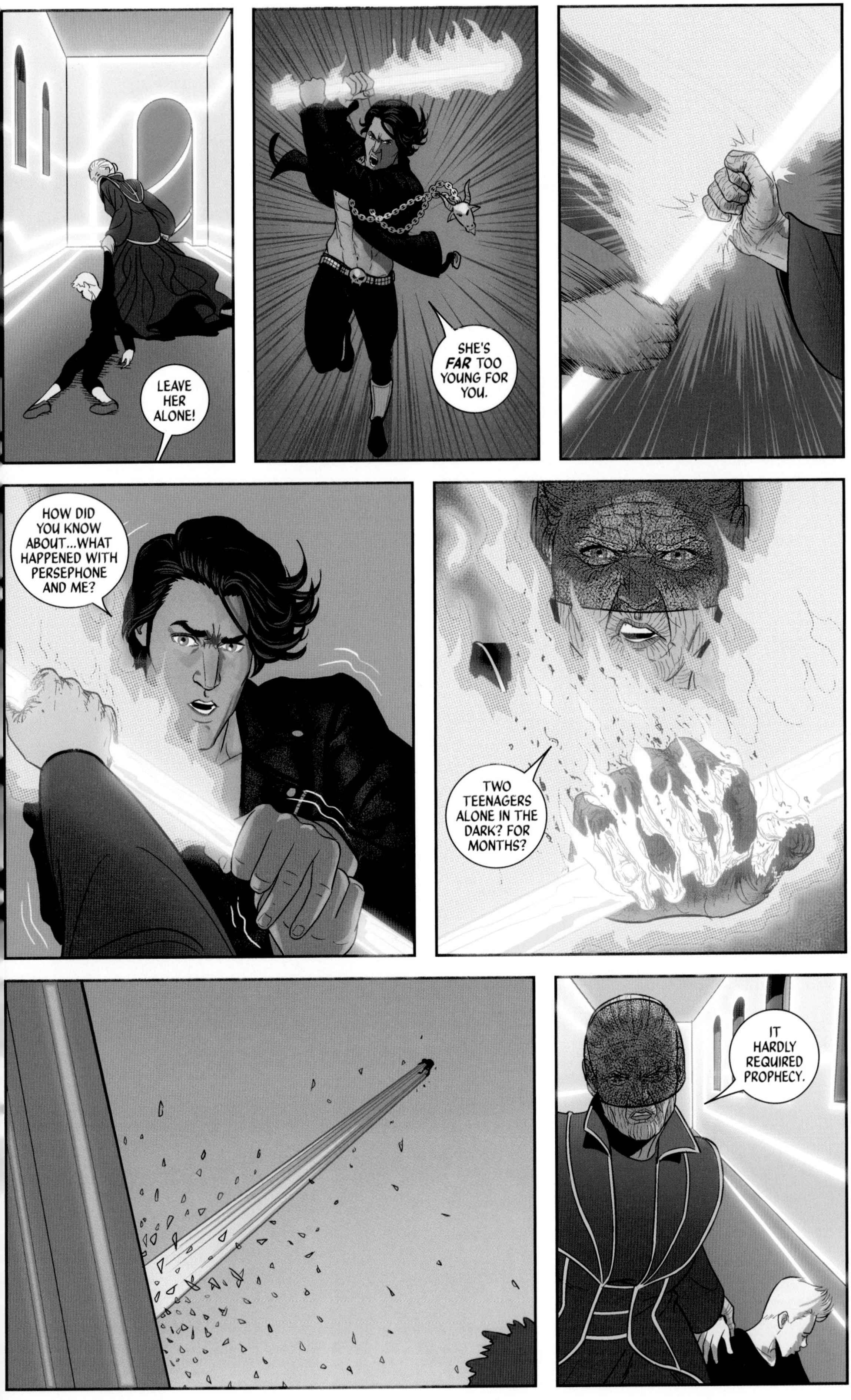
LEAVE HER ALONE!
SHE'S FAR TOO YOUNG FOR YOU.
HOW DID YOU KNOW ABOUT...WHAT HAPPENED WITH PERSEPHONE AND ME?
TWO TEENAGERS ALONE IN THE DARK? FOR MONTHS?
IT HARDLY REQUIRED PROPHECY.

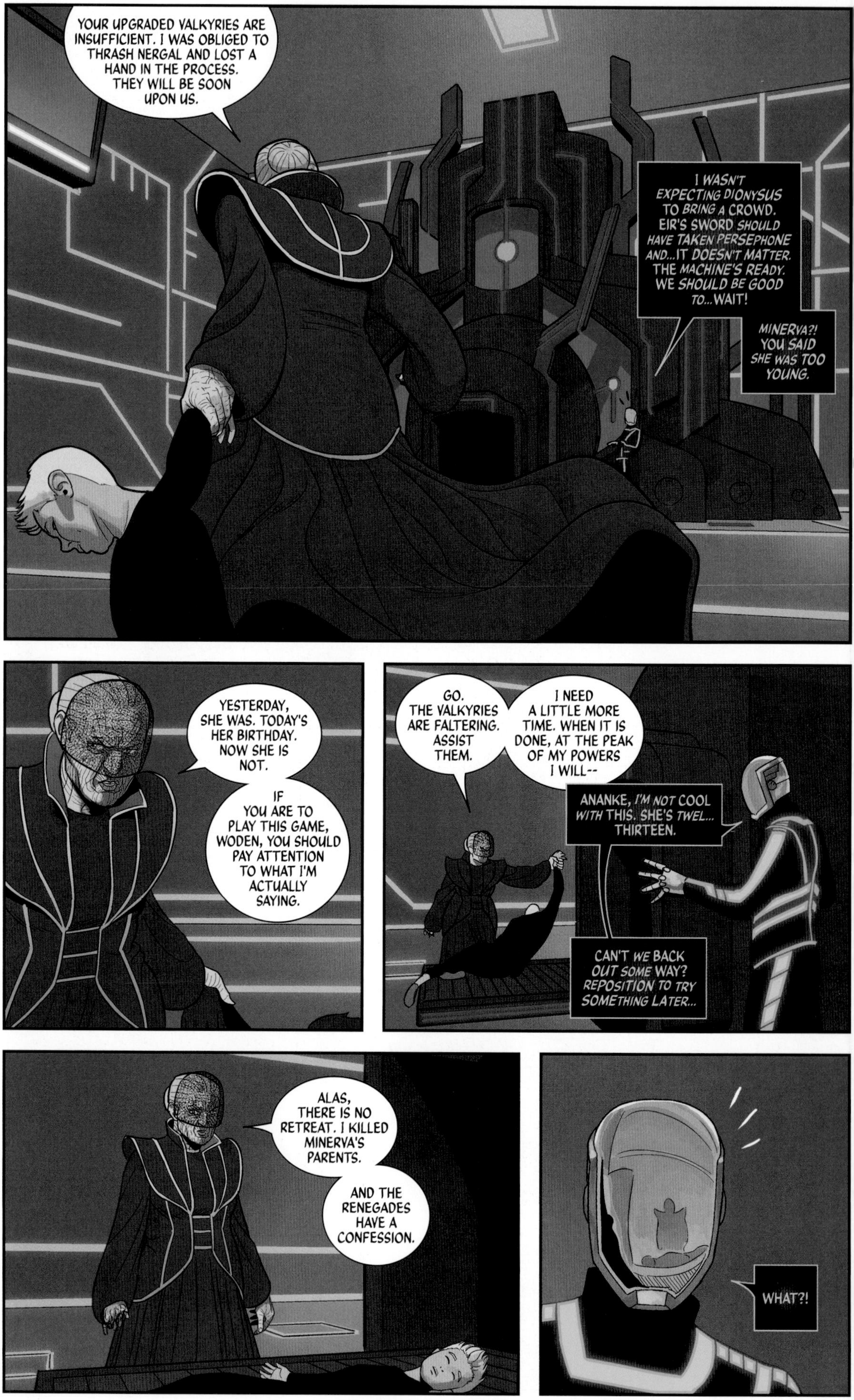
YOUR UPGRADED VALKYRIES ARE INSUFFICIENT. I WAS OBLIGED TO THRASH NERGAL AND LOST A HAND IN THE PROCESS. THEY WILL BE SOON UPON US.
I WASN'T EXPECTING DIONYSUS TO BRING A CROWD. EIR'S SWORD SHOULD HAVE TAKEN PERSEPHONE AND...IT DOESN'T MATTER. THE MACHINE'S READY. WE SHOULD BE GOOD TO...WAIT!
MINERVA?! YOU SAID SHE WAS TOO YOUNG.
YESTERDAY, SHE WAS. TODAY'S HER BIRTHDAY. NOW SHE IS NOT.
IF YOU ARE TO PLAY THIS GAME, WODEN, YOU SHOULD PAY ATTENTION TO WHAT I'M ACTUALLY SAYING.
GO. THE VALKYRIES ARE FALTERING. ASSIST THEM.
I NEED A LITTLE MORE TIME. WHEN IT IS DONE, AT THE PEAK OF MY POWERS I WILL--
ANANKE, I'M NOT COOL WITH THIS. SHE'S TWEL... THIRTEEN.
CAN'T WE BACK OUT SOME WAY? REPOSITION TO TRY SOMETHING LATER...
ALAS, THERE IS NO RETREAT. I KILLED MINERVA'S PARENTS.
AND THE RENEGADES HAVE A CONFESSION.
WHAT?!

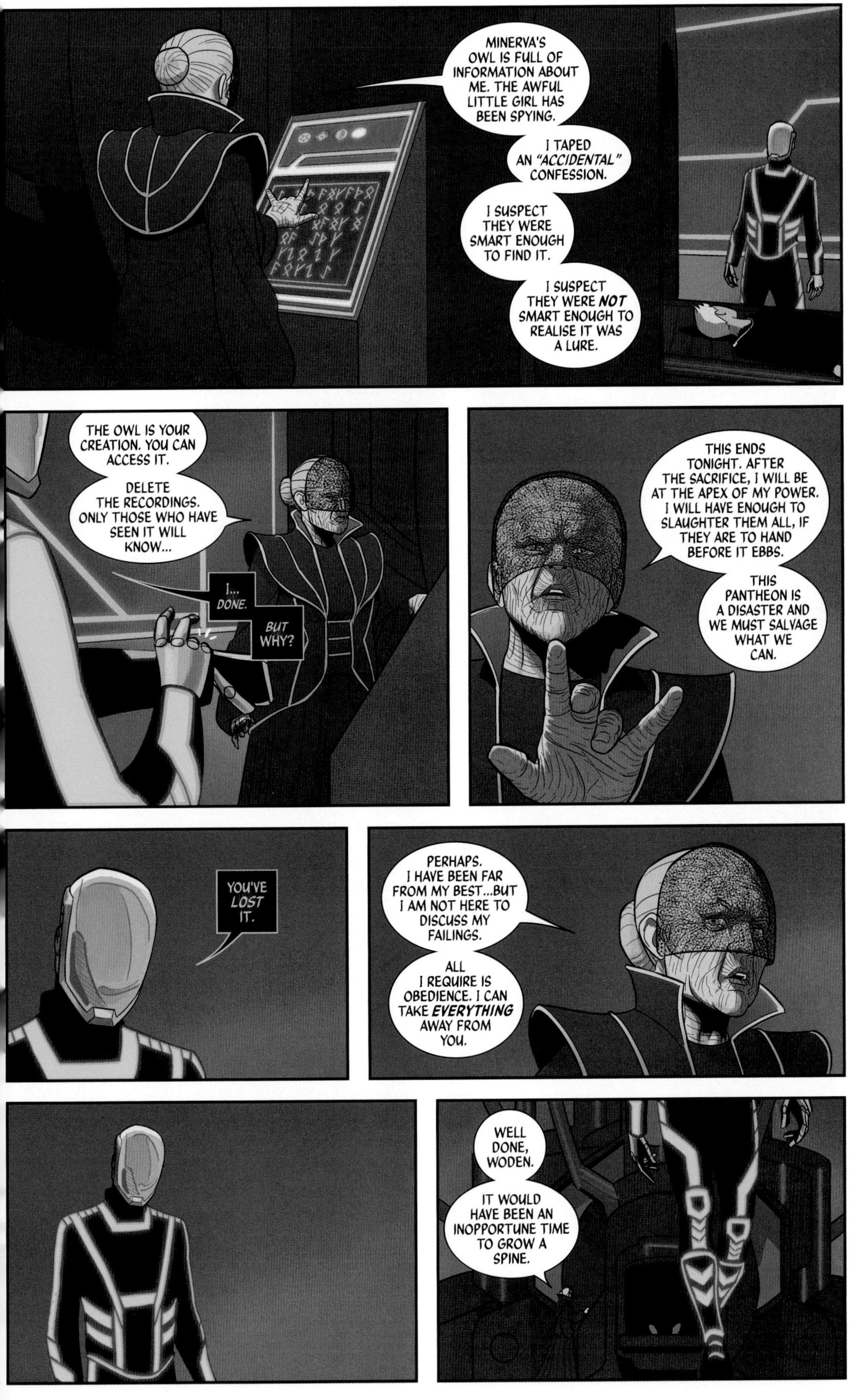
MINERVA'S OWL IS FULL OF INFORMATION ABOUT ME. THE AWFUL LITTLE GIRL HAS BEEN SPYING.
I TAPED AN "ACCIDENTAL" CONFESSION.
I SUSPECT THEY WERE SMART ENOUGH TO FIND IT.
I SUSPECT THEY WERE NOT SMART ENOUGH TO REALISE IT WAS A LURE.
THE OWL IS YOUR CREATION. YOU CAN ACCESS IT.
DELETE THE RECORDINGS. ONLY THOSE WHO HAVE SEEN IT WILL KNOW...
I... DONE.
BUT WHY?
THIS ENDS TONIGHT. AFTER THE SACRIFICE, I WILL BE AT THE APEX OF MY POWER. I WILL HAVE ENOUGH TO SLAUGHTER THEM ALL, IF THEY ARE TO HAND BEFORE IT EBBS.
THIS PANTHEON IS A DISASTER AND WE MUST SALVAGE WHAT WE CAN.
YOU'VE LOST IT.
PERHAPS. I HAVE BEEN FAR FROM MY BEST...BUT I AM NOT HERE TO DISCUSS MY FAILINGS.
ALL I REQUIRE IS OBEDIENCE. I CAN TAKE EVERYTHING AWAY FROM YOU.
WELL DONE, WODEN.
IT WOULD HAVE BEEN AN INOPPORTUNE TIME TO GROW A SPINE.

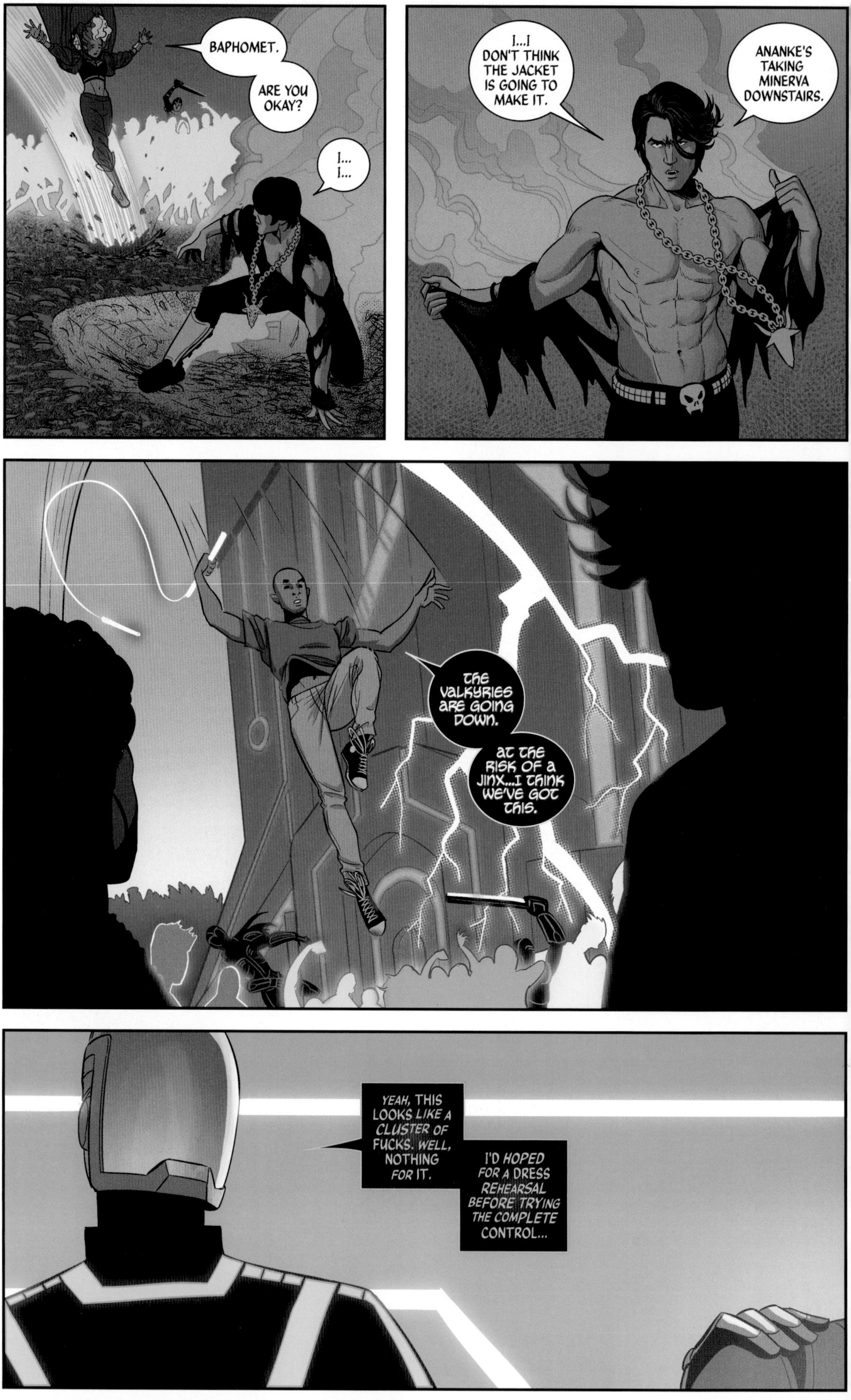
BAPHOMET.
ARE YOU OKAY?
I... I...
I...I DON'T THINK THE JACKET IS GOING TO MAKE IT.
ANANKE'S TAKING MINERVA DOWNSTAIRS.
THE VALKYRIES ARE GOING DOWN.
AT THE RISK OF A JINX...I THINK WE'VE GOT THIS.
YEAH, THIS LOOKS LIKE A CLUSTER OF FUCKS. WELL, NOTHING FOR IT.
I'D HOPED FOR A DRESS REHEARSAL BEFORE TRYING THE COMPLETE CONTROL...

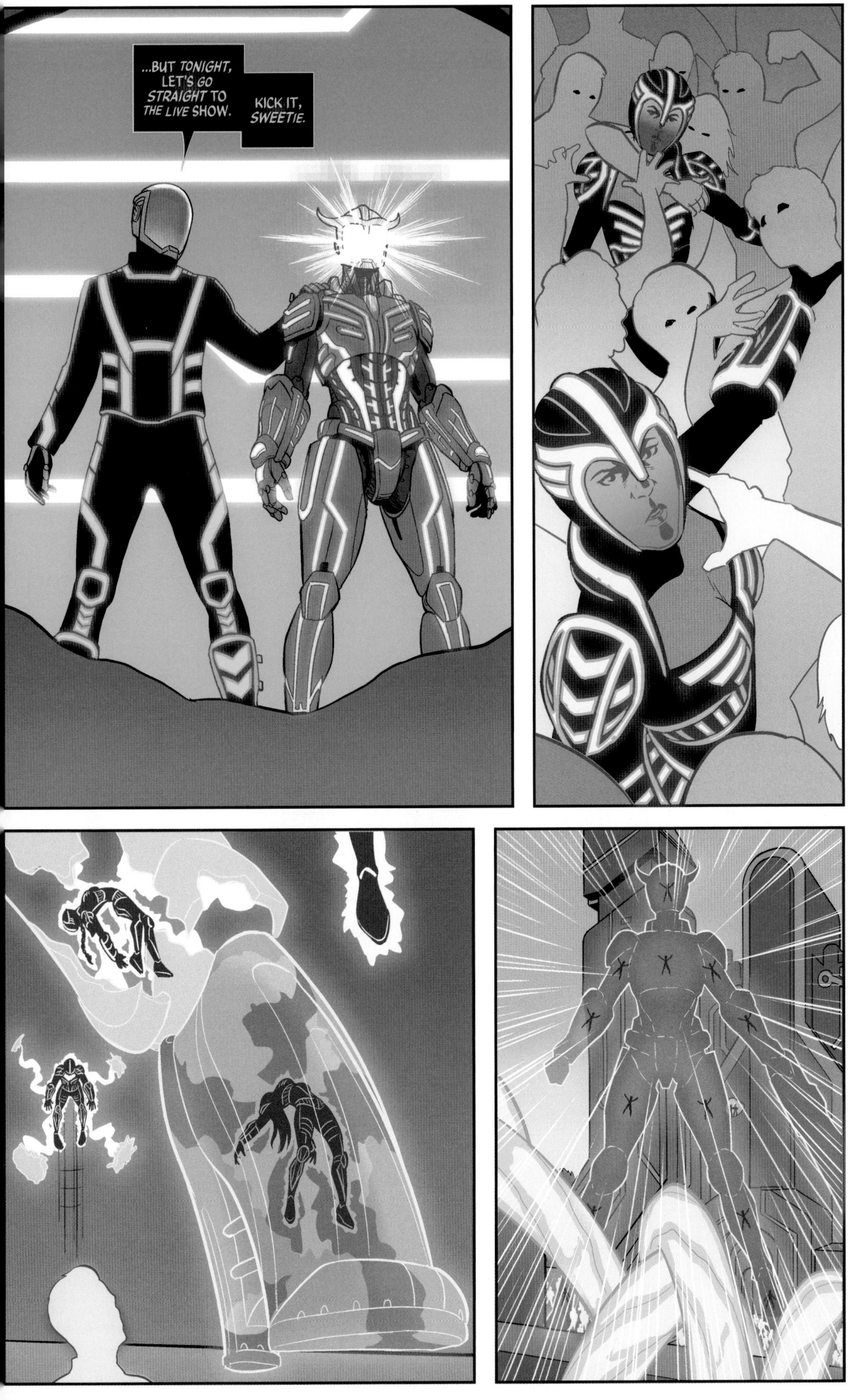
...BUT TONIGHT, LET'S GO STRAIGHT TO THE LIVE SHOW.
KICK IT, SWEETIE.

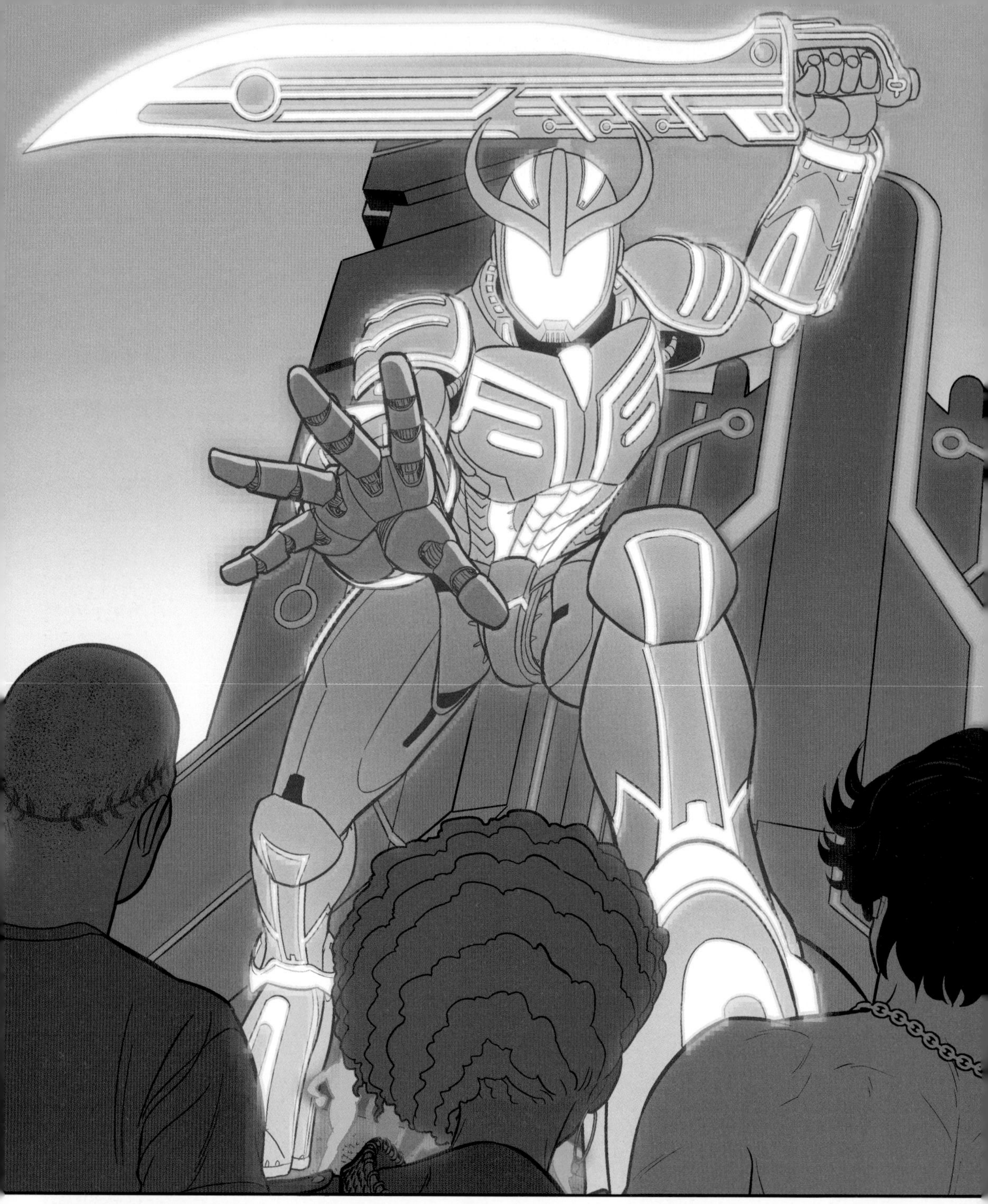

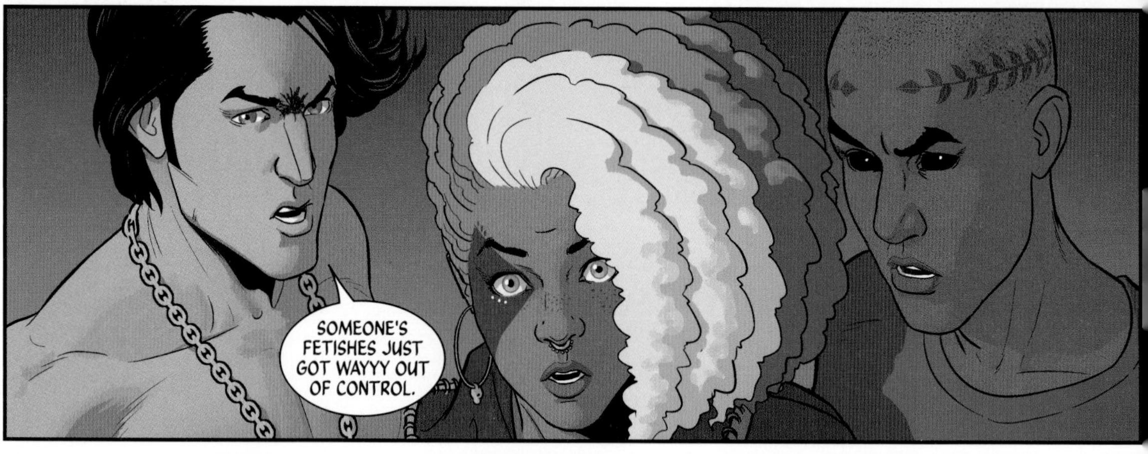
SOMEONE'S FETISHES JUST GOT WAYYY OUT OF CONTROL.

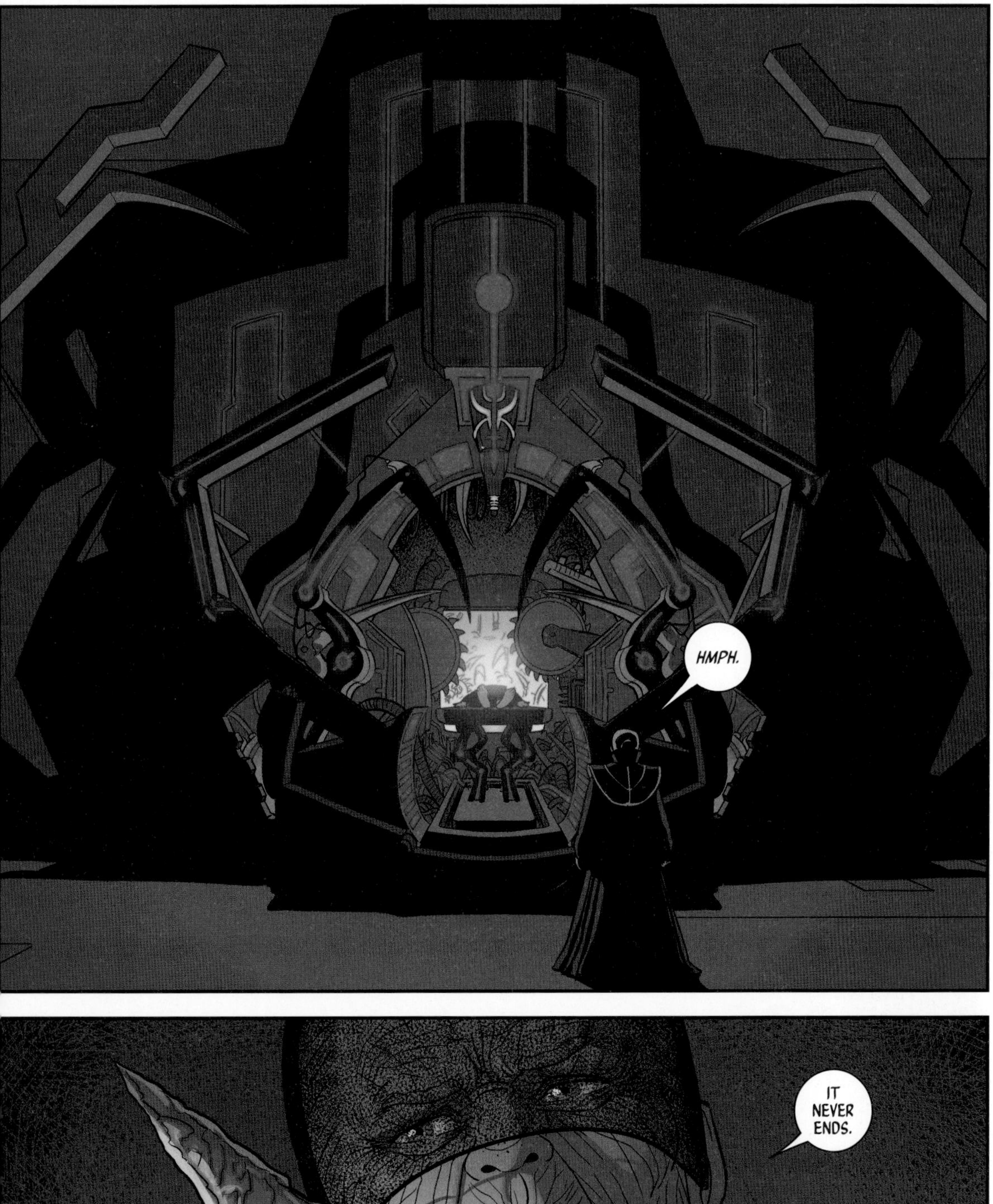
HMPH.

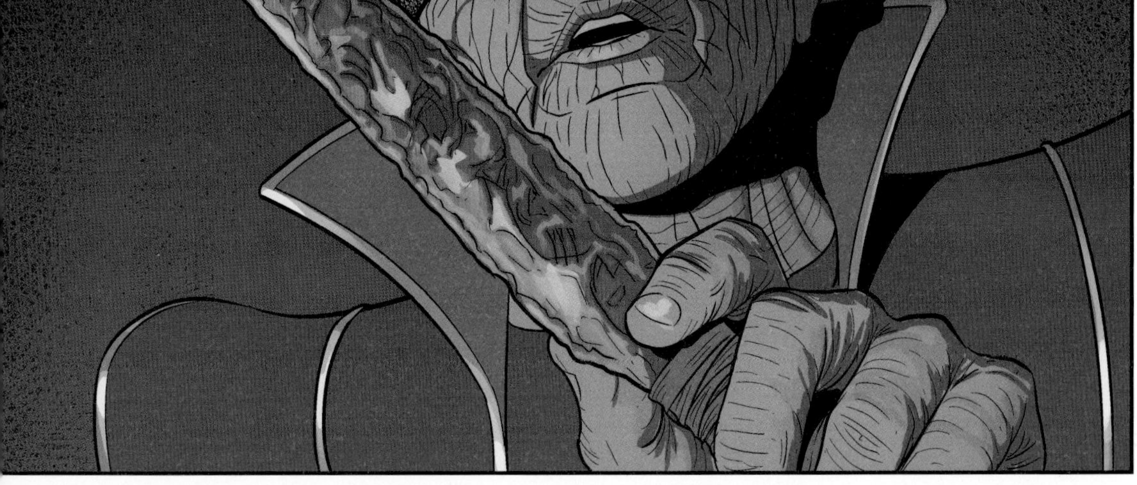
IT NEVER ENDS.

BAD BLOOD

24 SEPTEMBER 2014

THE
WICKED
+
THE DIVINE

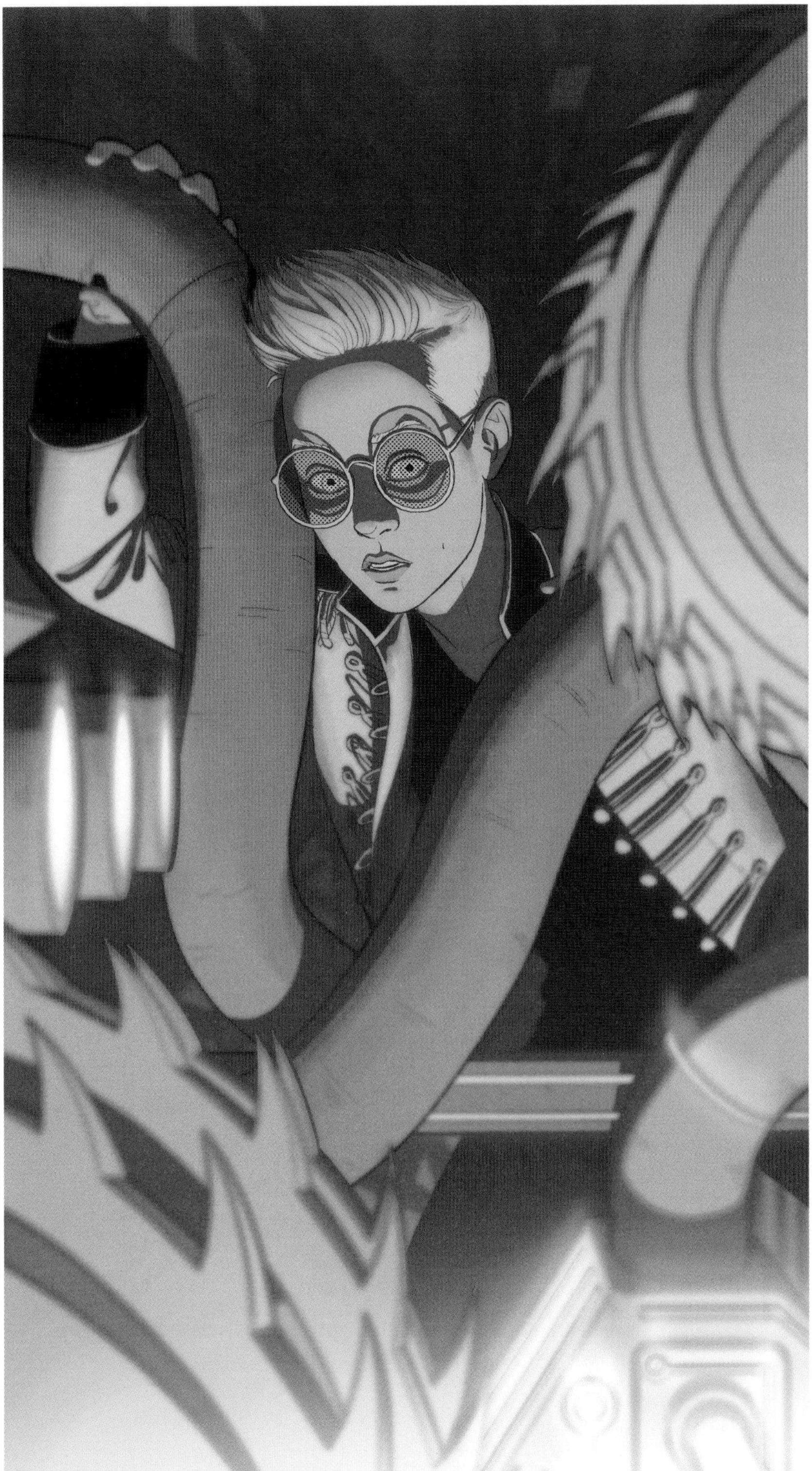

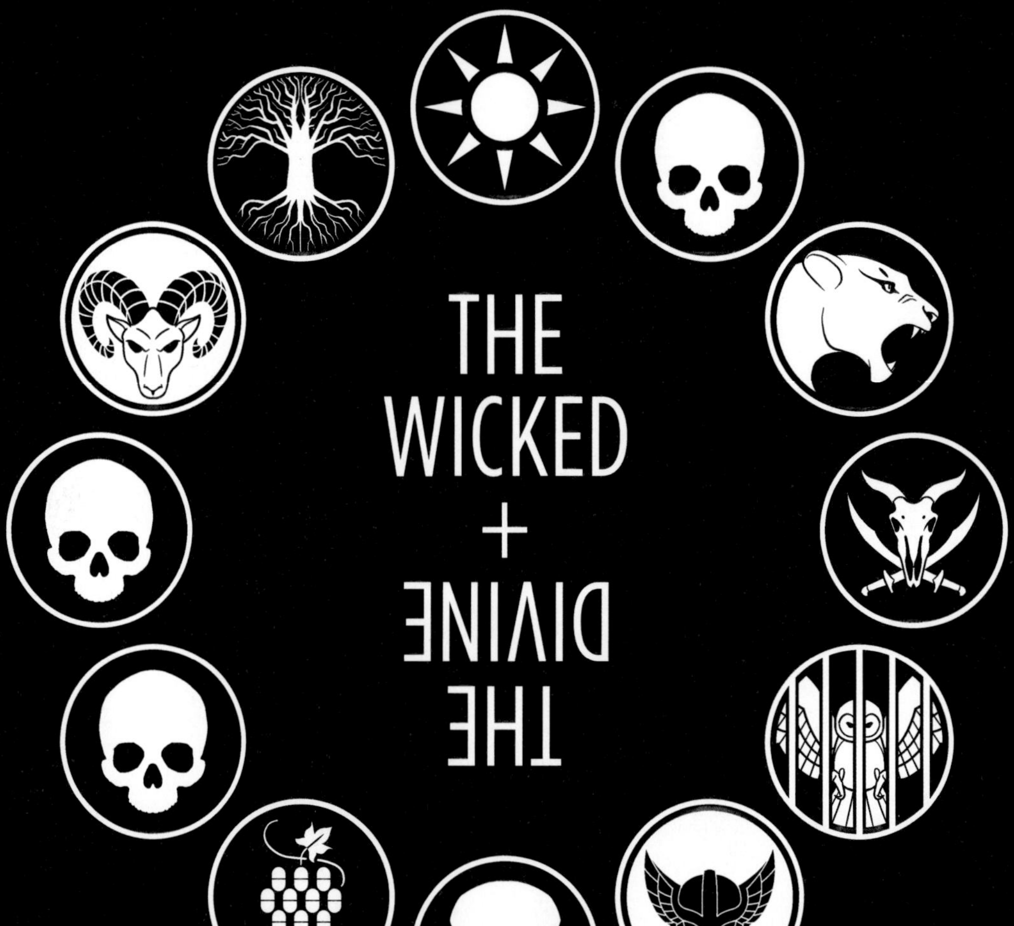
THE
WICKED
+
THE
DIVINE

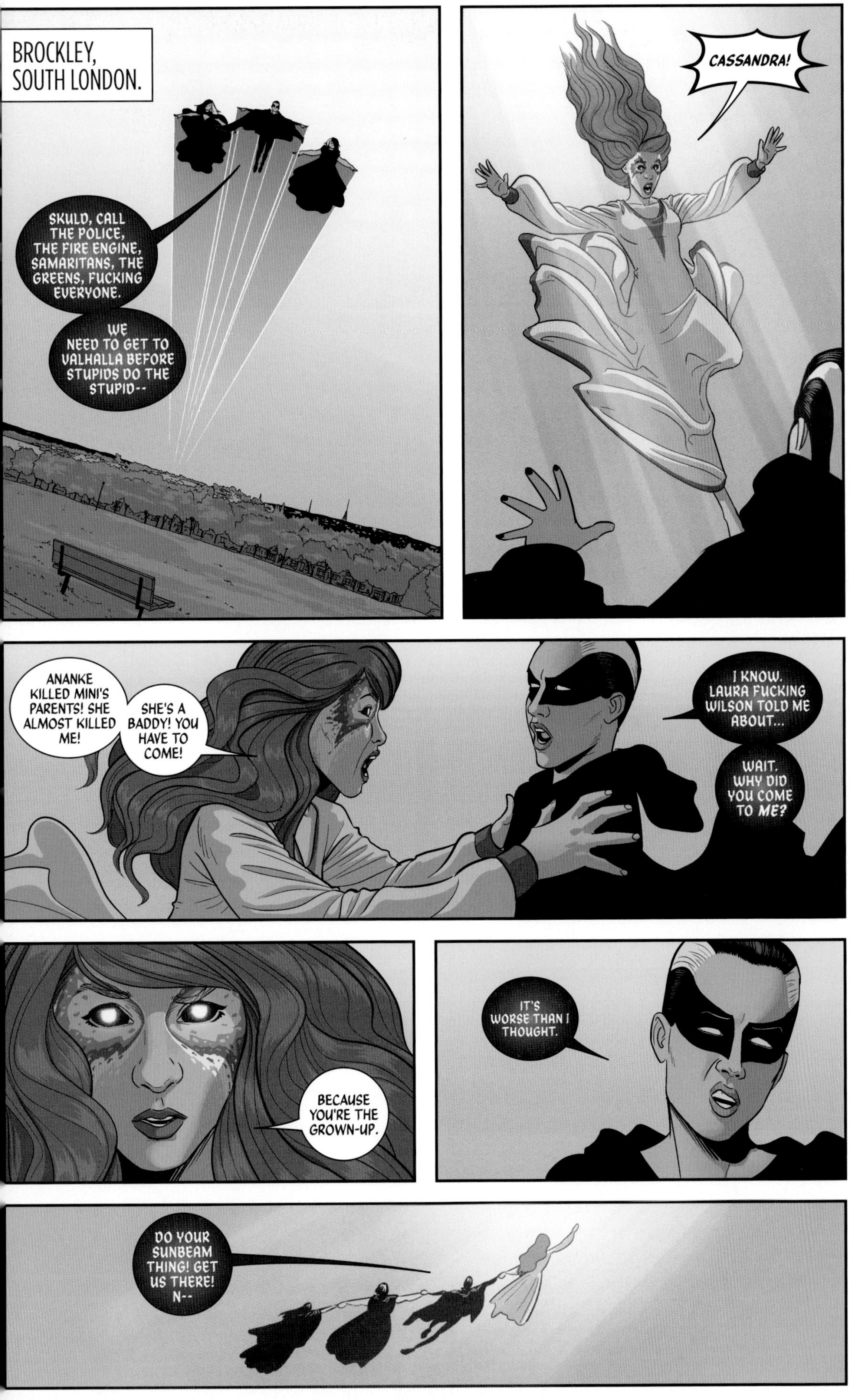

BROCKLEY, SOUTH LONDON.
SKULD, CALL THE POLICE, THE FIRE ENGINE, SAMARITANS, THE GREENS, FUCKING EVERYONE.
WE NEED TO GET TO VALHALLA BEFORE STUPIDS DO THE STUPID--
CASSANDRA!
ANANKE KILLED MINI'S PARENTS! SHE ALMOST KILLED ME!
SHE'S A BADDY! YOU HAVE TO COME!
I KNOW. LAURA FUCKING WILSON TOLD ME ABOUT...
WAIT. WHY DID YOU COME TO ME?
BECAUSE YOU'RE THE GROWN-UP.
IT'S WORSE THAN I THOUGHT.
DO YOUR SUNBEAM THING! GET US THERE! N--

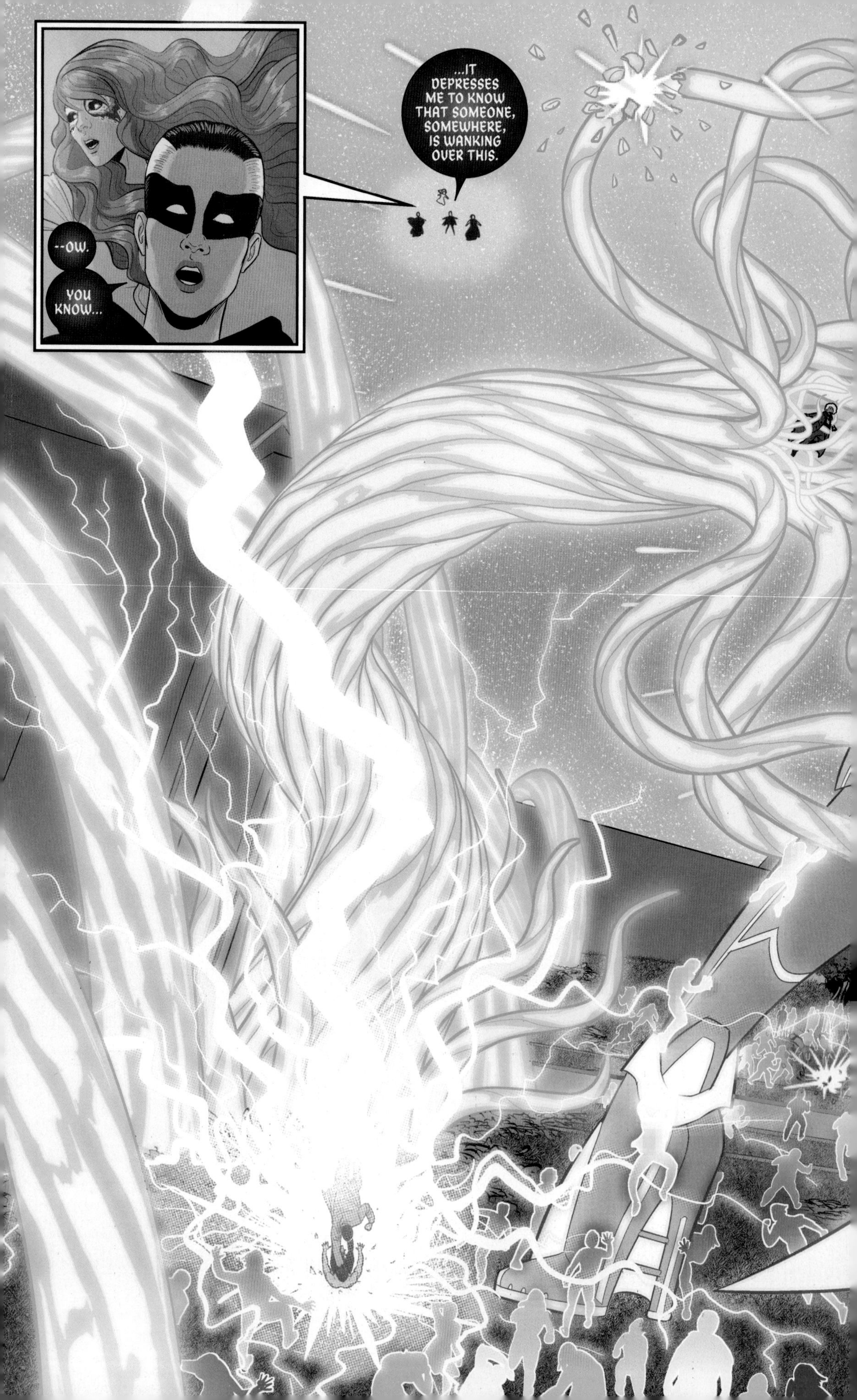
--OW.
YOU KNOW...
...IT DEPRESSES ME TO KNOW THAT SOMEONE, SOMEWHERE, IS WANKING OVER THIS.

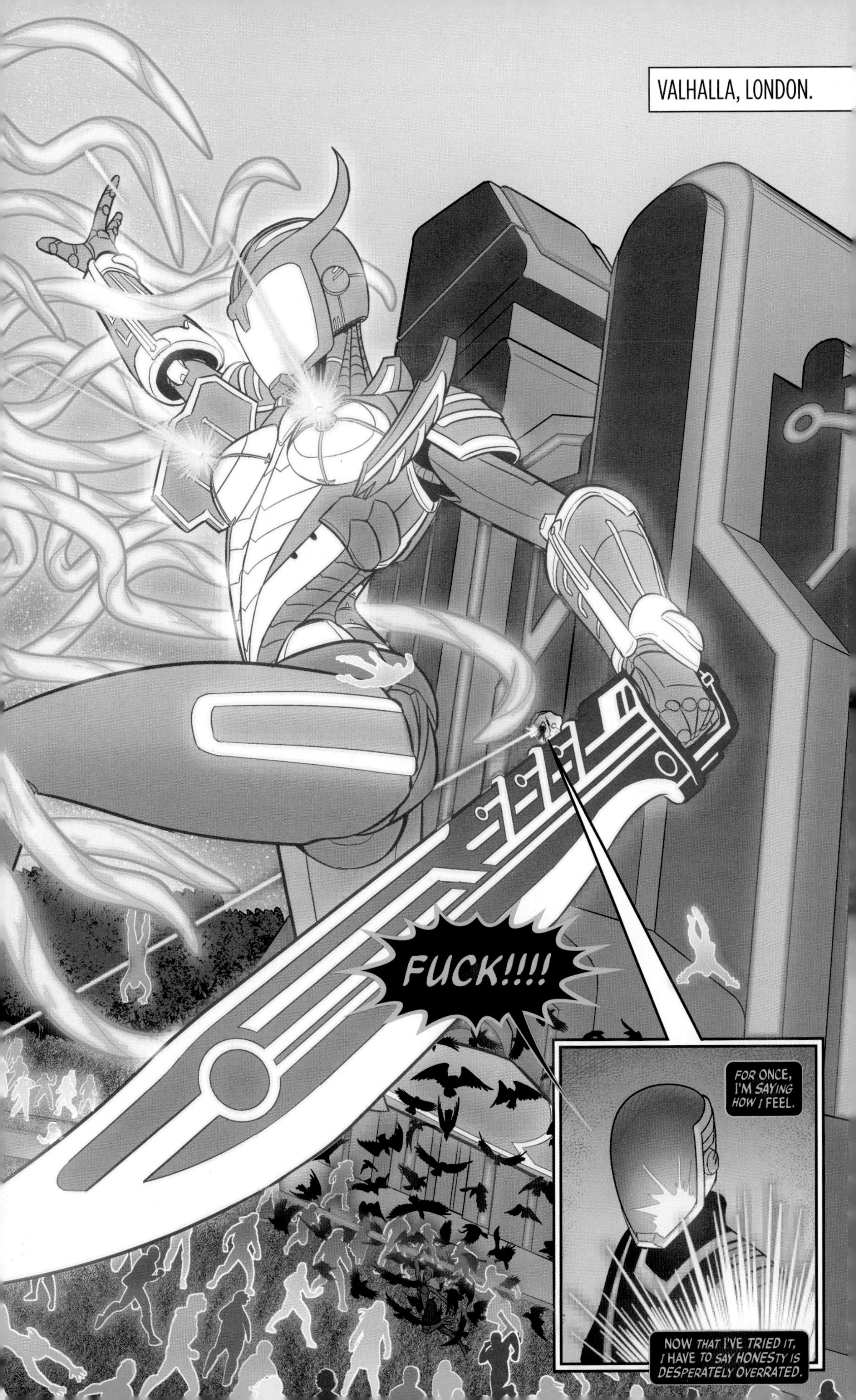
VALHALLA, LONDON.
FUCK!!!!
FOR ONCE, I'M SAYING HOW I FEEL.
NOW THAT I'VE TRIED IT, I HAVE TO SAY HONESTY IS DESPERATELY OVERRATED.

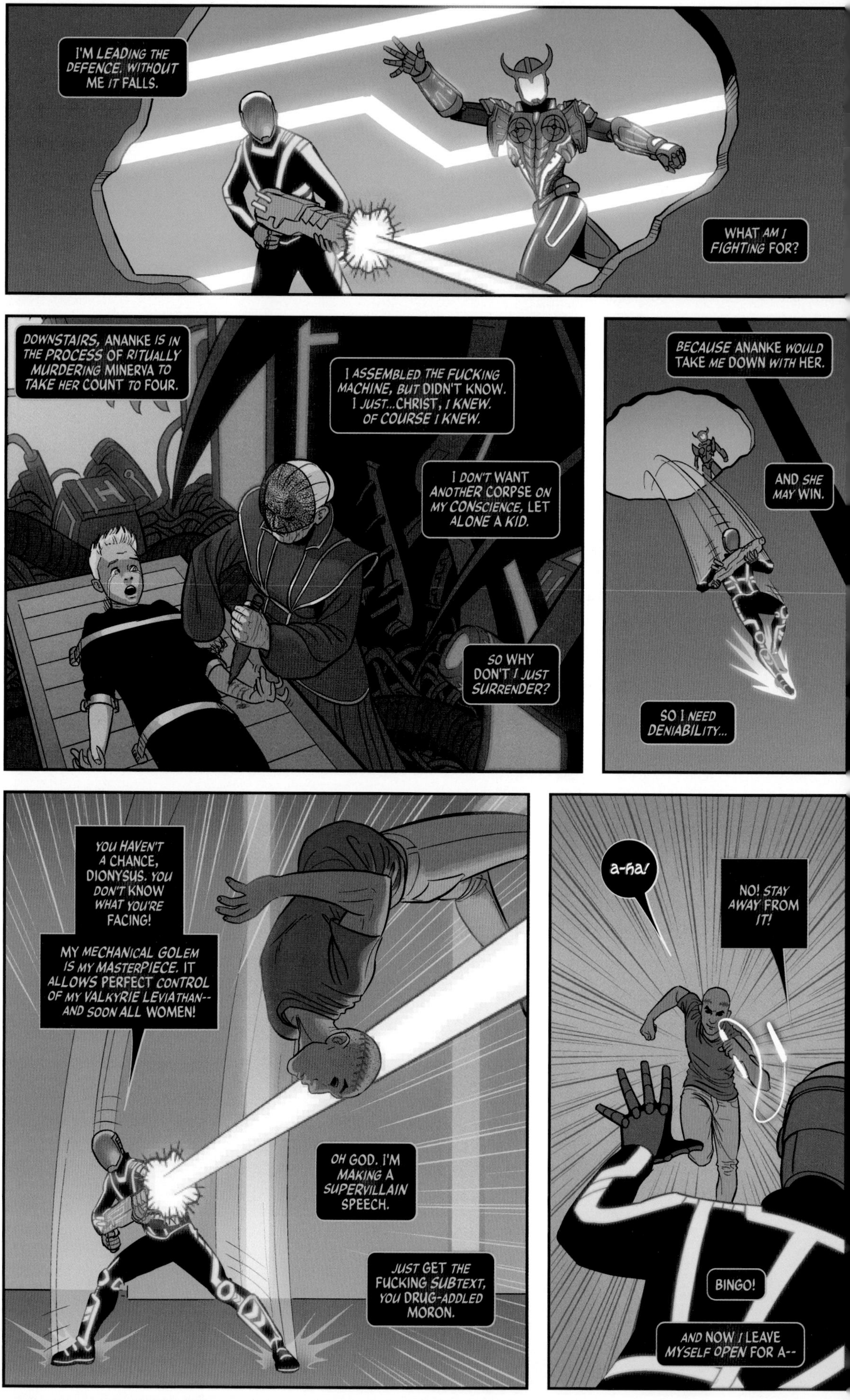
I'M LEADING THE DEFENCE. WITHOUT ME IT FALLS.
WHAT AM I FIGHTING FOR?
DOWNSTAIRS, ANANKE IS IN THE PROCESS OF RITUALLY MURDERING MINERVA TO TAKE HER COUNT TO FOUR.
I ASSEMBLED THE FUCKING MACHINE, BUT DIDN'T KNOW. I JUST...CHRIST, I KNEW. OF COURSE I KNEW.
I DON'T WANT ANOTHER CORPSE ON MY CONSCIENCE, LET ALONE A KID.
SO WHY DON'T I JUST SURRENDER?
BECAUSE ANANKE WOULD TAKE ME DOWN WITH HER.
AND SHE MAY WIN.
SO I NEED DENIABILITY...
YOU HAVEN'T A CHANCE, DIONYSUS. YOU DON'T KNOW WHAT YOU'RE FACING!
MY MECHANICAL GOLEM IS MY MASTERPIECE. IT ALLOWS PERFECT CONTROL OF MY VALKYRIE LEVIATHAN--AND SOON ALL WOMEN!
OH GOD. I'M MAKING A SUPERVILLAIN SPEECH.
JUST GET THE FUCKING SUBTEXT, YOU DRUG-ADDLED MORON.
A-HA!
NO! STAY AWAY FROM IT!
BINGO!
AND NOW I LEAVE MYSELF OPEN FOR A--

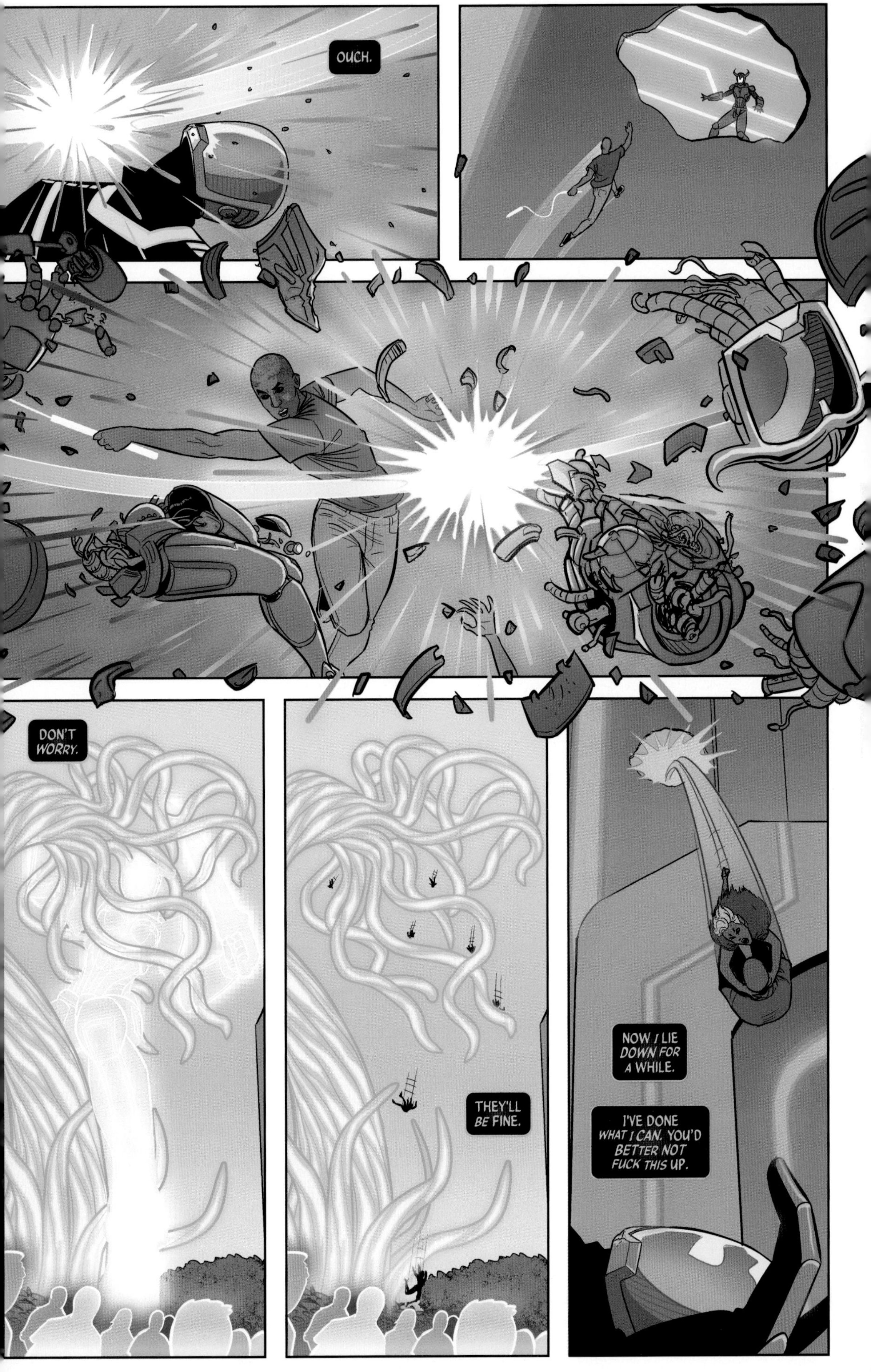
OUCH.
DON'T WORRY.
THEY'LL BE FINE.
NOW I LIE DOWN FOR A WHILE.
I'VE DONE WHAT I CAN. YOU'D BETTER NOT FUCK THIS UP.

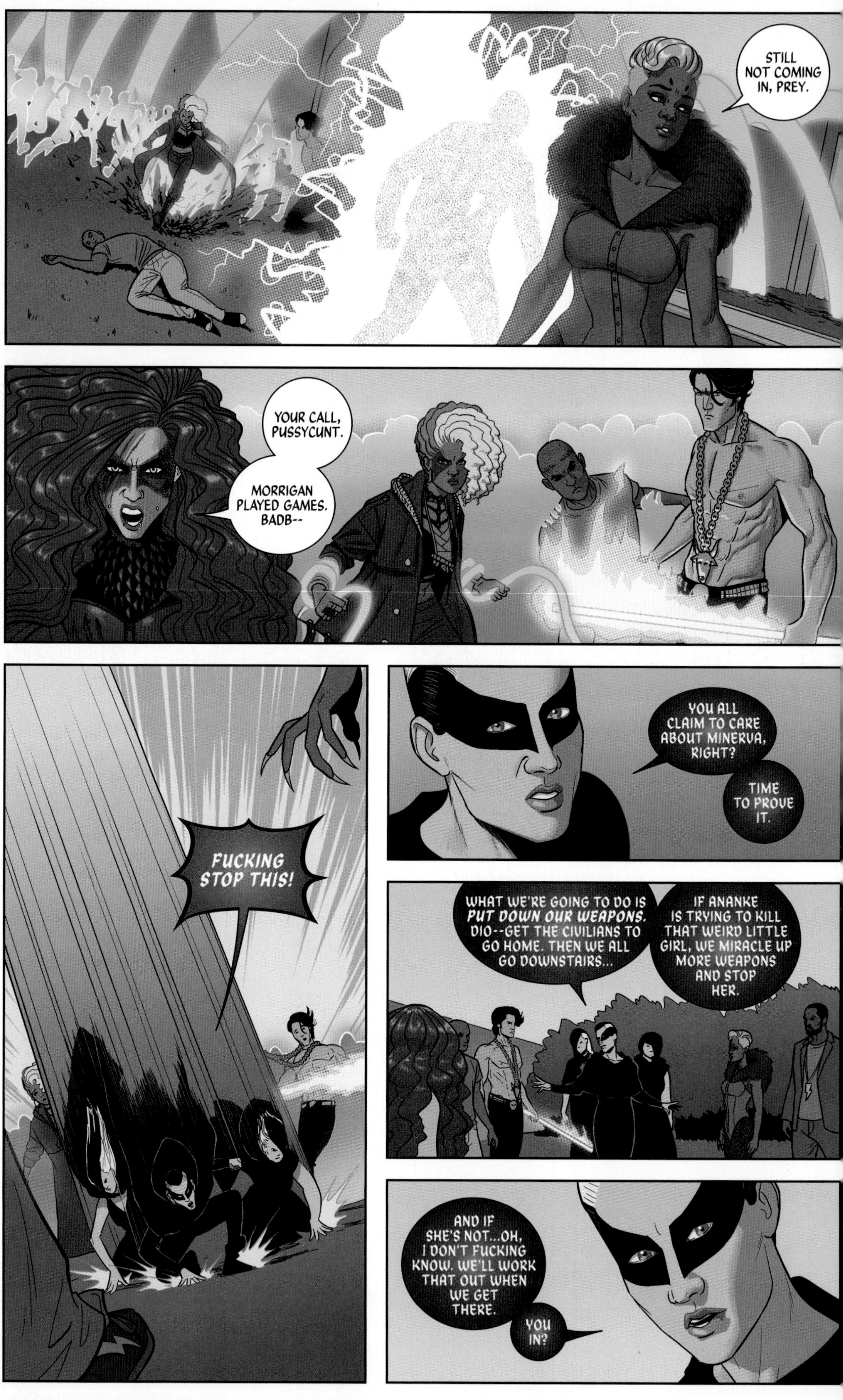
STILL NOT COMING IN, PREY.
YOUR CALL, PUSSYCUNT.
MORRIGAN PLAYED GAMES. BADB--
FUCKING STOP THIS!
YOU ALL CLAIM TO CARE ABOUT MINERVA, RIGHT?
TIME TO PROVE IT.
WHAT WE'RE GOING TO DO IS PUT DOWN OUR WEAPONS. DIO--GET THE CIVILIANS TO GO HOME. THEN WE ALL GO DOWNSTAIRS...
IF ANANKE IS TRYING TO KILL THAT WEIRD LITTLE GIRL, WE MIRACLE UP MORE WEAPONS AND STOP HER.
AND IF SHE'S NOT...OH, I DON'T FUCKING KNOW. WE'LL WORK THAT OUT WHEN WE GET THERE.
YOU IN?

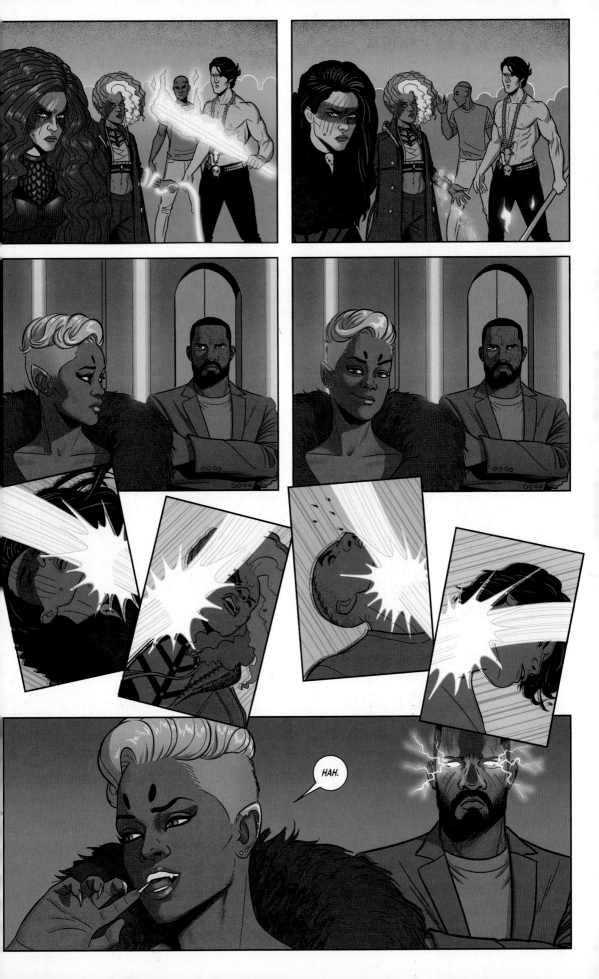

HAH.

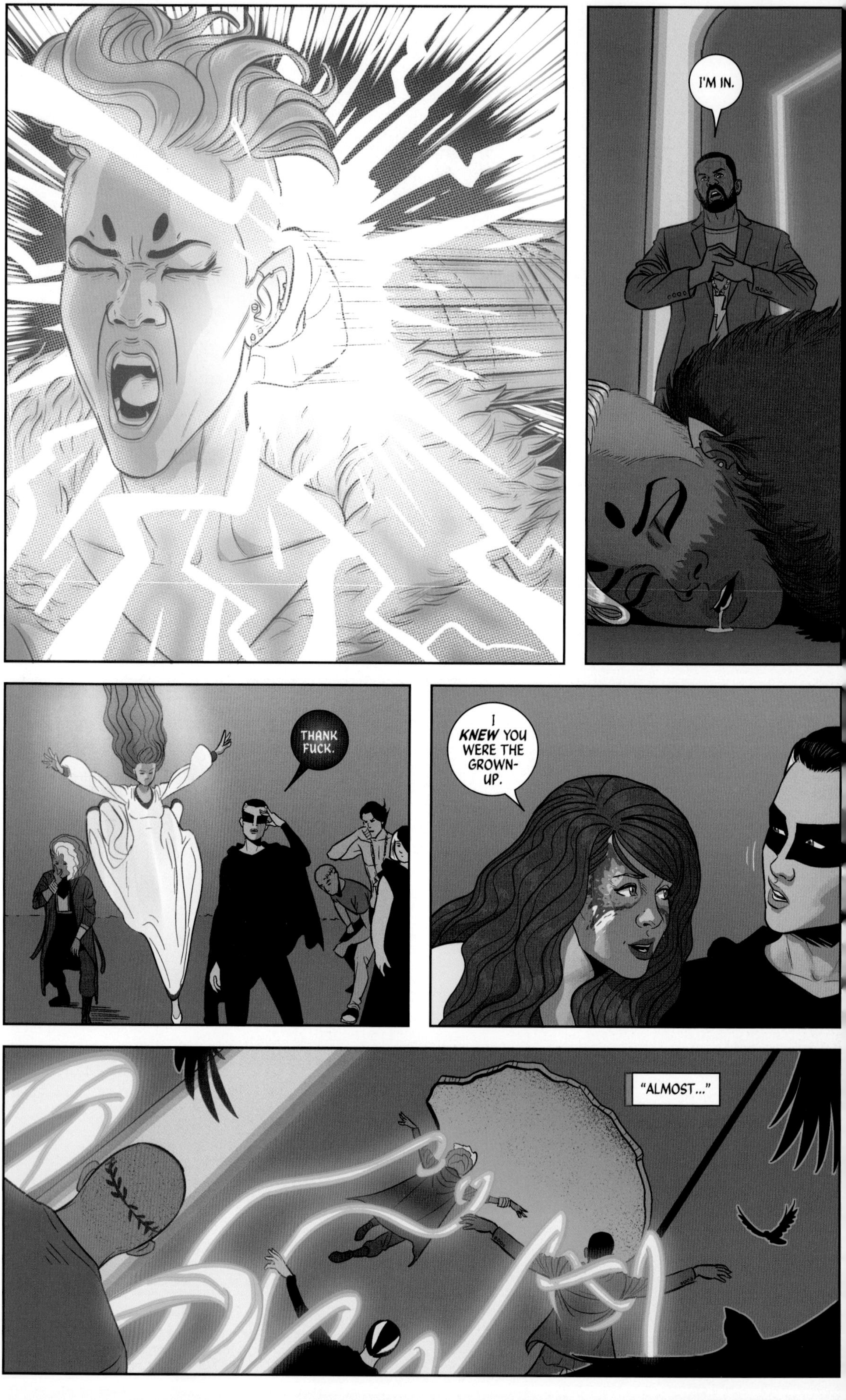
I'M IN.
THANK FUCK.
I KNEW YOU WERE THE GROWN-UP.
"ALMOST..."

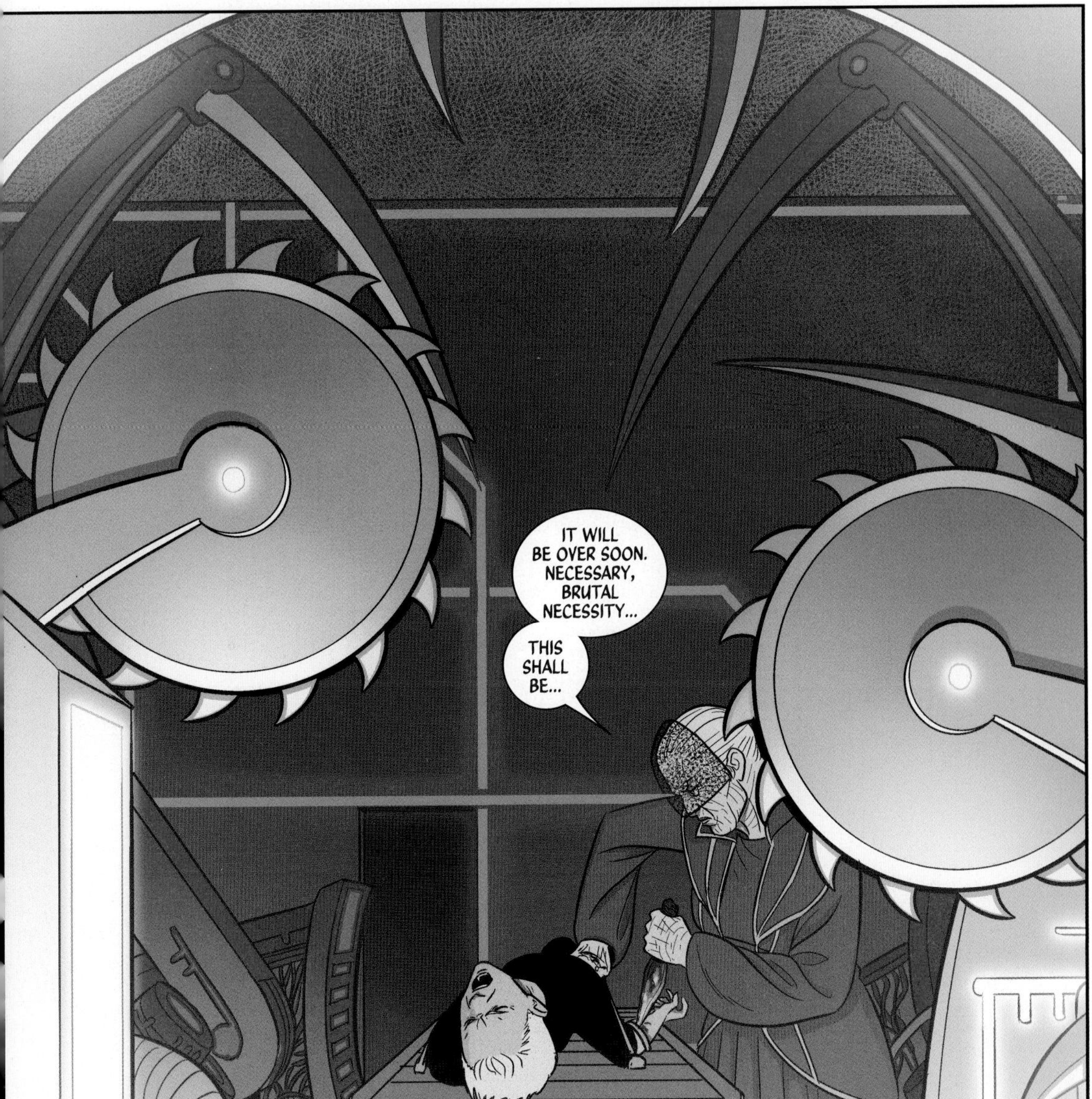
IT WILL BE OVER SOON. NECESSARY, BRUTAL NECESSITY...
THIS SHALL BE...

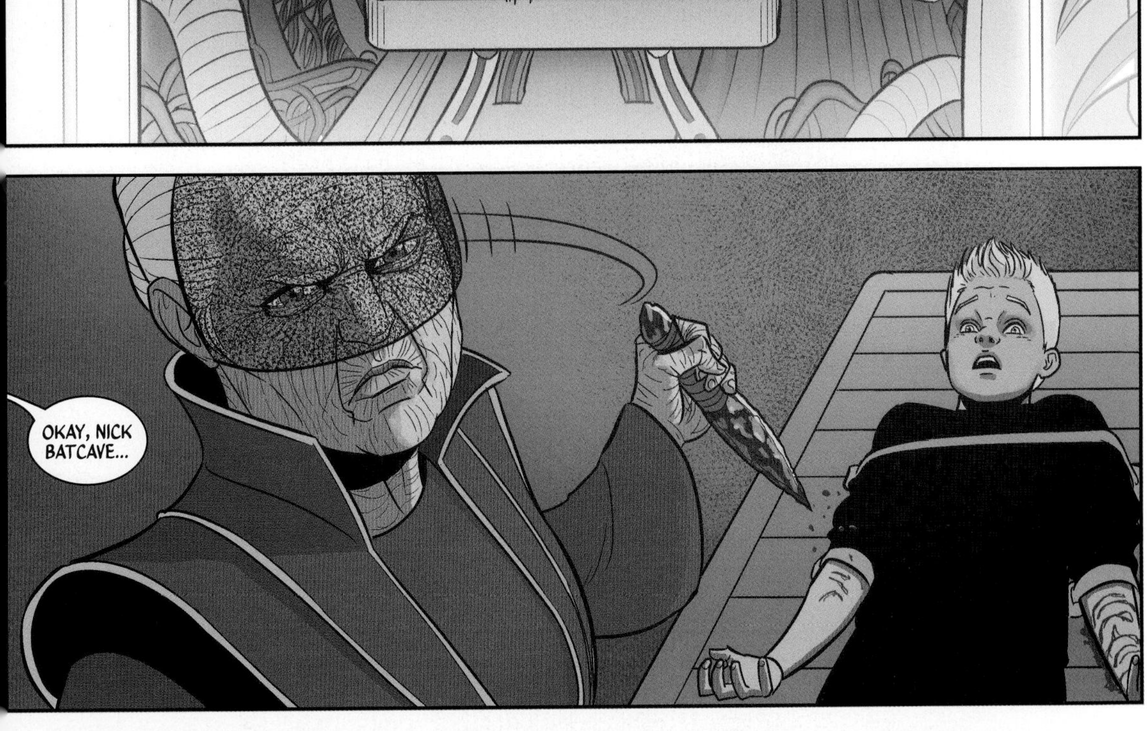
OKAY, NICK BATCAVE...

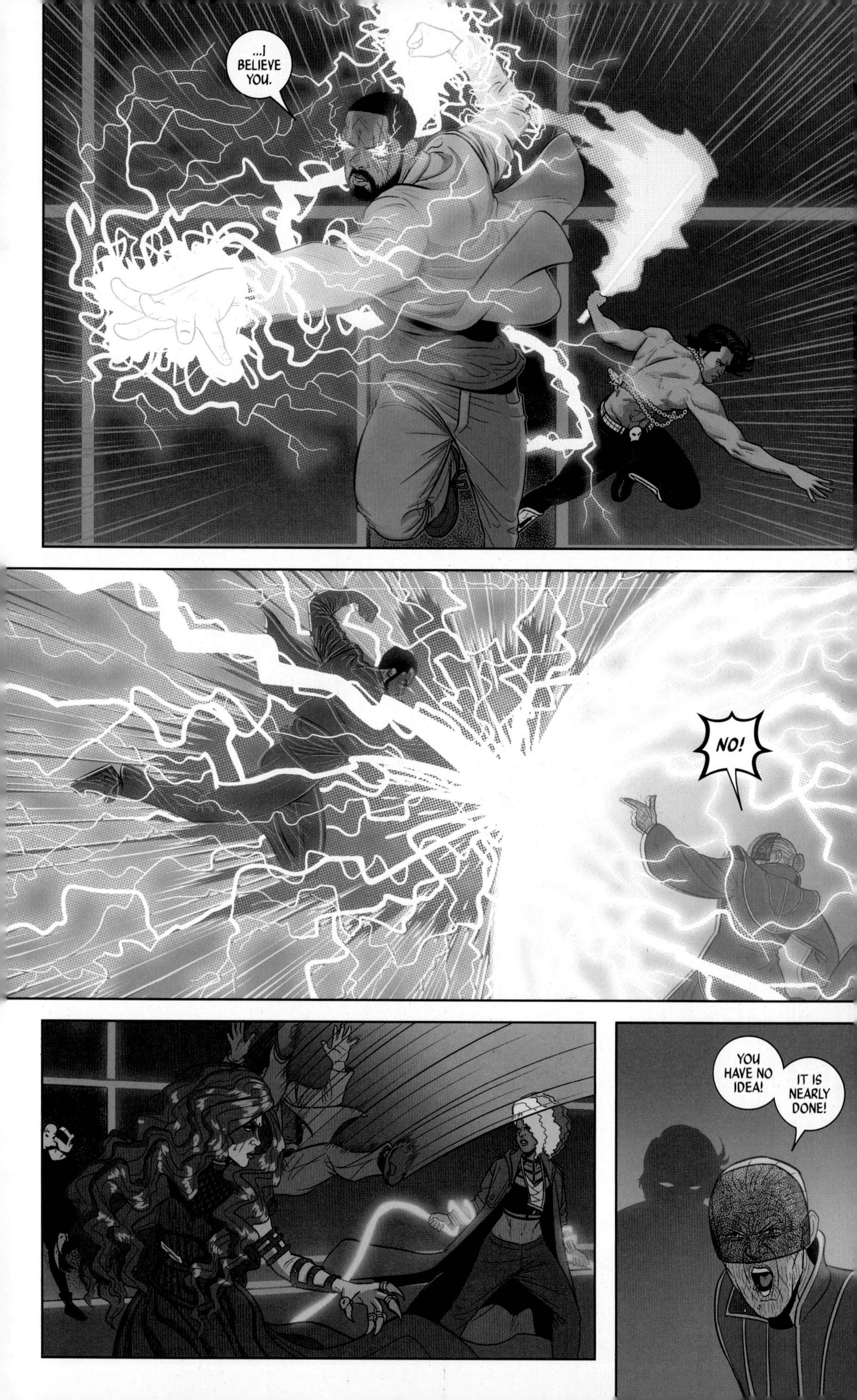

...I BELIEVE YOU.
NO!
YOU HAVE NO IDEA!
IT IS NEARLY DONE!

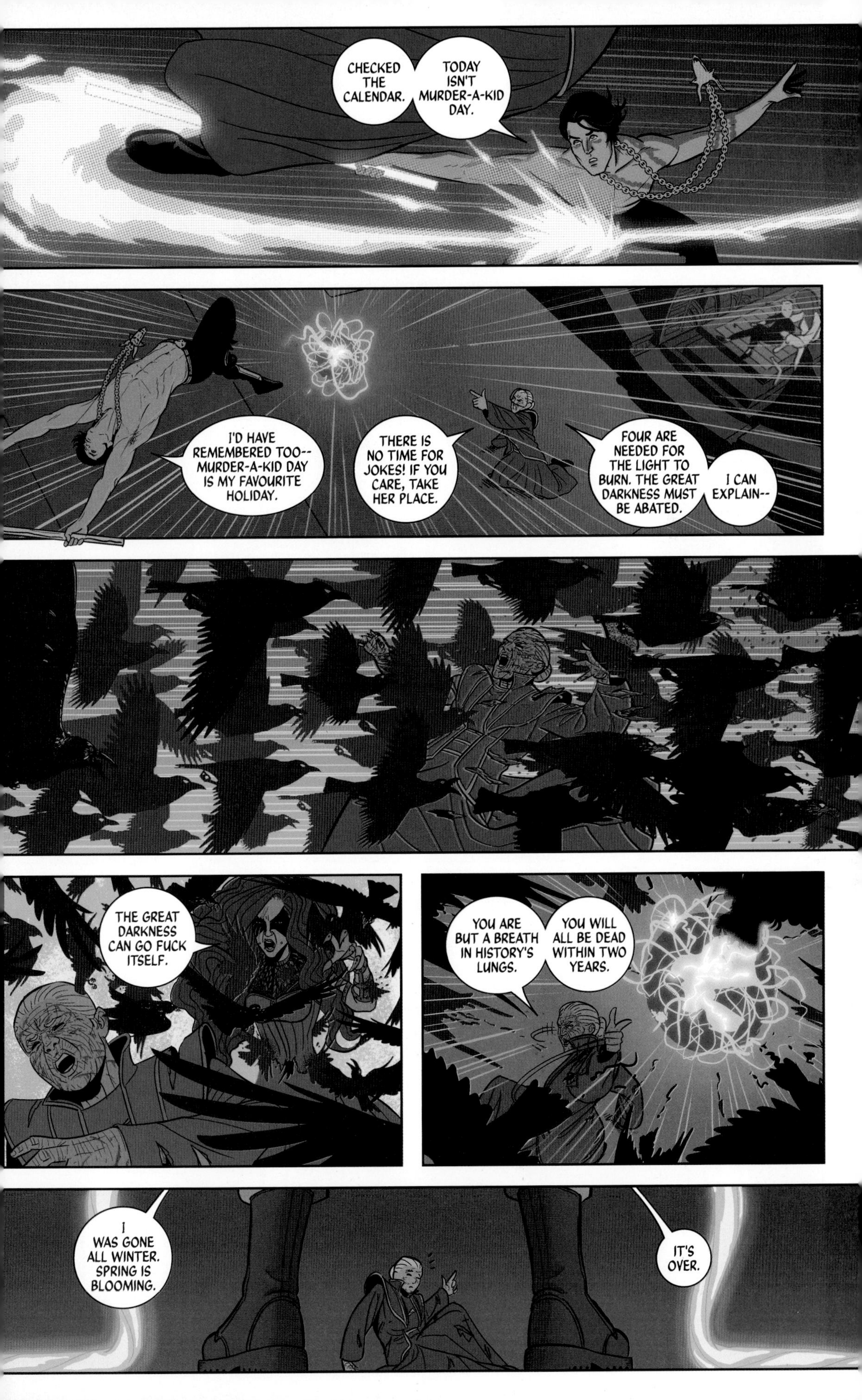
CHECKED THE CALENDAR.
TODAY ISN'T MURDER-A-KID DAY.
I'D HAVE REMEMBERED TOO-- MURDER-A-KID DAY IS MY FAVOURITE HOLIDAY.
THERE IS NO TIME FOR JOKES! IF YOU CARE, TAKE HER PLACE.
FOUR ARE NEEDED FOR THE LIGHT TO BURN. THE GREAT DARKNESS MUST BE ABATED.
I CAN EXPLAIN--
THE GREAT DARKNESS CAN GO FUCK ITSELF.
YOU ARE BUT A BREATH IN HISTORY'S LUNGS.
YOU WILL ALL BE DEAD WITHIN TWO YEARS.
I WAS GONE ALL WINTER. SPRING IS BLOOMING.
IT'S OVER.

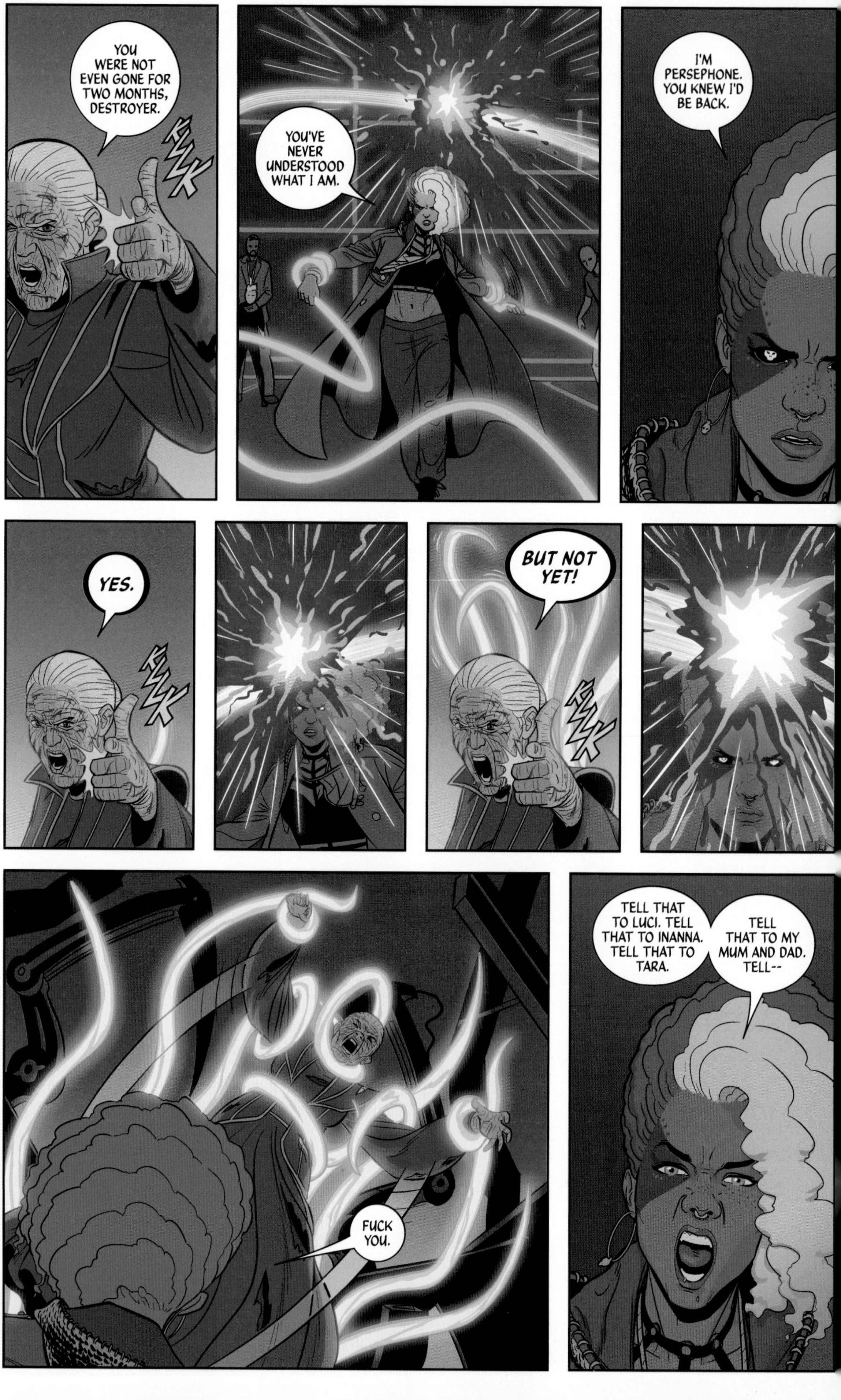

YOU WERE NOT EVEN GONE FOR TWO MONTHS, DESTROYER.
KLIK
YOU'VE NEVER UNDERSTOOD WHAT I AM.
I'M PERSEPHONE. YOU KNEW I'D BE BACK.
YES.
KLIK
BUT NOT YET!
KLIK
FUCK YOU.
TELL THAT TO LUCI. TELL THAT TO INANNA. TELL THAT TO TARA.
TELL THAT TO MY MUM AND DAD. TELL--

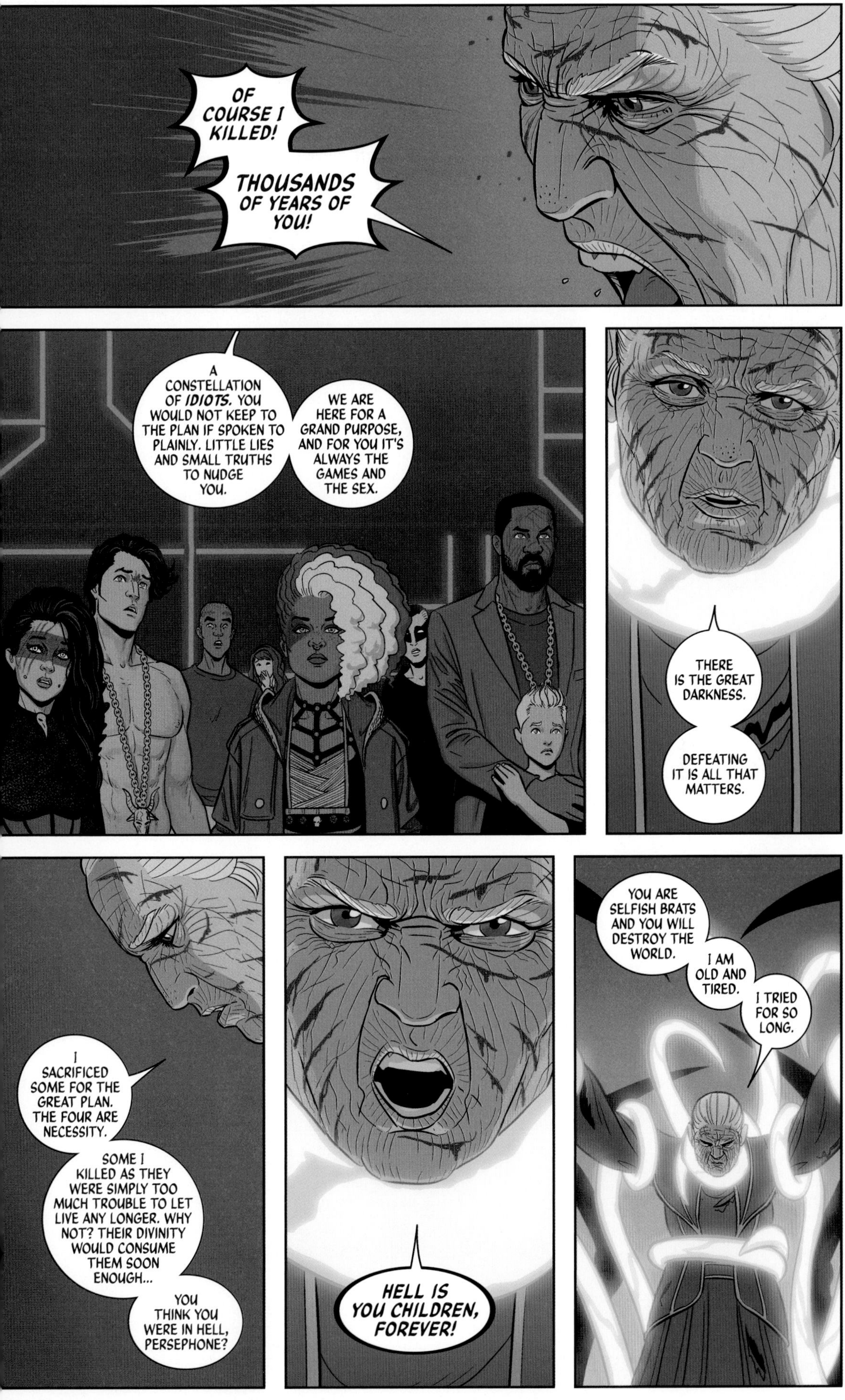
OF COURSE I KILLED!
THOUSANDS OF YEARS OF YOU!
A CONSTELLATION OF IDIOTS. YOU WOULD NOT KEEP TO THE PLAN IF SPOKEN TO PLAINLY. LITTLE LIES AND SMALL TRUTHS TO NUDGE YOU.
WE ARE HERE FOR A GRAND PURPOSE, AND FOR YOU IT'S ALWAYS THE GAMES AND THE SEX.
THERE IS THE GREAT DARKNESS.
DEFEATING IT IS ALL THAT MATTERS.
I SACRIFICED SOME FOR THE GREAT PLAN. THE FOUR ARE NECESSITY.
SOME I KILLED AS THEY WERE SIMPLY TOO MUCH TROUBLE TO LET LIVE ANY LONGER. WHY NOT? THEIR DIVINITY WOULD CONSUME THEM SOON ENOUGH...
YOU THINK YOU WERE IN HELL, PERSEPHONE?
HELL IS YOU CHILDREN, FOREVER!
YOU ARE SELFISH BRATS AND YOU WILL DESTROY THE WORLD.
I AM OLD AND TIRED.
I TRIED FOR SO LONG.

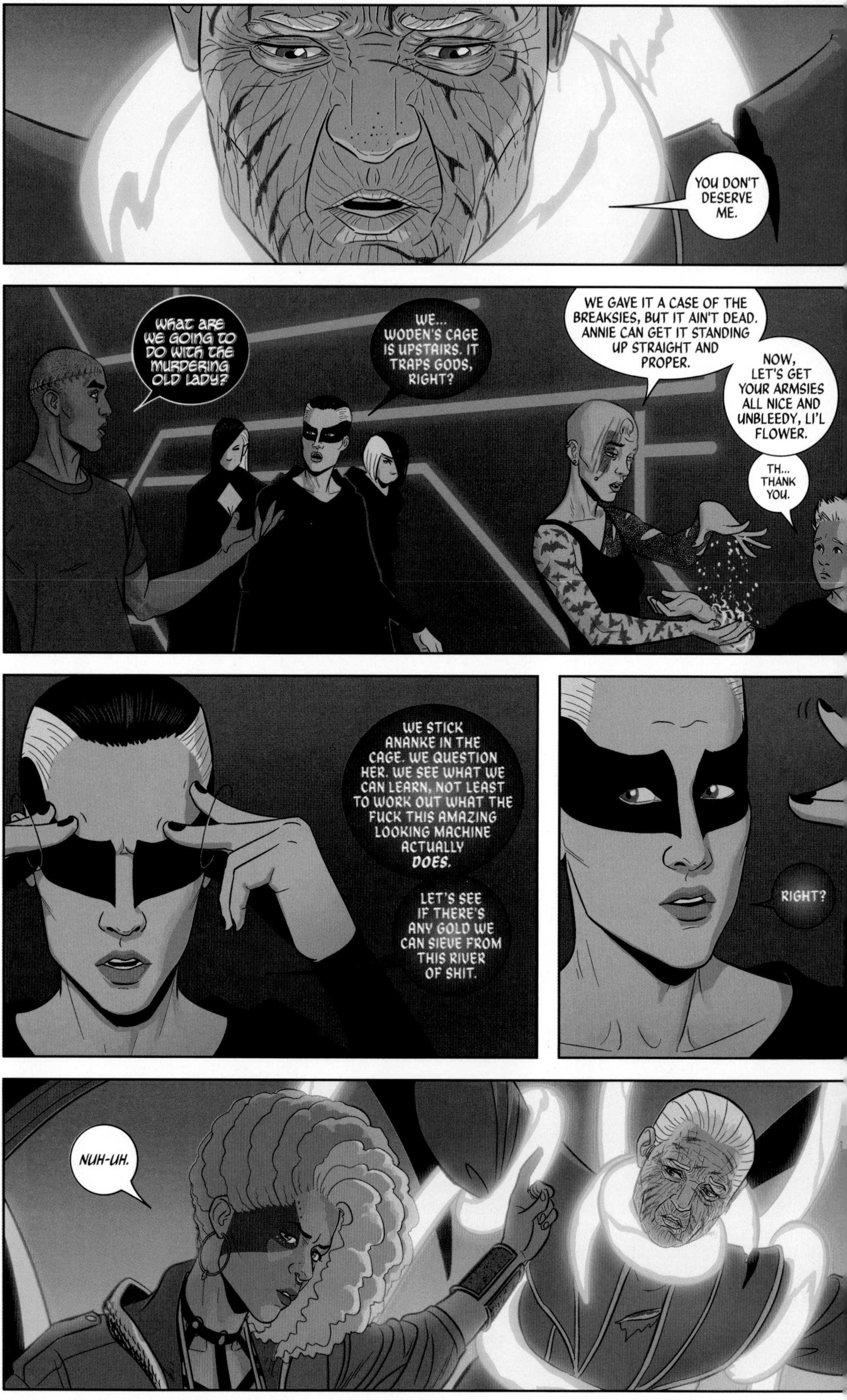

YOU DON'T DESERVE ME.
WHAT ARE WE GOING TO DO WITH THE MURDERING OLD LADY?
WE... WODEN'S CAGE IS UPSTAIRS. IT TRAPS GODS, RIGHT?
WE GAVE IT A CASE OF THE BREAKSIES, BUT IT AIN'T DEAD. ANNIE CAN GET IT STANDING UP STRAIGHT AND PROPER.
NOW, LET'S GET YOUR ARMSIES ALL NICE AND UNBLEEDY, LI'L FLOWER.
TH... THANK YOU.
WE STICK ANANKE IN THE CAGE. WE QUESTION HER. WE SEE WHAT WE CAN LEARN, NOT LEAST TO WORK OUT WHAT THE FUCK THIS AMAZING LOOKING MACHINE ACTUALLY *DOES.*
LET'S SEE IF THERE'S ANY GOLD WE CAN SIEVE FROM THIS RIVER OF SHIT.
RIGHT?
NUH-UH.

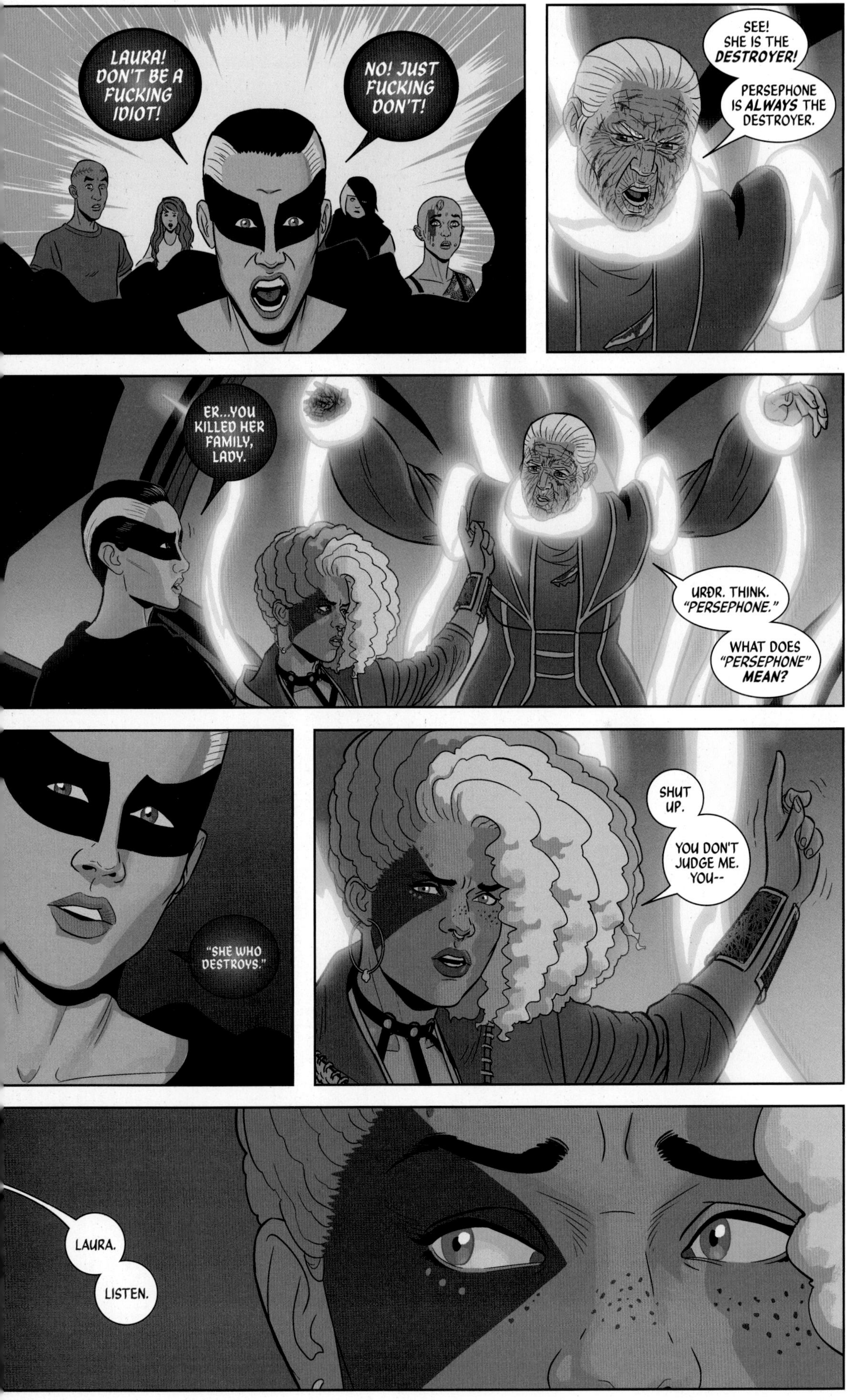
LAURA! DON'T BE A FUCKING IDIOT!
NO! JUST FUCKING DON'T!
SEE! SHE IS THE DESTROYER!
PERSEPHONE IS ALWAYS THE DESTROYER.
ER...YOU KILLED HER FAMILY, LADY.
URÐR. THINK. "PERSEPHONE."
WHAT DOES "PERSEPHONE" MEAN?
"SHE WHO DESTROYS."
SHUT UP.
YOU DON'T JUDGE ME. YOU--
LAURA.
LISTEN.

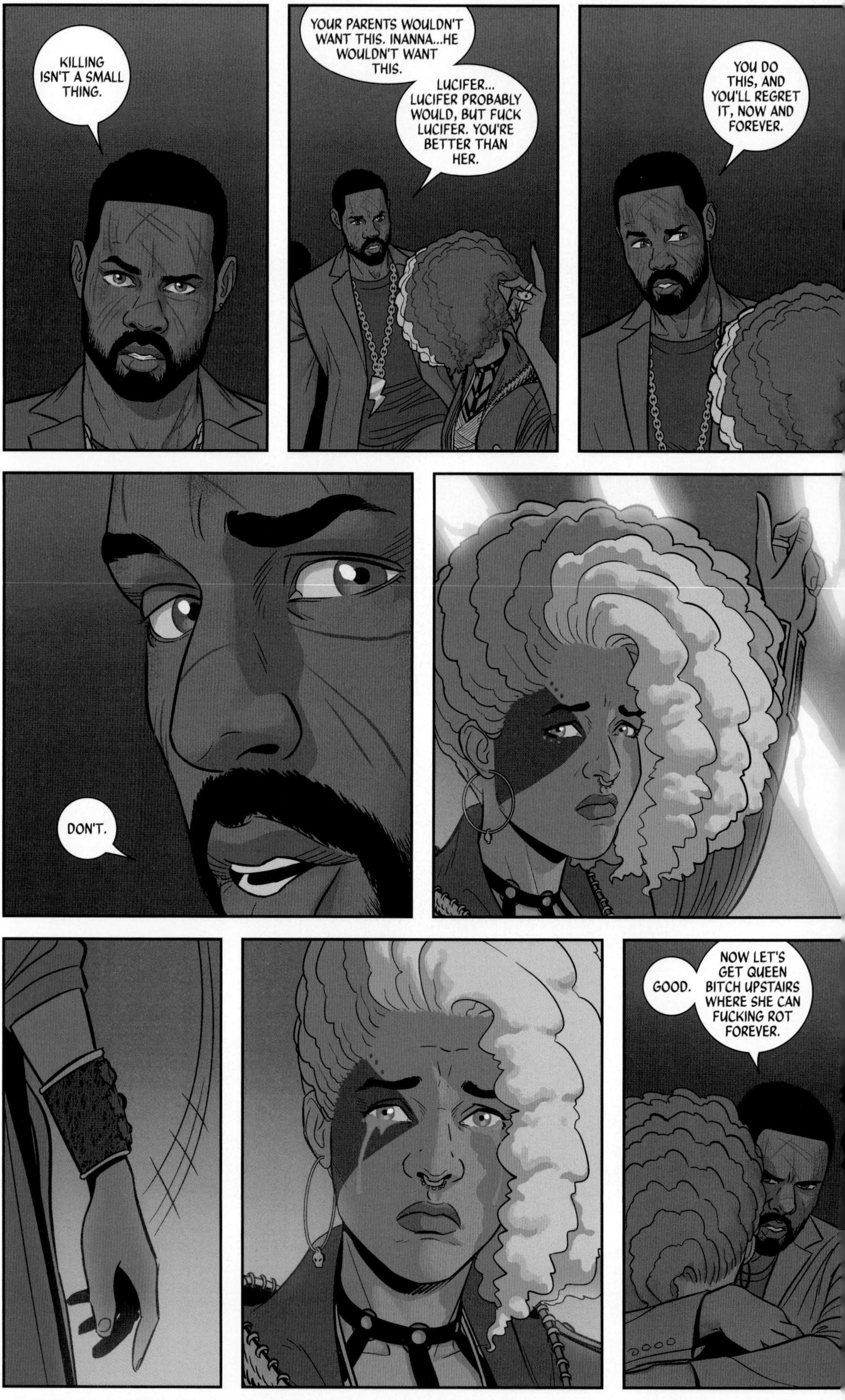
KILLING ISN'T A SMALL THING.
YOUR PARENTS WOULDN'T WANT THIS. INANNA...HE WOULDN'T WANT THIS.
LUCIFER... LUCIFER PROBABLY WOULD, BUT FUCK LUCIFER. YOU'RE BETTER THAN HER.
YOU DO THIS, AND YOU'LL REGRET IT, NOW AND FOREVER.
DON'T.
GOOD.
NOW LET'S GET QUEEN BITCH UPSTAIRS WHERE SHE CAN FUCKING ROT FOREVER.

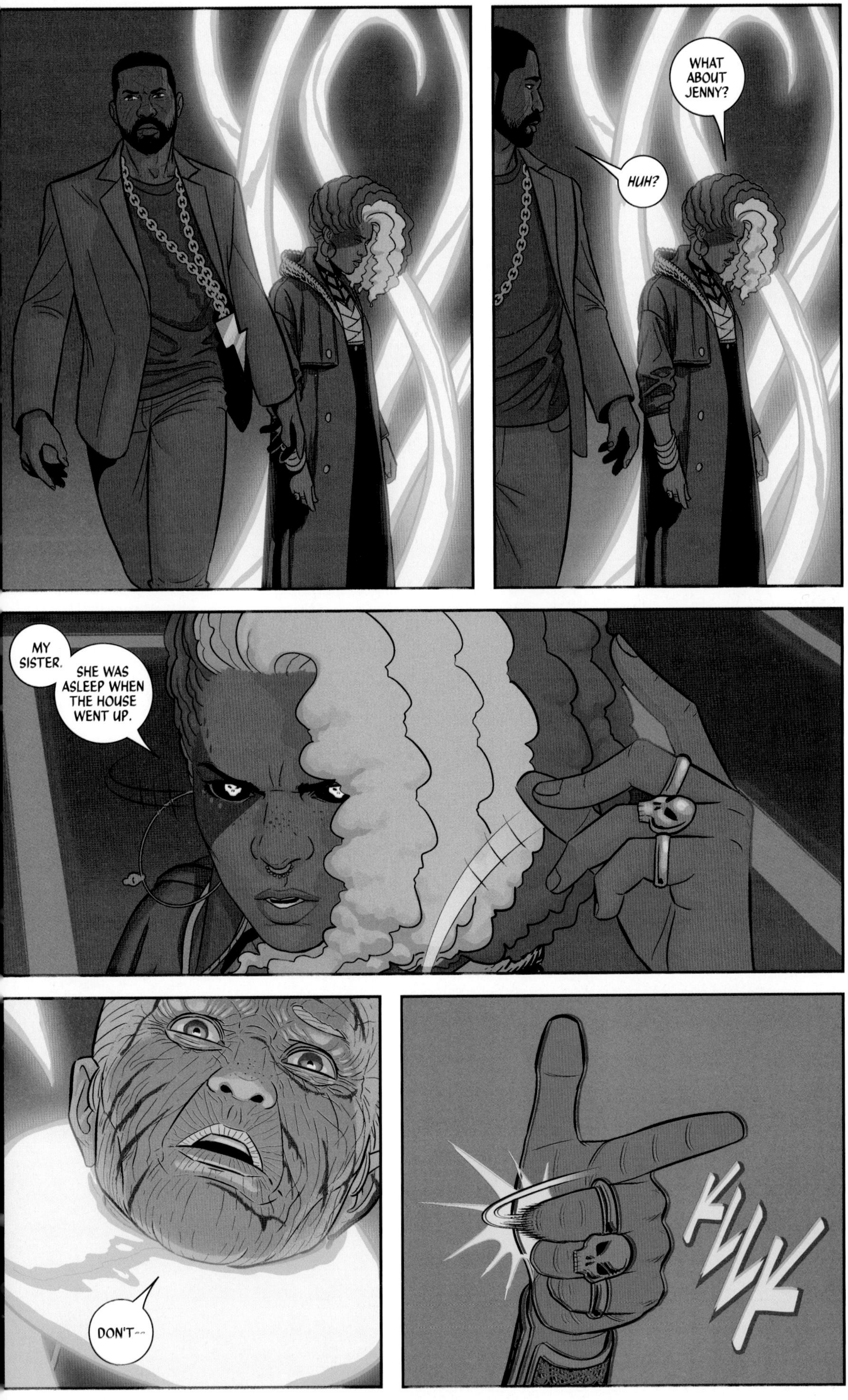
WHAT ABOUT JENNY?
HUH?
MY SISTER.
SHE WAS ASLEEP WHEN THE HOUSE WENT UP.
DON'T--
KLLK

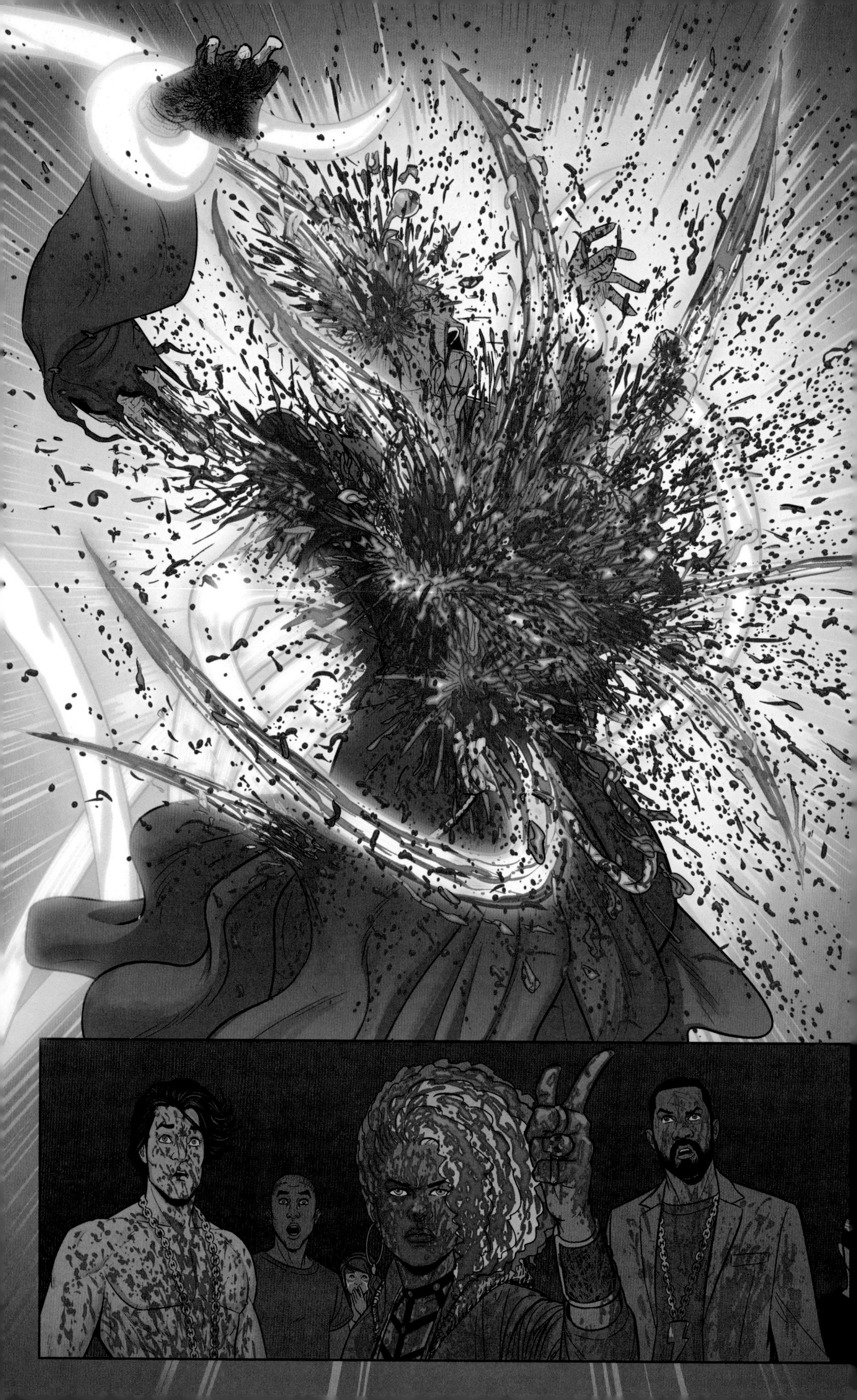

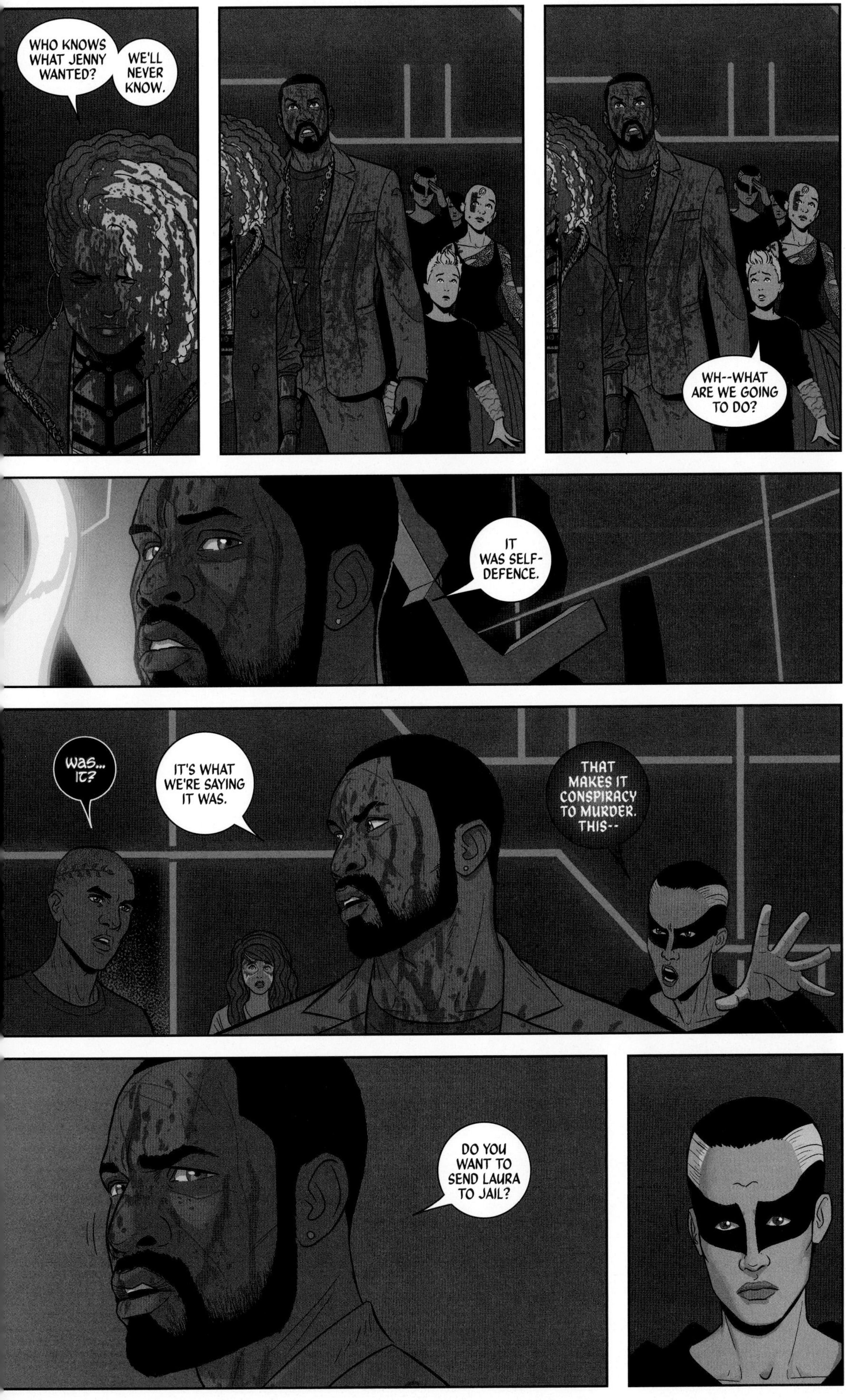
WHO KNOWS WHAT JENNY WANTED?
WE'LL NEVER KNOW.
WH--WHAT ARE WE GOING TO DO?
IT WAS SELF-DEFENCE.
Was... it?
IT'S WHAT WE'RE SAYING IT WAS.
THAT MAKES IT CONSPIRACY TO MURDER. THIS--
DO YOU WANT TO SEND LAURA TO JAIL?

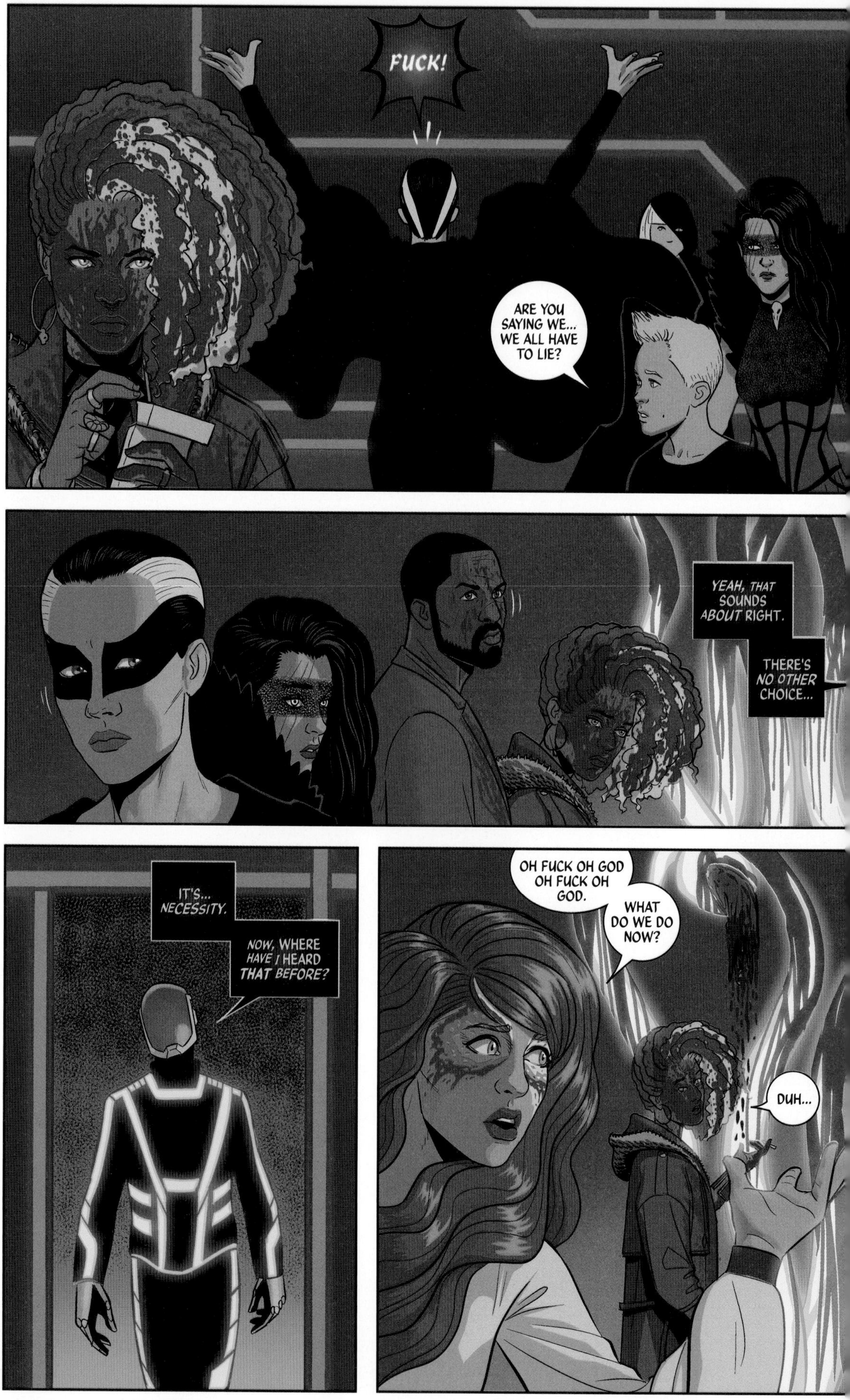
FUCK!
ARE YOU SAYING WE... WE ALL HAVE TO LIE?
YEAH, THAT SOUNDS ABOUT RIGHT.
THERE'S NO OTHER CHOICE...
IT'S... NECESSITY.
NOW, WHERE HAVE I HEARD THAT BEFORE?
OH FUCK OH GOD OH FUCK OH GOD.
WHAT DO WE DO NOW?
DUH...

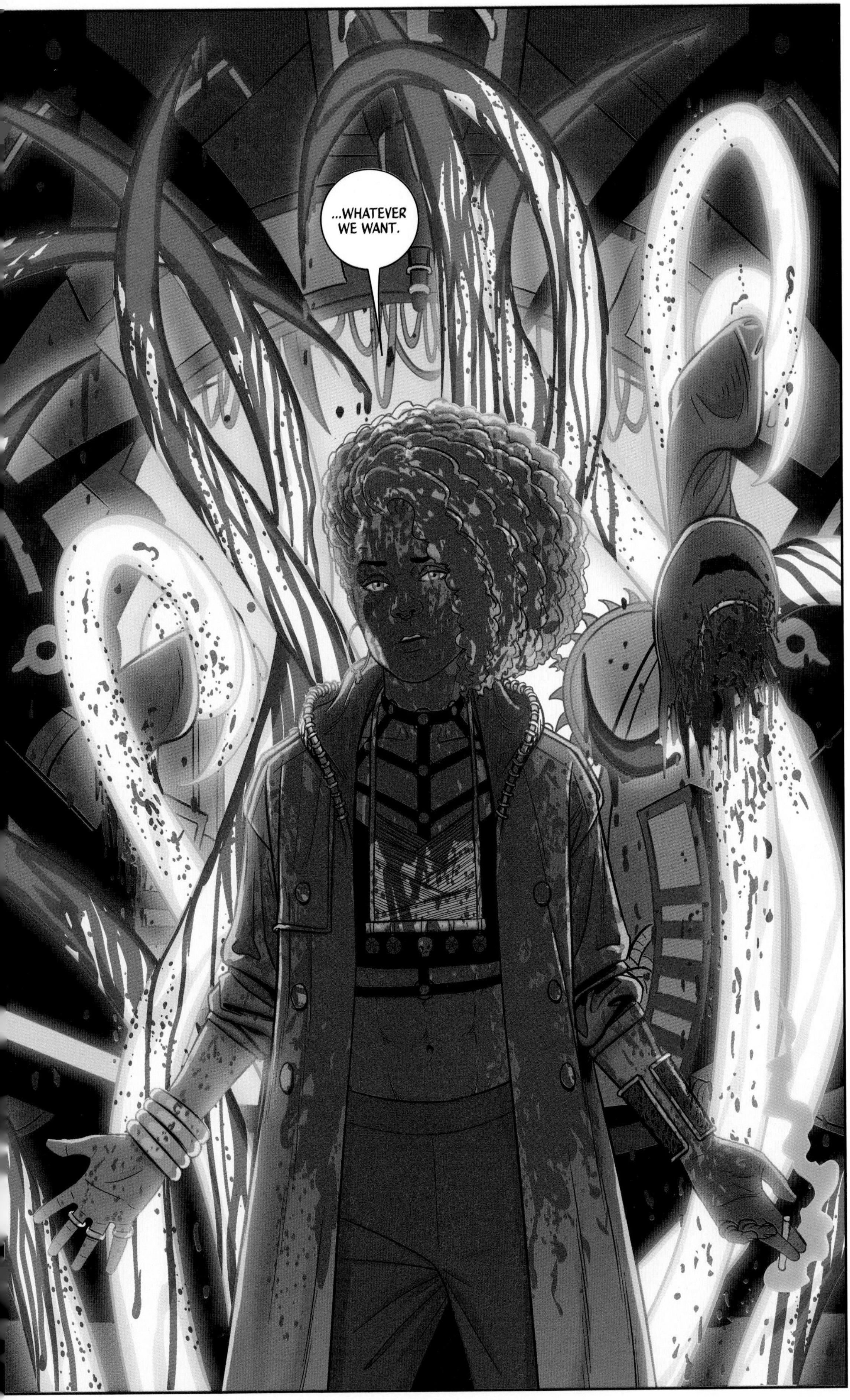
...WHATEVER WE WANT.

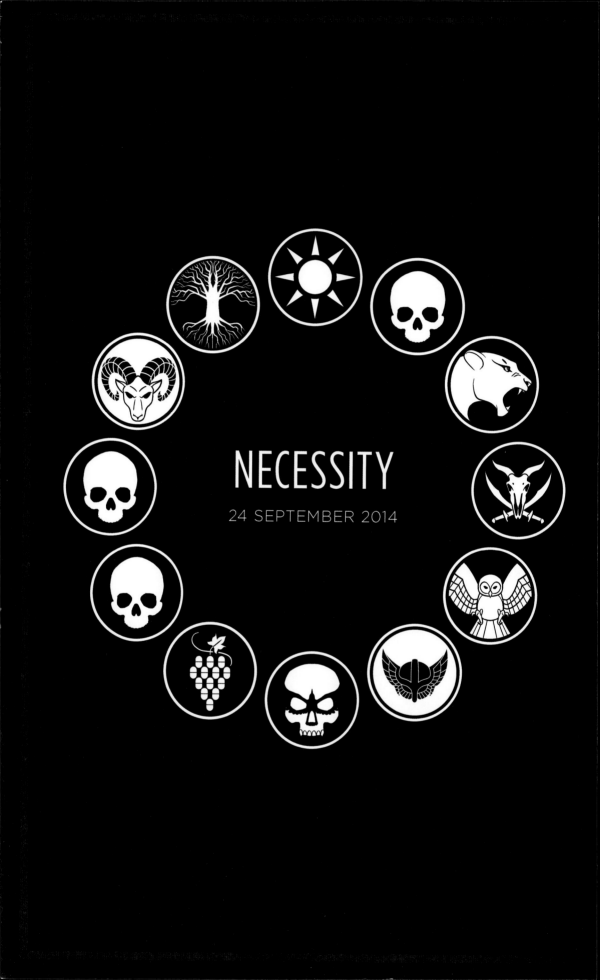

NECESSITY

24 SEPTEMBER 2014

THE
WICKED

+

ƎNIΛIᗡ
ƎHT

NEXT:
IMPERIAL PHASE
(PART 1)

VARIANT ART

We've definitely fallen in love with doing alternate covers and extra-curricular imagery created by some of our most talented peers. Treating them as icons is very much part of the point of the exercise. Equally, occasionally we like completing a visual motif. In this case, with Persephone's return, Jamie wanted to do one more head shot, closing the loop we started with the Laura portrait on the cover of issue 1. Once more we return and all that.

Matthew Wilson, Jamie McKelvie
Issue 18 ECCC cover

Matthew Wilson, Jamie McKelvie
Issue 18 cover

Kris Anka
Issue 19 cover

Jenny Frison
Issue 20 cover

David Aja
Issue 21 cover

Olly Moss
Issue 22 cover

Jamie McKelvie
Bookplate made for Forbidden Planet

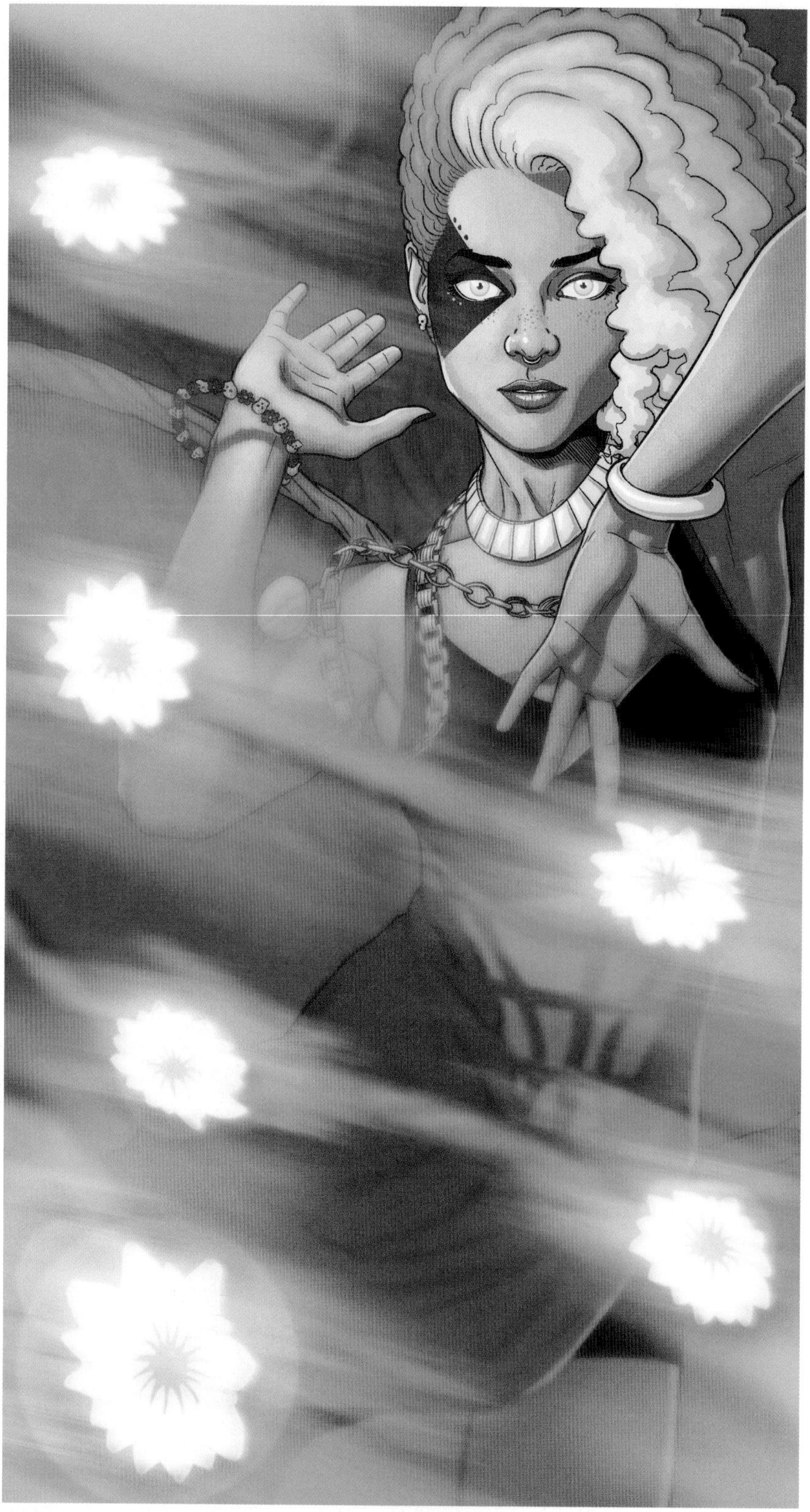

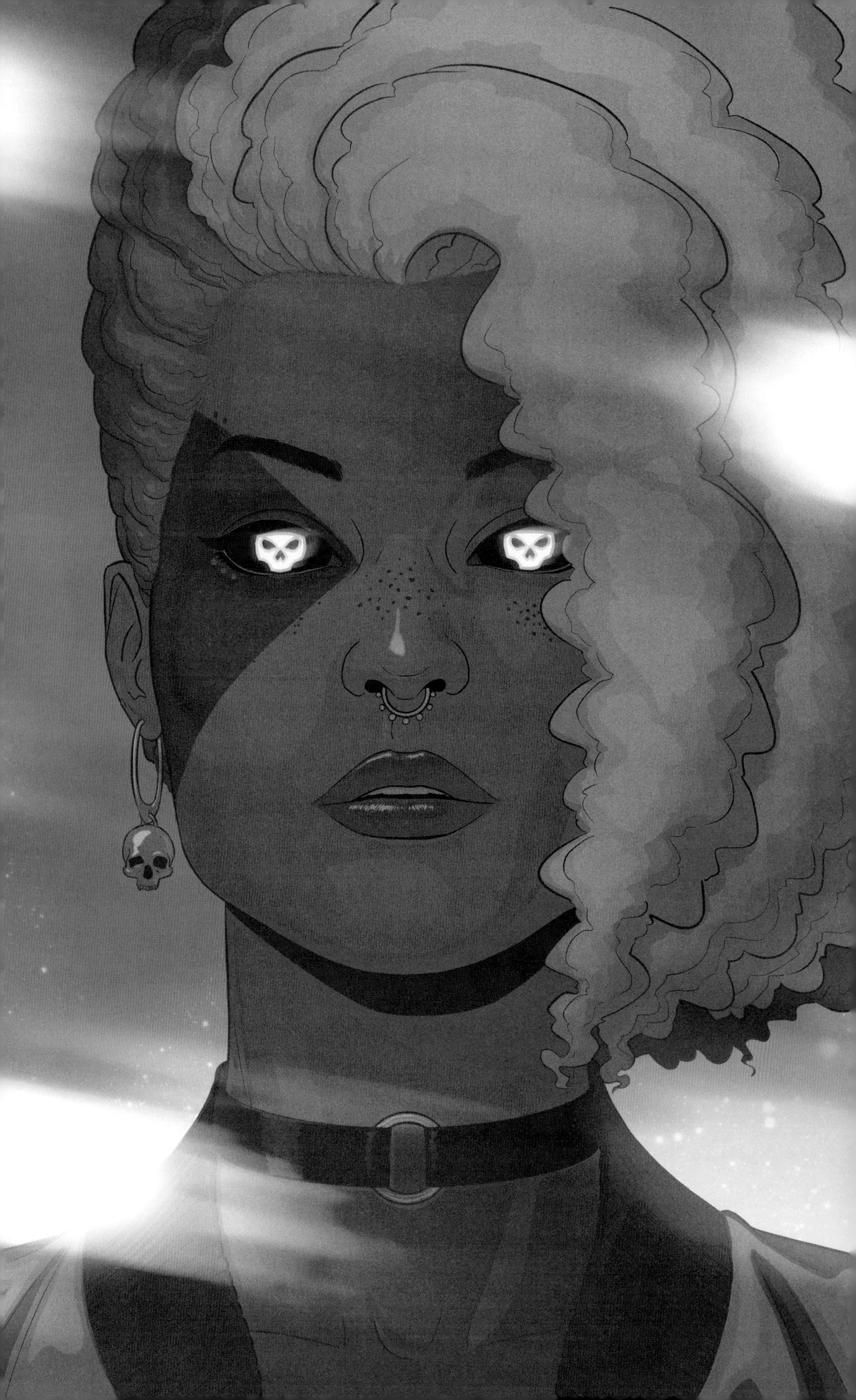

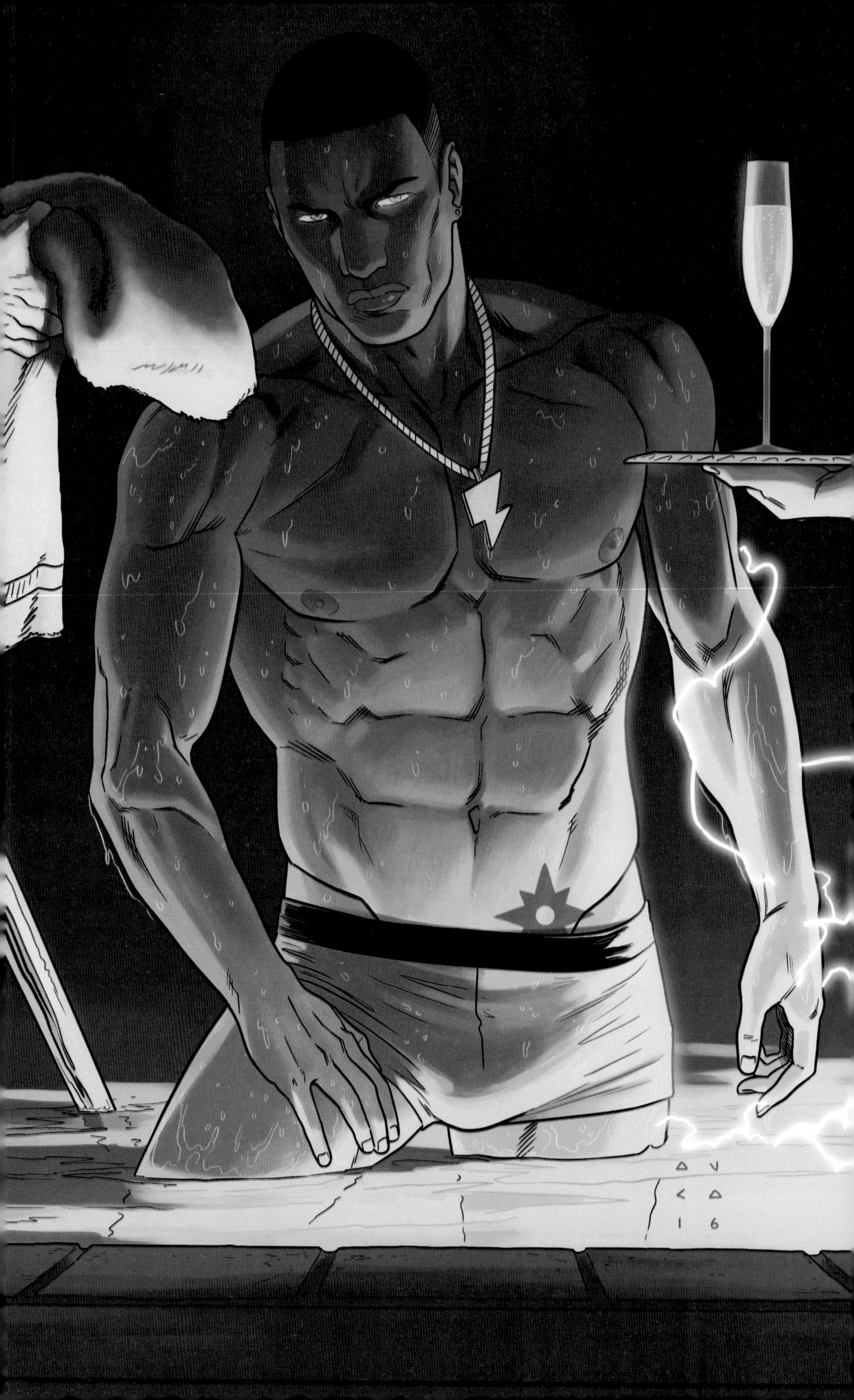

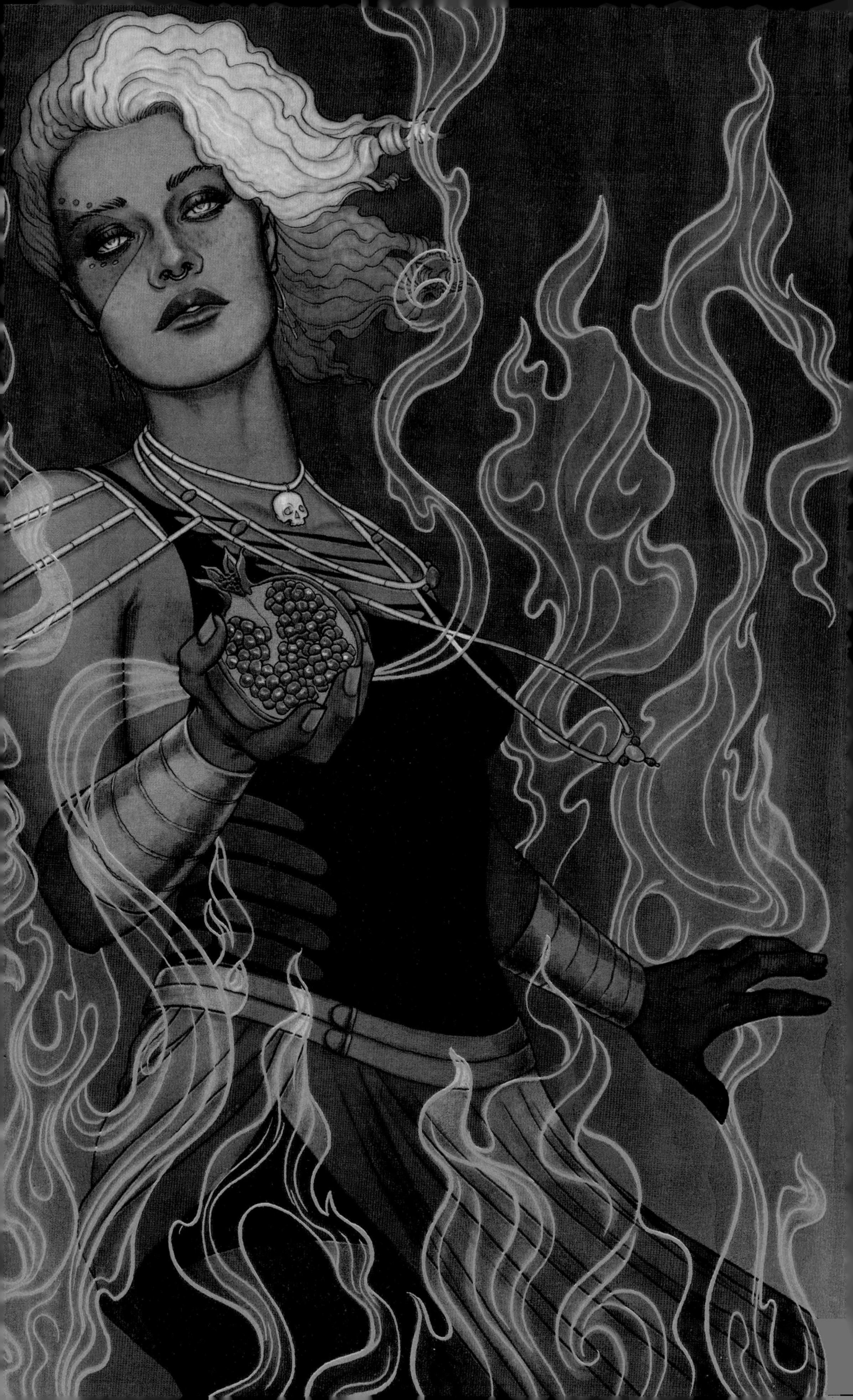

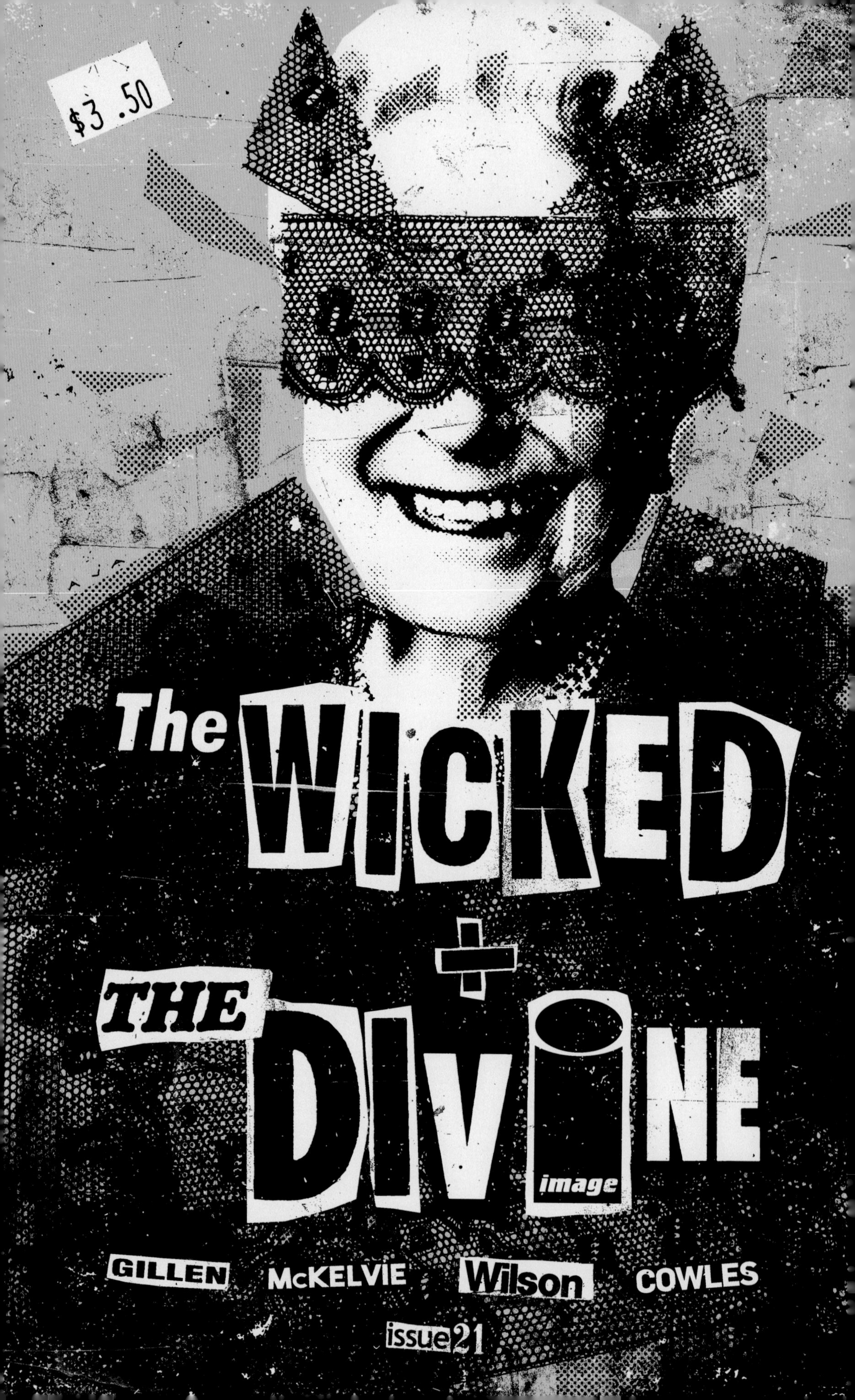
$3 .50
The WICKED + THE DIVINE
image
GILLEN McKELVIE Wilson COWLES
issue 21

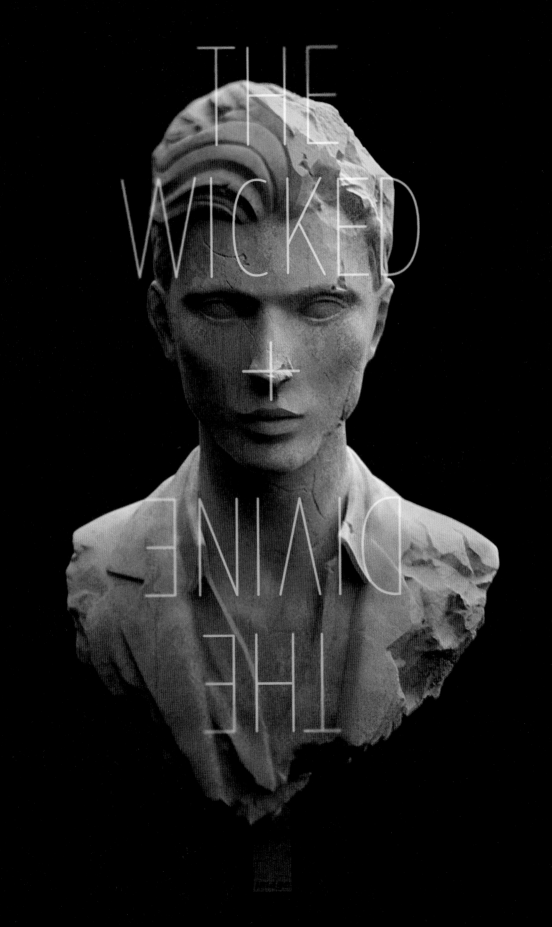

GILLEN   McKELVIE   WILSON   COWLES

THE
WICKED
+
THE
DIVINE

MAKING OF

As the title suggests, this arc is the most action-packed so far, and probably of the whole series. It very much harks back to some of the work we did on our *Young Avengers* for Marvel. As such, it's a good time to show how we do this thing called comics. We alternate between full script and Marvel Method (i.e. a loose outline which has dialogue added after the fact) depending on the effect we're looking for. Also, in a moment of honesty, it should be noted that any scripts may be edited to remove any future spoilers. We do a lot of foreshadowing, as you may have noticed.

Each of our examples follows the process of the comic. We have Kieron's script, Jamie's pencils and inks, followed by Dee's flats (which delineates area of colour for future elaboration) then Matt's colours. There's a final stage we've included where there's small tweaks Jamie (and occasionally Kieron) calls for after the pass. There's also all manner of other chat that happens around all this, of course, but we'd have to give you access to our email, IM, slack, etc to see all that. So (er) we're not.

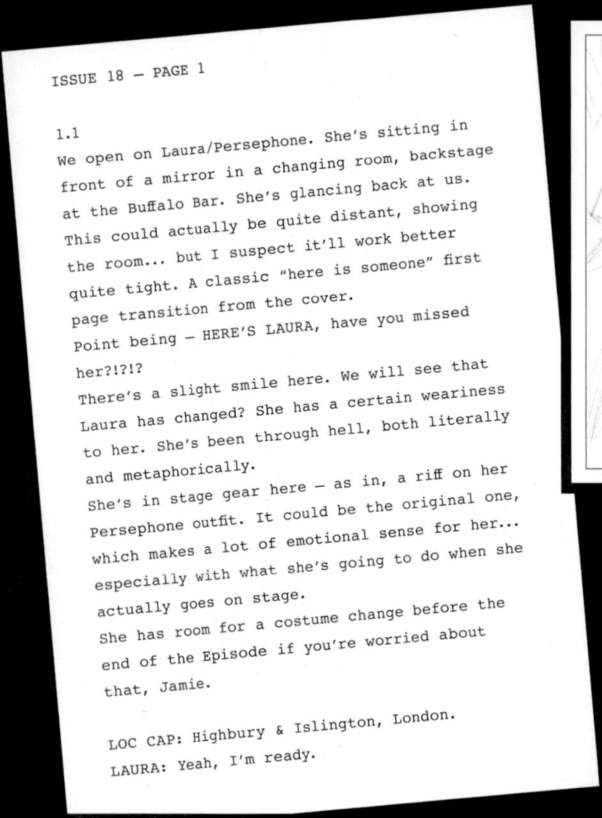

ISSUE 18 — PAGE 1

1.1
We open on Laura/Persephone. She's sitting in front of a mirror in a changing room, backstage at the Buffalo Bar. She's glancing back at us. This could actually be quite distant, showing the room... but I suspect it'll work better quite tight. A classic "here is someone" first page transition from the cover.
Point being – HERE'S LAURA, have you missed her?!?!?
There's a slight smile here. We will see that Laura has changed? She has a certain weariness to her. She's been through hell, both literally and metaphorically.
She's in stage gear here – as in, a riff on her Persephone outfit. It could be the original one, which makes a lot of emotional sense for her... especially with what she's going to do when she actually goes on stage.
She has room for a costume change before the end of the Episode if you're worried about that, Jamie.

LOC CAP: Highbury & Islington, London.
LAURA: Yeah, I'm ready.

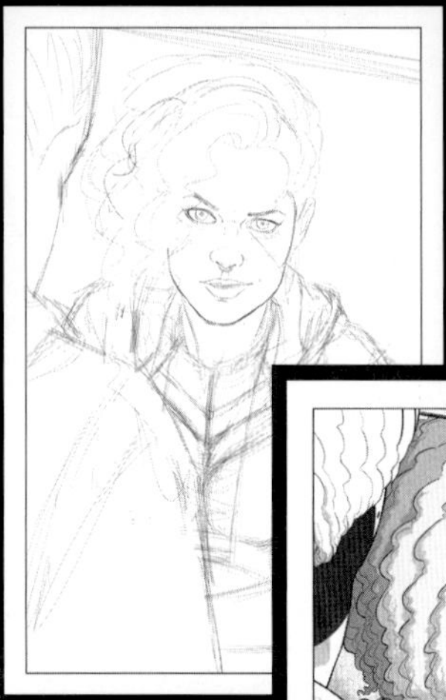

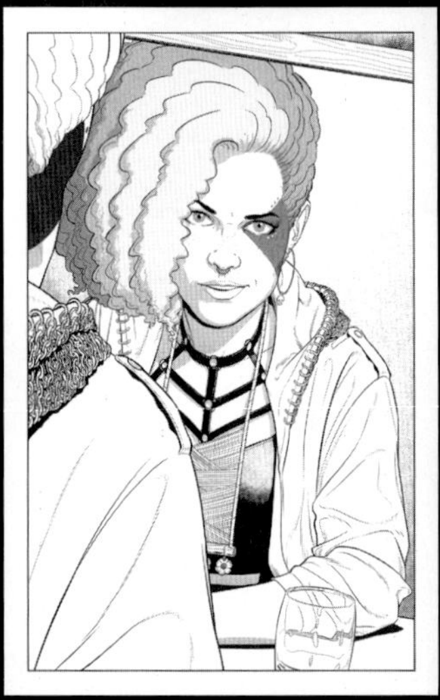

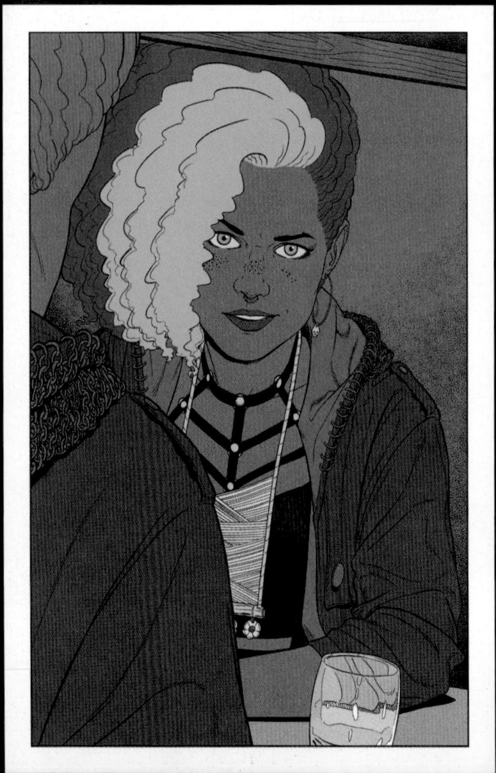

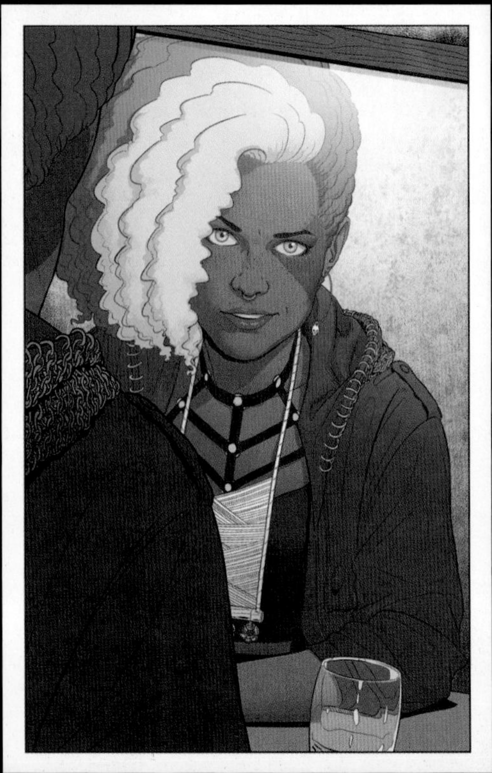

ISSUE 19 – PAGE 12

Let's Marvel Method this, though it's almost certainly a three panel page – maybe we can do something clever with small panels though. This is very much a dramatic fight scene we should perhaps try and work out clever stuff with.

And there's an ELECTRICITY BURST arc flying out of the owl. Everyone goes flying...

And standing there, crackling, fists clenched, is Baal. Can we have him wearing shades? Oh god, I want him wearing shades so I'm going to write it, and you can go with it or not. Largest panel on the page, I suspect. Everyone spread in all directions, coming to.

And tight on Baal, either removing the glasses or tipping them down so you can see his eyes. "Round Two." His other hand is raised, with a KLLK!

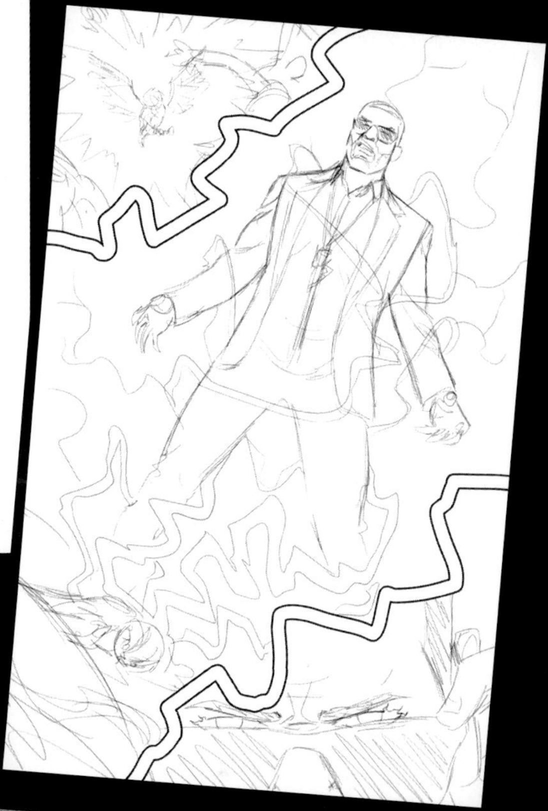

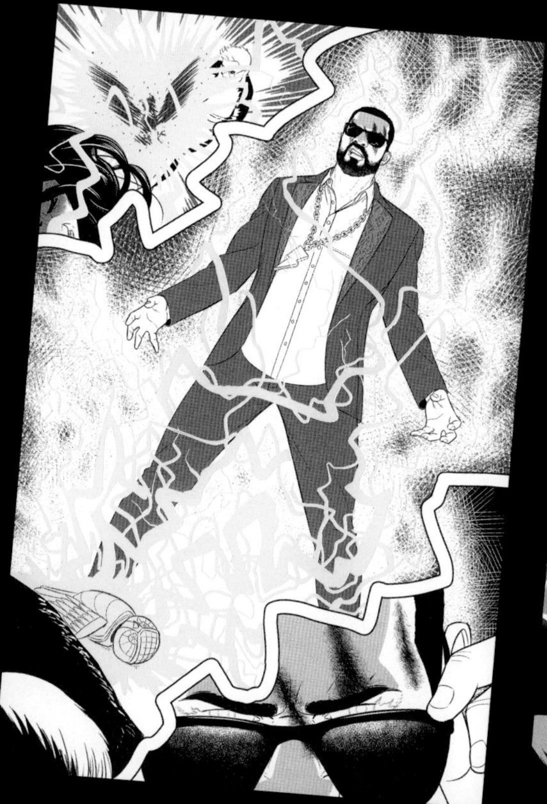

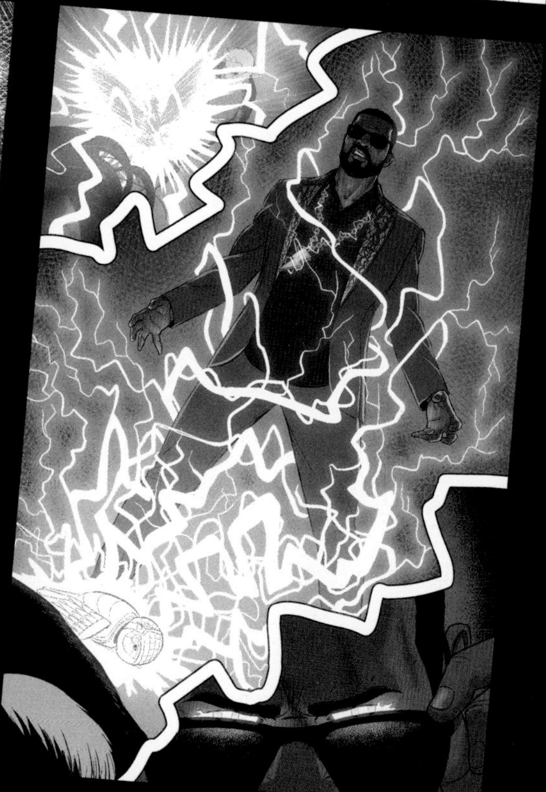

ISSUE 19 – PAGE 14

And she transforms to Badb: "Because I'm tearing out your fucking tongue."

Screaming brutally, she warps into a mass of crows and ravens. We did a little of this last time, but that was in a much smaller grid. We may not have even see it – here we do, and here we get that awfulness of Badb's face being half-raven and transforming into raven, and raven with teeth. Hell, we probably have accelerated to them having metal-edged wings. They are dark and increasingly dark, flying across the room...

And Baal is engulfed by the slashing, biting ravens... as as is Minerva.

From the blackness, Minerva screams.

We may want to do something clever here, in terms of layout, in a Young Avengers way. Raven panels? I dunno. I suspect an awesome raven attack would do, especially if we linger on how strange these ravens are getting. And, yes, they're crows, but for some reason I keep on writing ravens.

Minerva drops away from the melee, as Badb's raven swarm and Baal falls backwards. He's dropped her. We can see Minerva has a bunch of thin cuts. Baal will probably insult her noting this is irresponsible... which is entirely correct.

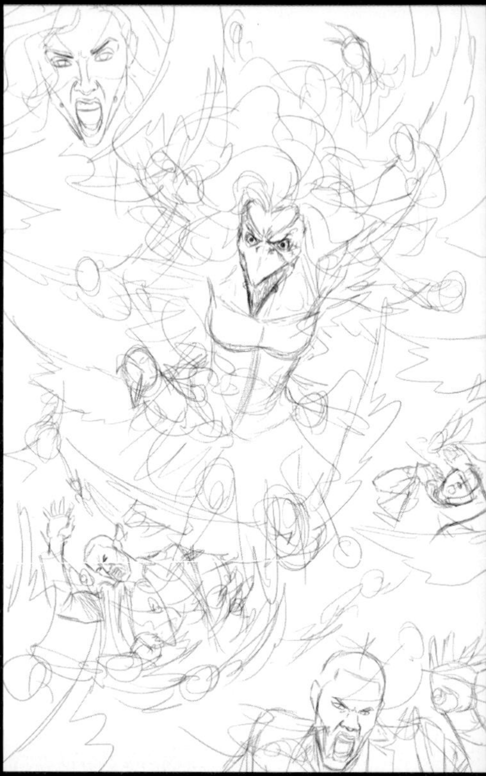

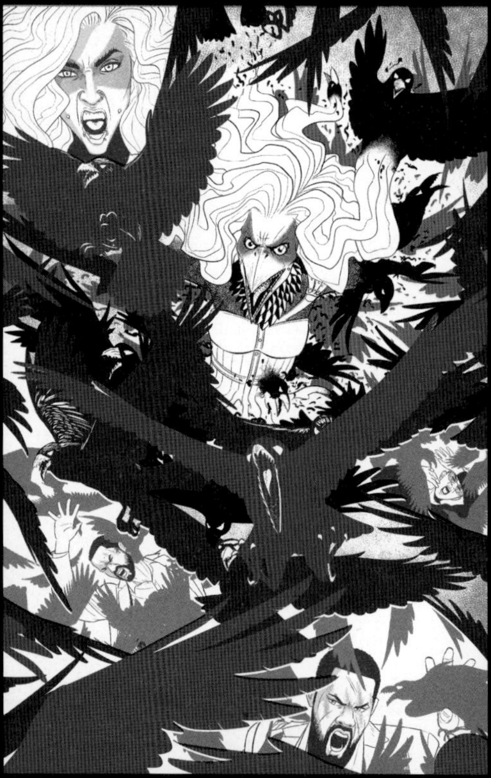

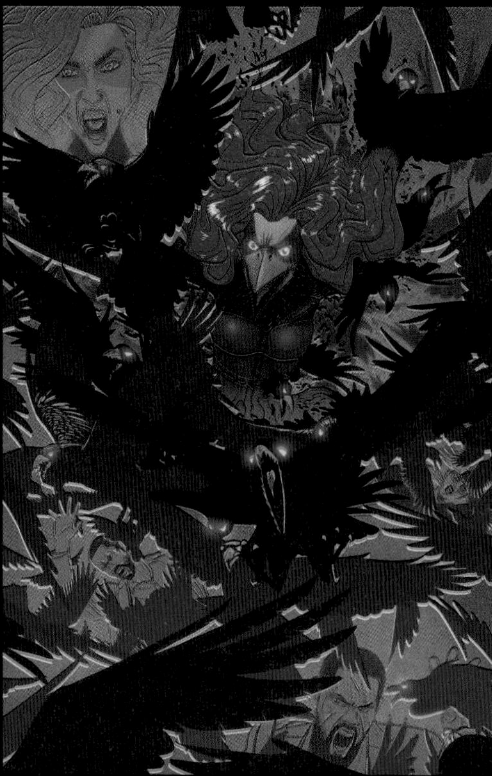

ISSUE 20 – PAGE 22

22.1

And big dramatic reveal on our boy, Baphomet, looking at himself in amazement.

Like all the changes, this is Baphomet as his most baphomet-y. He is his rock and roll god, fire dripping off him, surrounded by the circle.

We could have details here – most of them have some element around him. Perhaps the floor he lands on has transformed into skulls... as in a layer of burning skulls across the floor? Or maybe rather than landing on his feet, he's landing on a throne made of skull, in the full on Khorne-y way?

Basically, a moment of him loving it...

ANANKE: We meet again...

ANANKE: ...Nergal.

22.2

And Baphomet bounces up, growling angrily. Ananke is caught by surprise by the strength of the outburst.

ANANKE: I missed y--

BAPHOMET: **NERGAL? (SHOUTED)**

BAPHOMET: **ARE YOU TAKING THE PISS? (SHOUTED)**

22.3

Back in the real world. Laura, frowning. This is... a different sort of expression from where she was. She's not been jolted out of her depression or something, but at least it's something different to think about. This would be where we would start to bring up the colour, if we wanted.

LAURA: What's wrong with being Nergal?

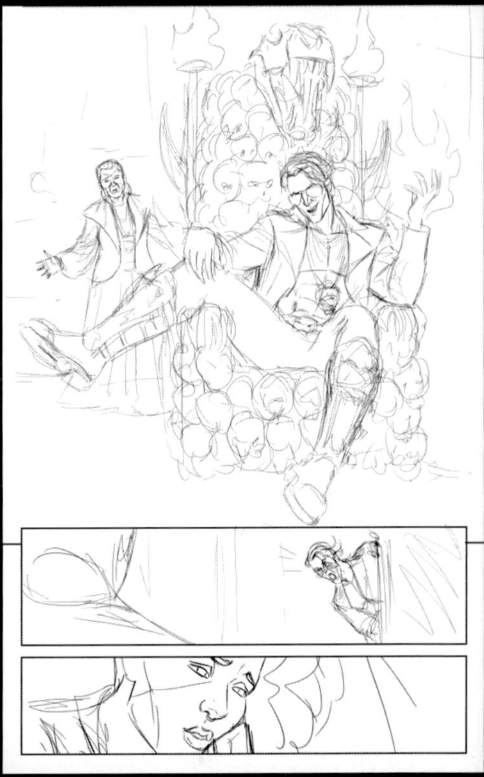

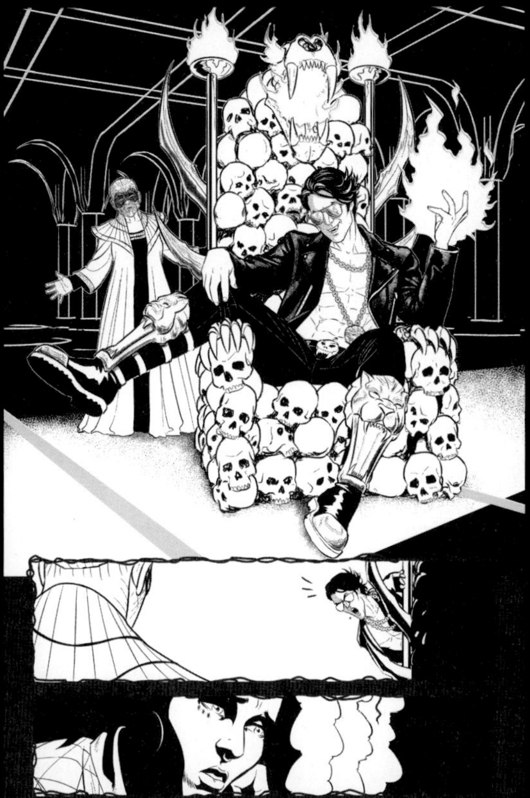

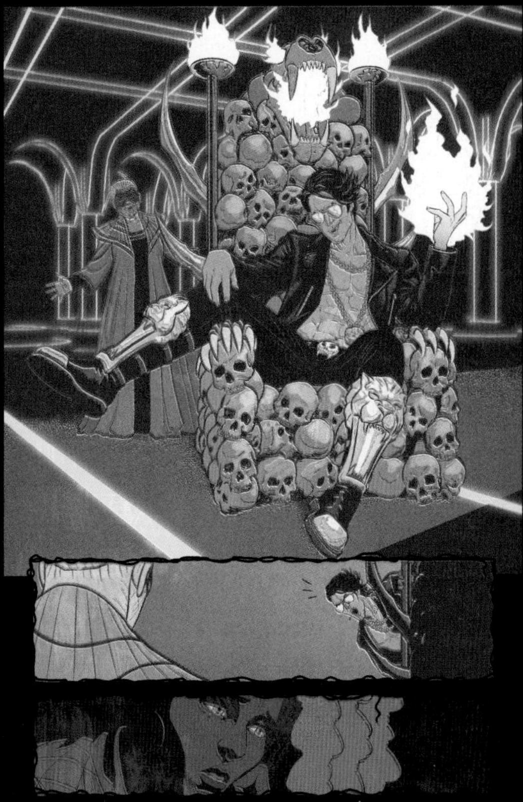

ISSUE 21 – PAGE 21

21.1
And we're on the view of the machine, opened up in all its magnificence. In the centre of this swirls of sinister light and colour is our Minerva, bound suspended in mid air, arms and legs at 45 degrees. She's still unconscious. Cogs whirl nearby, slowly turning. This is a rube goldberg monster machine, and the light makes everything strange...
Ananke is standing before it, watching, with her back to us...
ANANKE: Hmph.

21.2
And on Ananke. In her hand is a knife. Stone knife. Obsidian would be my preference, which is *very old indeed*.
I'd add symbols to the blade, related to the Pantheon. Perhaps the symbol we used for ANANKE in issue 20?
She tests the edge on the palm of the remaining flesh of her burned hand. A drop of blood forms between the blade and her flesh.
ANANKE: Will this never end?

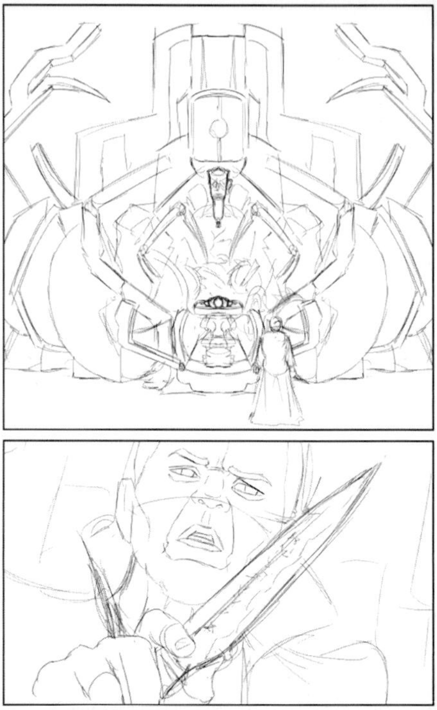

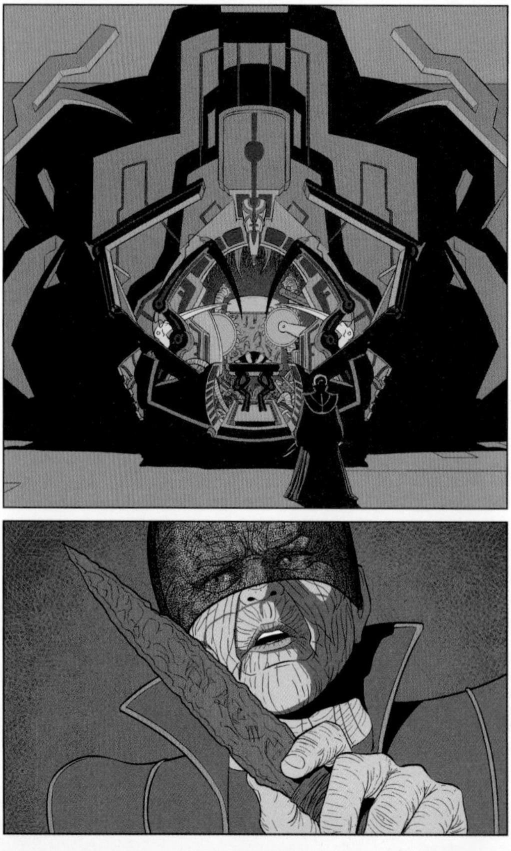

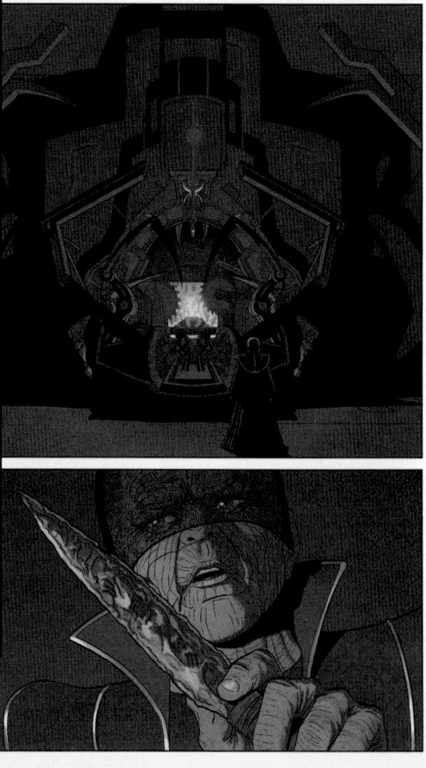

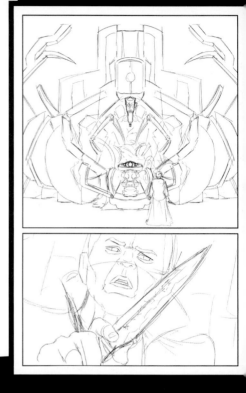

ISSUE 22

PAGE 2-3

Double page spread, with two inserts. One insert is top left, one is bottom right.
And this spread is... hard. It should be hard. We've set up an awesome fight last issue, and we're just not going to do it. We don't have space, and I probably wouldn't do a proper fight anyway. This is tableau-based storytelling, trying to create a place to explore, a place to make everyone's imagination to go wild in. This is the page we want all over the Internet. But basically, the job is to get all the awesome of VOLTRON VALKYRIE vs EVERYTHING into a panel of UTTER FUCKING CHAOS.
Sorry, guys.

2-3.1

The top left insert.
And we're on Amaterasu and Cass, fading into existence, wind rushing past them.
They're all kind of shocked.
(The other two Norns will be here too, though don't necessarily need to be on panel.)
LOC CAP: Valhalla, London.
CASS: Oh god.

2-3.2

The main DPS.
The battle outside Valhalla.
In the centre is THE VOLTRON VALKYRIE, enormous, with the Crowd swarming up its legs like raver ants. It swings its club, sending people flying. They crackle a little – Dionysus' protective magics and their own energies. Its Skyscraper stilettos press into the ground. It is mainly fighting Persephone, who has summoned up masses of crystal vines too do so – her as a tiny figure in this mass of writhing crystaline material, almost a cthuloid creature of vines. The Valkyrie-Voltron's breasts/bra are currently TWO ENORMOUS MINIGUNS firing tiny blasts that look like translucent glowing angels. (To stress – the whole "The good guys look like bad guys" this is very much there. In this fight, we're rooting for Cthulhu.)
Yes, it's likely the bad guys will lose... but it's still a mess.
Work in the other gods around this whole fucking mess – Sakhmet vs the Morrigan. Baal moves, crackling lighting, dancing with Baphomet. Woden is in the second hole in the wall (where Baph came through), firing his gun... and standing beside his PINK VALKYRIE.
Chaos! Glorious chaos!

Cass/Amaterasu are tiny figures in the sky high above this clusterfuck
– use Amaterasu's halo to guide the eye.
Sorry, guys. This is the poster.

CASS: It depresses me to know that someone, somewhere is wanking over this.

2-3.3

Second insert.
We're tight on Woden, firing one of his guns.
WODEN: **FUCK!!!!**
(SHOUTED)
CAP: For once, I'm saying how I feel.
CAP: Now I've tried it, I have to say honesty is **desperately** overrated.

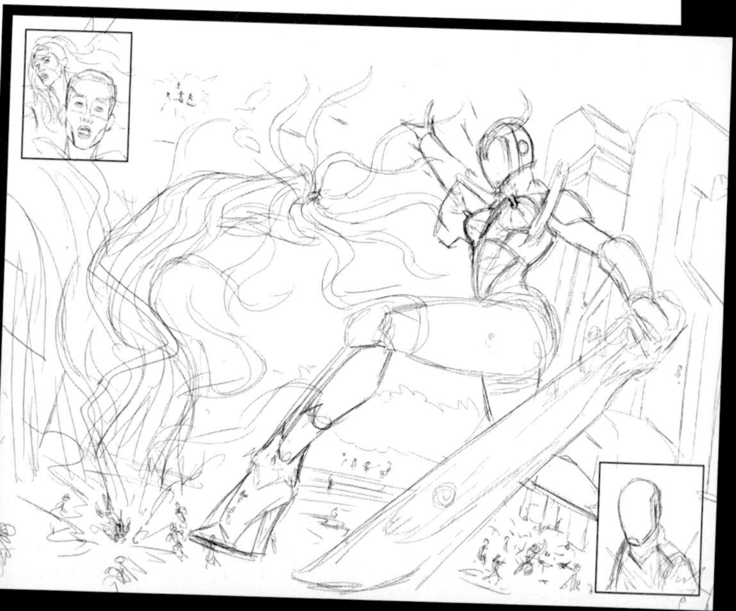

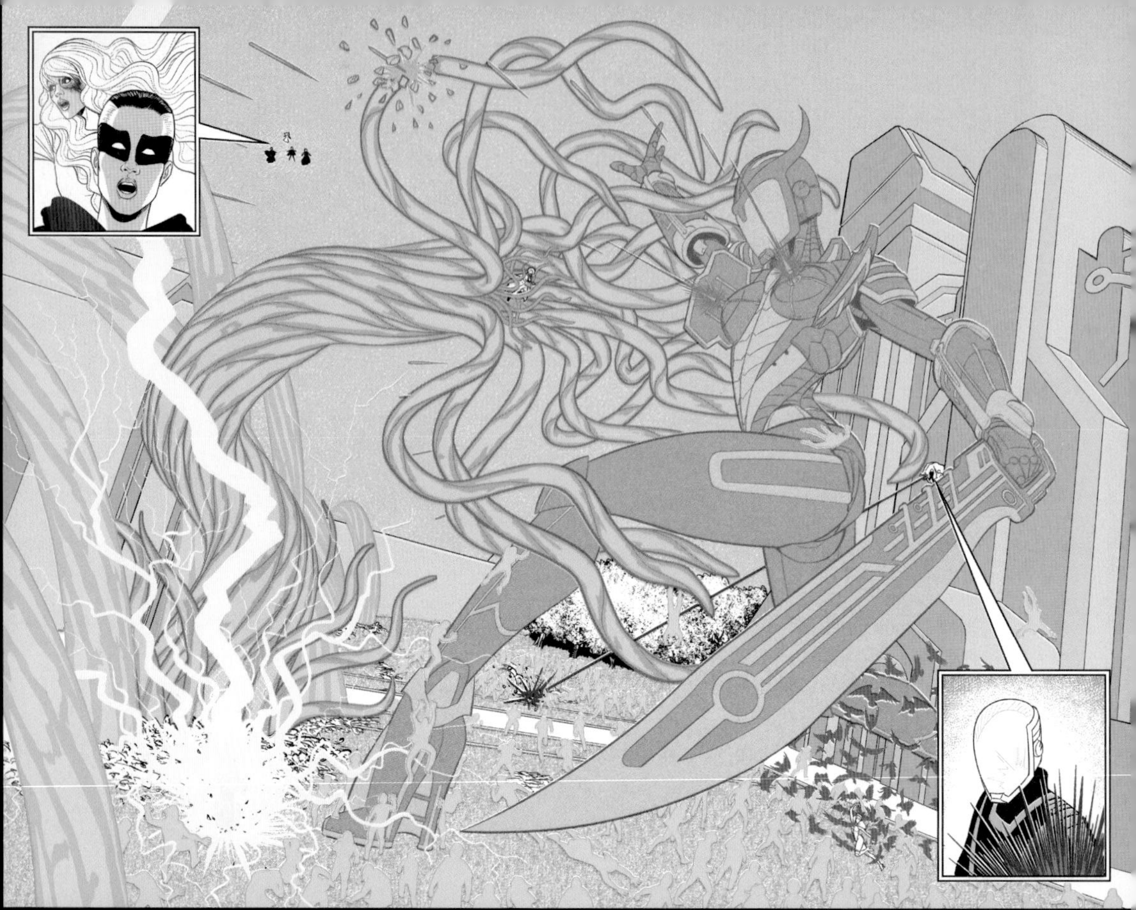

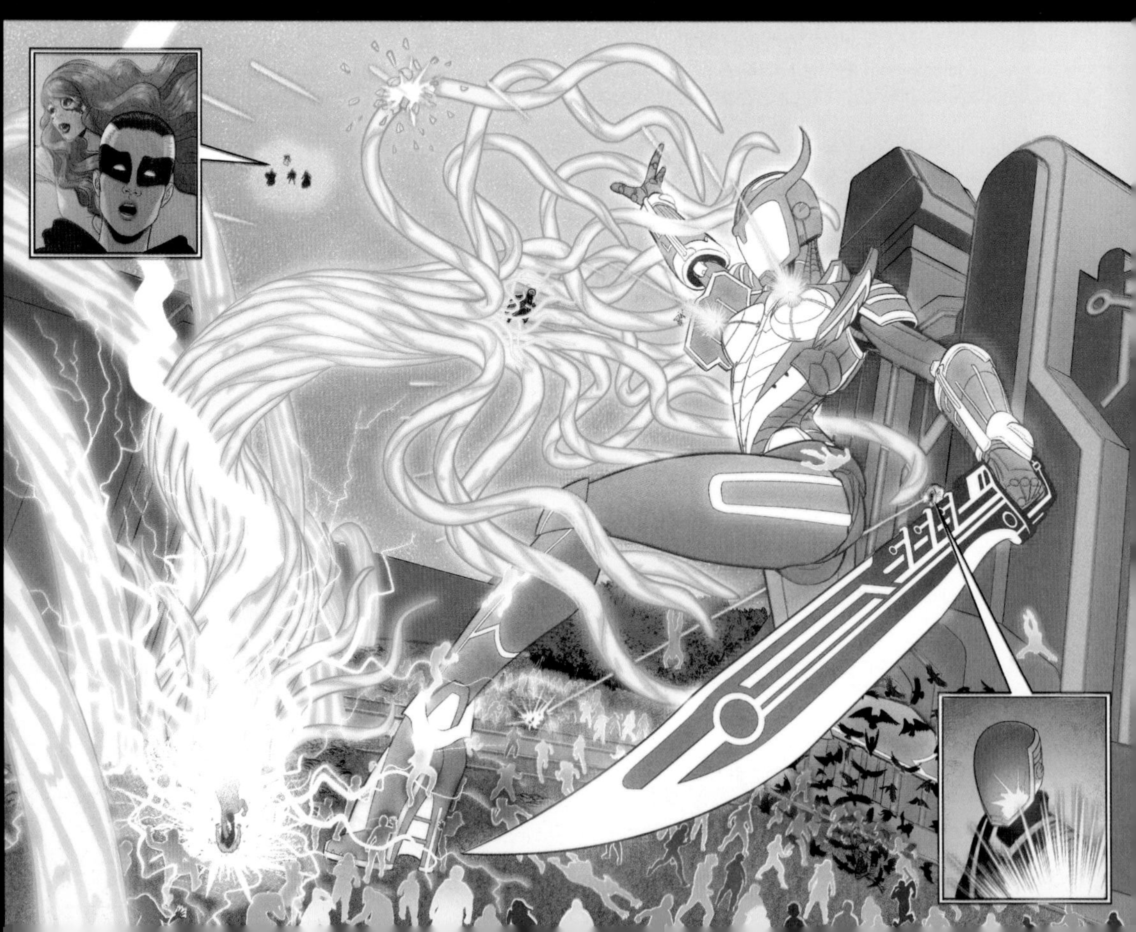

We set up a mailing list for Dionysus way back in issue 7, just because the flyer which introduced Dionysus really felt like it needed to include one. We had no idea what we were going to do with it. Since then, we use it for an occasional in-character stream-of-consciousness download from Dionysus. This was sent out the day issue 22 came out, to mirror Dionysus' in-world recruiting of his crowd.

From: Dionysus <dionyssiankissstory@gmail.com>
Subject: UNDERGROUND DIONYSUS KISS STORY PARTY XXVIII After Party

Okay, that's a lie. There's no actual after party. It's more of a party in a "We're playing *World of Warcraft* and we're off to beat up a dragon" way than anything I'd actually enjoy doing in 2014.

Morrigan has just turned into Badb, and made a hissing noise at me for writing that. I didn't mean it like that. Now she's telling me to hurry up, but she's not exactly making me relax. I didn't know that crows could hiss, but BREAKING NEWS! it is not a relaxing noise.

Cut to the chase. I need your help. Anyone on this mailing list around London and can get to Valhalla in the next half hour or so? This is to you. Everyone else, get back to bed or get back to whatever you were doing.

I've already got the XVIII crowd with me, except those who dropped out. More came than I thought which... I dunno. I'm humbled. Sometimes it feels like I'm giving too much, but this just shows that you give, and stuff comes back. Or maybe everyone just wants to feel like a superhero for once.

I'm getting off point: we need to storm our way into Valhalla and need every hand we can get. And who has more hands than the dancefloor that marches like a man?

This could be dangerous. How dangerous? I don't know. But you have to believe me, this is life and death. If we don't pull this off, I'm pretty sure... okay, I don't want to write it. Writing makes it real, and making it real may stop me. I'm basically running on autopilot here, guys. Well, autopilot and energy drinks.

It's odd. It's like a state of grace. Every step I'm making feels right. We have to do this. That makes it easier? The choice has been removed. There's only action. It's like dancing, and step follows step follows step.

Okay, I'm getting spacey and Morrigan is doing growly beakface.

So — storming a place full of gods. I can't promise you'll be fine, but... we do have an edge. You know my parties? Ever noticed what *doesn't* happen there? Pain. No one gets hurt. People fall over and there's no bruises. No sprains even. That's me. That's what I give you when you're in my crowd. I promise, I won't take it too far when we go in. If it looks like something is going to hurt *any* of you, and I'll pull out. You're all precious.

I'm not into violence. But i'm into life, and sometimes you got to fight for your right to party. We want the night to last forever and have something happy in it. If we don't do something quickly, this night ends for a little girl and there's nothing happy any more.

Hope to see some of you soon, and see everyone else soon after that. But if I don't? I love you all.

Peace out.
Dio

(Over) As issue 18 was our big comeback, with Jamie and Matt returning to the book, we wanted to make some serious noise. We had the idea of cutting a "trailer" of images from the issue, in t manner of a movie. Here's what we came up with...

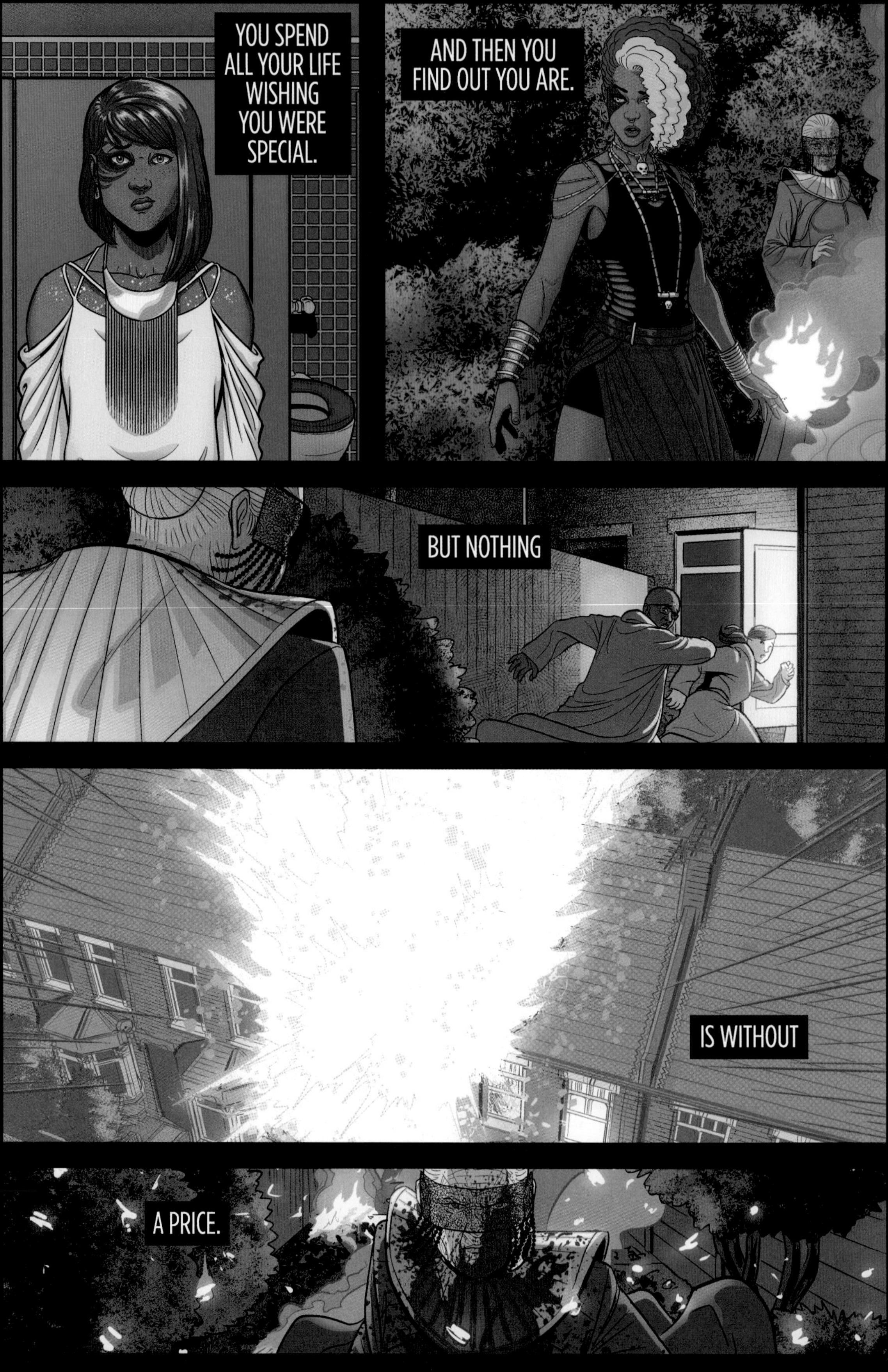
YOU SPEND ALL YOUR LIFE WISHING YOU WERE SPECIAL.
AND THEN YOU FIND OUT YOU ARE.
BUT NOTHING
IS WITHOUT
A PRICE.

AND NOW?

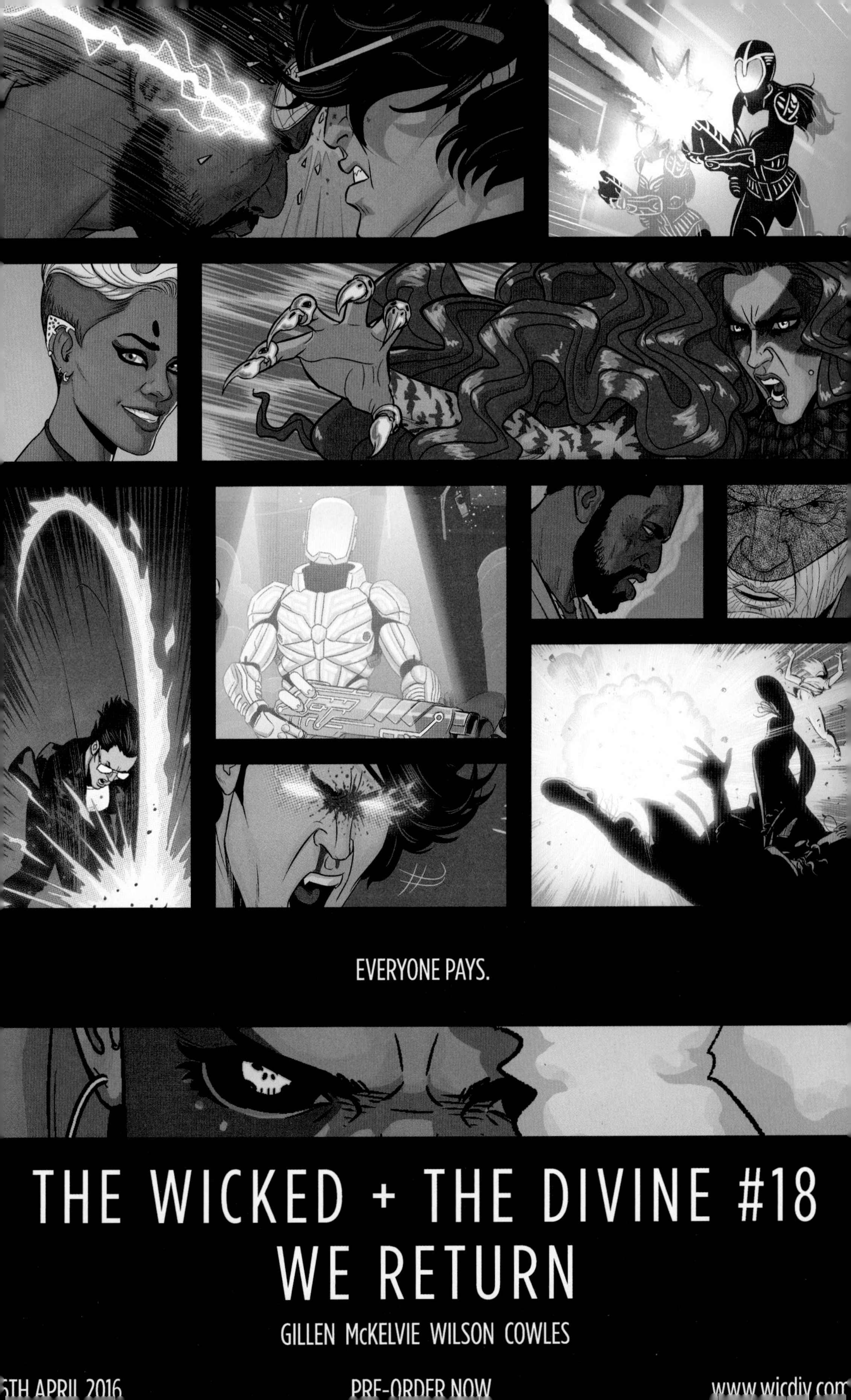

EVERYONE PAYS.
THE WICKED + THE DIVINE #18
WE RETURN
GILLEN McKELVIE WILSON COWLES
TH APRIL 2016
PRE-ORDER NOW
www.wicdiy.com

ALSO BY THE CREATORS

THE WICKED + THE DIVINE

VOL. 1: THE FAUST ACT
#1—5 COLLECTED

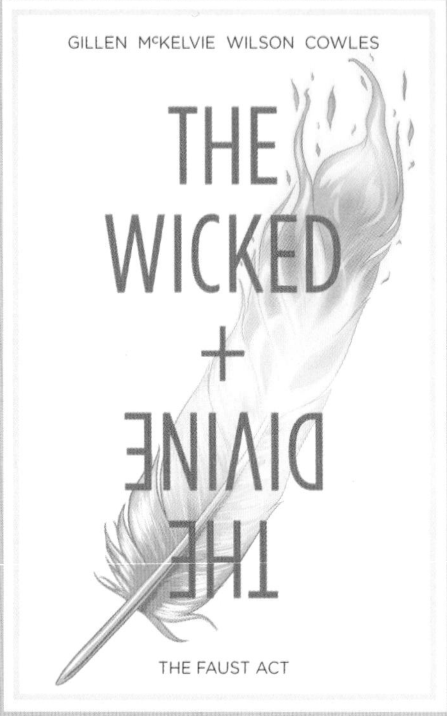
GILLEN McKELVIE WILSON COWLES
THE WICKED + DIVINE THE
THE FAUST ACT

VOL. 2: FANDEMONIUM
#6—11 COLLECTED

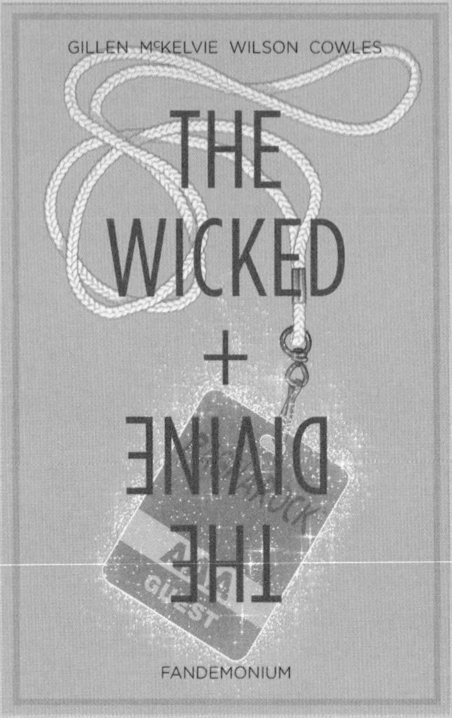
GILLEN McKELVIE WILSON COWLES
THE WICKED + DIVINE THE
GUEST
FANDEMONIUM

VOL. 3: COMMERCIAL SUICIDE
#12—17 COLLECTED

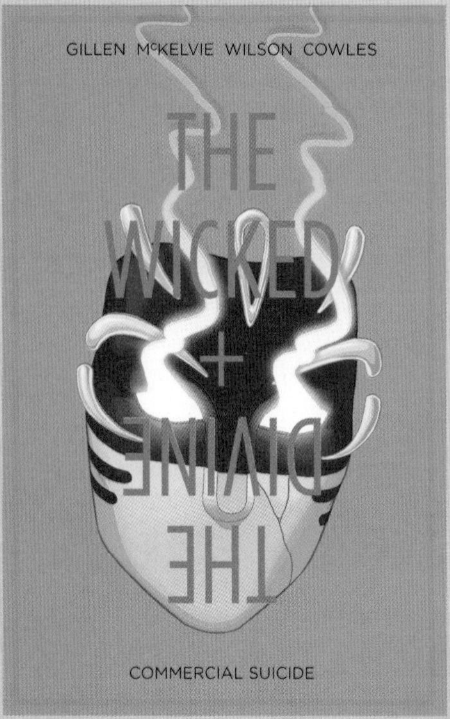
GILLEN McKELVIE WILSON COWLES
THE WICKED + DIVINE THE
COMMERCIAL SUICIDE

THE WICKED AND THE DIVINE:
BOOK ONE #1—11 COLLECTED

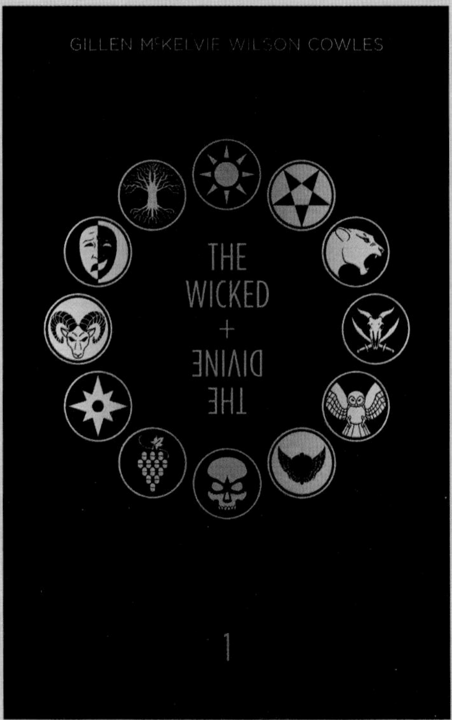
GILLEN McKELVIE WILSON COWLES
THE WICKED + DIVINE THE
1

PHONOGRAM

VOL. 1:
RUE BRITANNIA

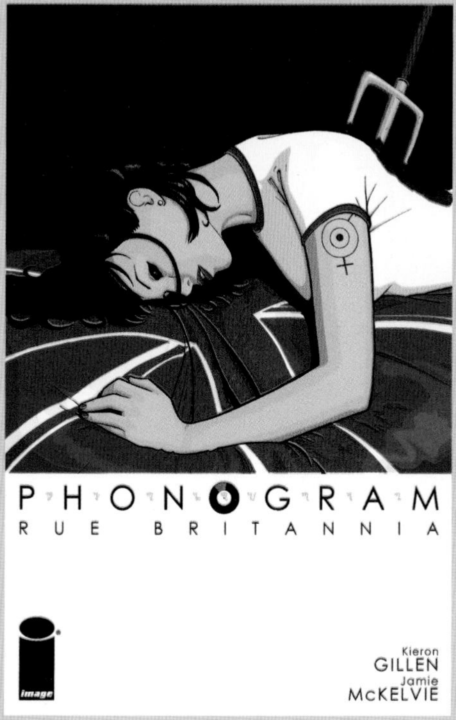
PHONOGRAM
RUE BRITANNIA
Kieron
GILLEN
Jamie
McKELVIE

VOL. 2:
THE SINGLES CLUB

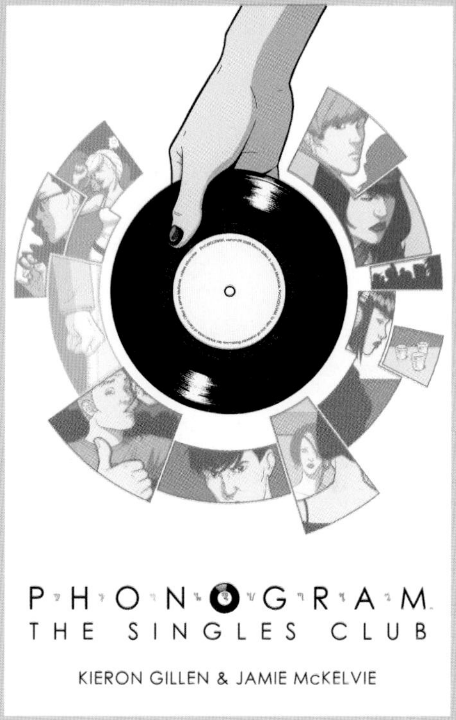
PHONOGRAM
THE SINGLES CLUB
KIERON GILLEN & JAMIE McKELVIE

VOL. 3:
THE IMMATERIAL GIRL

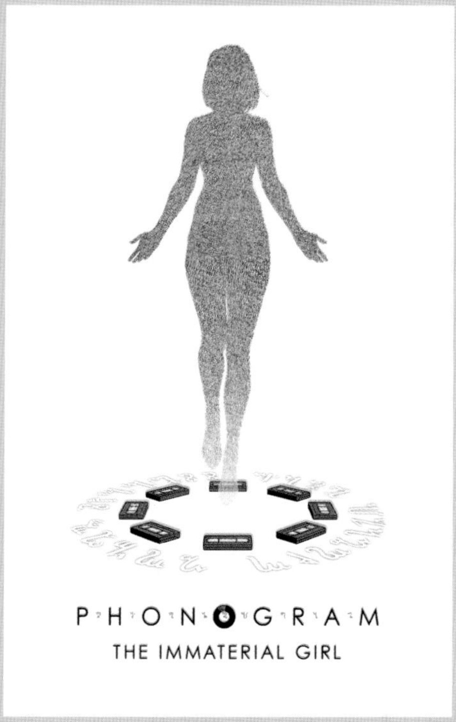
PHONOGRAM
THE IMMATERIAL GIRL

FOR FURTHER INFORMATION ON
THE WICKED + THE DIVINE:

www.wicdiv.com

major news, new issues, merchandise.

#WicDiv

the hashtag on twitter for WicDiv Discussion

WicDiv

the general tag on tumblr for the community.

bit.ly/WicDivPlaylist

the ever-updated Spotify Playlist for the series.

ALSO BY THE CREATORS

SUBURBAN GLAMOUR

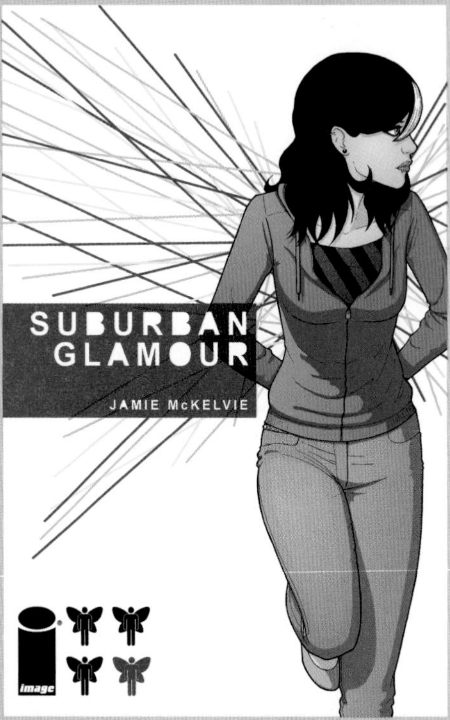
SUBURBAN GLAMOUR
JAMIE McKELVIE

THREE

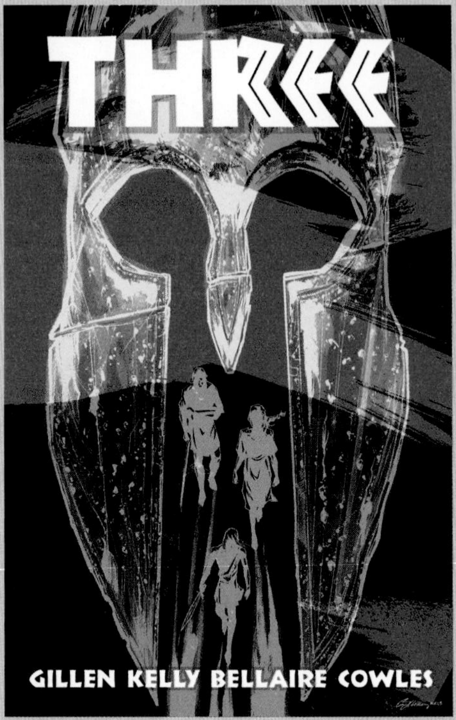
THREE
GILLEN KELLY BELLAIRE COWLES

OTHER TITLES

BY KIERON GILLEN, JAMIE MCKELVIE AND MATT WILSON

YOUNG AVENGERS:
STYLE > SUBSTANCE

YOUNG AVENGERS:
ALTERNATIVE CULTURE

YOUNG AVENGERS:
MIC-DROP AT THE EDGE
OF TIME AND SPACE

WRITTEN BY KIERON GILLEN

ÜBER
(Volumes 1–5)

MERCURY HEAT
(Volumes 1-2)

STAR WARS:
DARTH VADER

THOR: ULTIMATE
COLLECTION

JOURNEY INTO
MYSTERY: THE
COMPLETE COLLECTION
(Volume 1)

JOURNEY INTO
MYSTERY: THE
COMPLETE COLLECTION
(Volume 2)

SIEGE: BATTLEWORLD

WOLVERINE: ORIGIN II

And lots more, but that's enough for now, methinks.

DRAWN BY JAMIE MCKELVIE

LONG HOT SUMMER
(with Eric Stephenson)

X-MEN SEASON ONE
(with Dennis Hopeless)

And smaller work divided widely in other places.

COLOURED BY MATT WILSON

PAPER GIRLS

CRY HAVOC

And millions and trillions of others, honestly, he's so busy it's kind of overwhelming.

NAILED IT!
nail wraps
espionage cosmetics

Limited Edition
Officially Licensed!

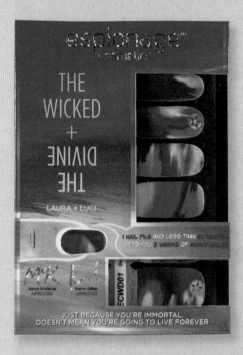

espionagecosmetics.com/WicDiv

EXCLUSIVE
THE WICKED + THE DIVINE
NAIL WRAPS

The first two of five exclusive *The Wicked + The Divine* nail wrap sets to be released by Espionage Cosmetics. Each side of this set of wraps features the iconography and distinct colours associated with WicDiv characters. With two sides to choose from, you can mix and match to your heart's content!

SET 1: Laura + Luci
SET 2: Baal + Inanna

FEATURES:

- Gloss finish
- Glow in the dark ink
- Silver foil accents
- Dual nail wrap design! Rock a different god on each hand!

Kieron Gillen is a writer who is a big scary animal.

Jamie McKelvie is an artist who isn't scared of any animal.

Matt Wilson is a colourist who has actually coloured a scary number of the comics Kieron and Jamie are posing in front of.

Photograph by Lindsey Byrnes